Electric Utility Resource Planning

Electric Utility Resource Planning
Past, Present and Future

JOSEPH FERRARI

ELSEVIER

Elsevier
Radarweg 29, PO Box 211, 1000 AE Amsterdam, Netherlands
The Boulevard, Langford Lane, Kidlington, Oxford OX5 1GB, United Kingdom
50 Hampshire Street, 5th Floor, Cambridge, MA 02139, United States

Notices
Knowledge and best practice in this field are constantly changing. As new research and experience broaden our understanding, changes in research methods, professional practices, or medical treatment may become necessary.

Practitioners and researchers must always rely on their own experience and knowledge in evaluating and using any information, methods, compounds, or experiments described herein. In using such information or methods they should be mindful of their own safety and the safety of others, including parties for whom they have a professional responsibility.

To the fullest extent of the law, neither the Publisher nor the authors, contributors, or editors, assume any liability for any injury and/or damage to persons or property as a matter of products liability, negligence or otherwise, or from any use or operation of any methods, products, instructions, or ideas contained in the material herein.

British Library Cataloguing-in-Publication Data
A catalogue record for this book is available from the British Library

Library of Congress Cataloging-in-Publication Data
A catalog record for this book is available from the Library of Congress

ISBN: 978-0-12-819873-5

For Information on all Elsevier publications
visit our website at https://www.elsevier.com/books-and-journals

Publisher: Joe Hayton
Acquisitions Editor: Graham Nisbet
Editorial Project Manager: Leticia M. Lima
Production Project Manager: Kamesh Ramajogi
Cover Designer: Christian Bilbow

Typeset by MPS Limited, Chennai, India

Working together
to grow libraries in
developing countries

www.elsevier.com • www.bookaid.org

Contents

Preface   *ix*

1. Introduction to electric utilities and how they plan for the future   1

Introduction   1
Electric utilities: the basics   2
The early history of the electric utility   4
The early stages of the evolution of cost approaches   7
Varying technology types that made up (and still make up) the generation mix
of most utilities   8
    Coal boiler plants   9
    Combustion turbines   10
    Combined-cycle combustion turbines   11
    Reciprocating engines (Recips)   12
    Hydro   14
    Nuclear   14
    Other   16
Long-range planning (also referred to as long-term planning or integrated
resource planning)   16
    Basics of utility long-range planning   18
    Major approaches to capacity expansion planning   25
    Approach 1—capital cost   25
    Approach 2—annual cost   26
    Approach 3—levelized cost of energy   26
    Approach 4—load duration curve-screening curve approach   27
    Approach 5—all source-load duration curve approach   27
    Approach 6—load duration curve-based capacity expansion models   29
    Approach 7—modified load duration curve-based capacity expansion models   31
    Approach 8—chronological capacity expansion models   32
Summary and timeline of capacity expansion planning approaches   33
References   35

2. Influx of variable renewable energy sources, the way things are going   39

Introduction   39
Policy and incentives driving change   41
Brief history of solar power   43

Brief history of wind power   45
Trends in installed solar and wind capacity and pricing   47
How solar and wind impact dispatch and pricing   50
Variability of solar and wind   53
Net load versus load   55
Challenges renewables impose on baseload generators   61
Effect of geographic diversity   62
Time scale is important   63
Solar and wind degradation rates   65
Baseload is going away, enter residual loads   67
Ramifications for resource planning   69
References   71

3. **Energy storage and conversion**   **73**

Basic principles of energy storage   74
Size and duration   75
Types of energy storage   78
    Pumped hydro   78
    Flywheels   79
    Thermal storage   81
    Other forms of thermal energy storage   81
    Battery energy storage   82
    Compressed air energy storage   88
    Liquid air energy storage   89
Trends in deployment of energy storage   90
Degradation issues   91
Reference metrics for common forms of energy storage   95
Resource planning considerations   95
    Is storage even in the integrated resource plan?   96
    The case for real-time considerations   97
    Chronological capacity expansion to value flexibility   99
    Mandates and subsidies   103
References   105

4. **Renewable fuels for long-term energy storage**   **109**

Introduction   109
Renewable fuels as long-term energy storage   110
What about biofuels?   112
    Direct combustion   113
    Recycled biofuels   114
    Synthetic biofuels   114

Resource planning considerations   115
Hydrogen   115
    Power to hydrogen   116
    Hydrogen to power   119
    Resource planning considerations for hydrogen   121
Direct air carbon capture   126
    High-temperature aqueous solution direct air capture   127
    Low-temperature solid sorbent direct air capture   128
    Resource planning considerations for direct air capture   128
Methanation: combining hydrogen and carbon   129
    Catalytic/thermochemical methanation   130
    Biological methanation   130
    Resource planning considerations for methanation   130
Final thoughts on renewable fuels   131
References   134

5. Long-term capacity expansion planning   139

Introduction   139
Costs in capacity expansion   140
    Operating expenditures   140
    Fixed operations and maintenance   140
    Capital expenditures   141
The supply stack and marginal cost   142
Net load and the supply stack   145
Real-time dispatch   145
Capacity factors   147
Screening curves   148
Load duration curve   151
    Using the load duration curve for long-term planning   152
Generic five-step capacity expansion framework, traditional approach   153
    Convergence contingent on reserve provision and reliability   155
    Production cost models   157
    Concerns related to traditional approaches, particularly for systems with
    variable renewable energy   158
    Importance of dynamic features   160
    Attempted fixes to the traditional approach   162
Advanced approaches—chronological long-term planning models   163
Capacity expansion models for regional and policy initiatives   167
Final considerations for resource planners and analysts   168
References   170

6. Illustrating concepts with examples   173

How flexibility reduces curtailment and maximizes the value of variable
renewable energy sources   173
The impact of increasing variable renewable energy penetration on day
ahead and real-time pricing   177
  Examples of variable renewable energy driving baseload and intermediate
  resources out of the market   183
  Resource planning considerations   184
Ancillary services   185
  Flexible capacity in organized markets   186
  Example from SPP (2014)   187
  Example from NYISO (2016)   187
  Example from ERCOT (2016)   188
  Example from SPP (2018)   190
  Example from CAISO (2019)   191
  Resource planning considerations   192
  Energy storage (and flexible capacity in general) in integrated resource plans   194
The future direction of integrated resource plans   197
References   200

7. Pathways to 100% decarbonization   203

Learning from the past   203
The definition of "100%": the importance of semantics   206
Pathways to 100%   207
  The path to 100% renewable   208
  The path to 100% carbon-free   214
  The path to 100% carbon-neutral (net-zero)   218
  Summary of the pathways to 100%   223
A comparison of different pathways using capacity expansion analyses   224
  New-build capacity by scenario   226
  Land use   226
  Generation, load, curtailment, and air emissions   227
  Timing of use of power to methane in the 100% carbon-neutral scenario   228
  Long-term storage potential of power to gas   229
  Costs   230
  Summary   231
Final thoughts on pathways to 100% and the importance of resource planning   232
References   234

Index   239

Preface

Electric utilities must continually reassess when and how they install new generation capacity to meet load reliably. For many years the pool of technologies utilities could choose from was rather narrow, and associated costs, performance, and other factors were well understood. Accordingly, they could use straightforward approaches toward valuation to make choices they were confident in and were easily understood by shareholders or regulators. These plans are most often contained in an integrated resource plan, or IRP. The IRP is a document prepared on a recurring basis that provides a roadmap of the utility's plans for capacity expansion, associated costs, and financial impacts, and a description of how valuations were performed to justify choices. While all utilities are not required to produce public versions of IRP documents, practically all electric utilities prepare these plans on a regular basis.

Today the electric power sector is being driven by a common desire to decarbonize, couched in terms of 100% renewable energy. Commitments are made to gradually phase out fossil fuels and replace energy production with solar, wind, hydroelectric, and other carbon-free energy sources, such as nuclear. Energy storage is required to time-shift overproduction of renewable energy to periods with lulls in the same. However, serious complications arise when trying to apply legacy resource planning approaches to more modern power systems. For example, equilibrium energy balance assumptions embodied in load-duration-curve capacity expansion approaches assume all resources are dispatchable and only generate only when needed. Clean power systems, in contrast, have large amounts of nondispatchable solar and wind, which have both seasonal fluctuations and volatile output, requiring new and more explicitly time-dependent approaches for planning purposes. The planning process is made even more complex by the much wider pool of technologies to choose from. For example, it was not too long ago that textbooks on energy economics described electricity as a commodity that had to be instantly consumed because it could not be stored. Today there are a host of renewable energy storage technologies each with different attributes, cost, performance, scaling capabilities, and so on. There is growing awareness of land use requirements for renewables, a new dimension that raises environmental concerns. The thought processes and mathematics behind legacy planning approaches are simply insufficient to support this new renewable dominated world.

While many electric utilities are exploring new and more dynamic planning approaches to form the basis of their IRPs, my observation has been that we "are not quite there" yet. Utilities use IRP planning approaches they are familiar with, and often this is what is expected from shareholders and regulators. But as we add more variable renewables, the outcomes often fall short of what was expected, evidenced by cost overruns, higher emissions, and reliability issues. Changing modeling paradigms can be a costly endeavor, involving learning curves not just for utilities, but also for policy makers and regulators. The cost is rather small, however, considering that the outcome will be a far more efficient and robust power system that will save ratepayers billions of dollars.

This book was written to provide guidance for the transition from simple legacy planning to more dynamic state-of-the-art approaches required for high renewable penetration. An overview of the origins of electric utilities and simple planning approaches used in the past sets the stage for how we got to where we are today. The evolution of solar, wind, and other renewable technologies as well as energy storage is presented, with discussion of how their unique features necessitate new planning approaches. New planning approaches are presented along with examples of utilities on the cutting edge of the planning space. Numerical examples are provided to demonstrate concepts. And finally, a review of different approaches to a 100% clean energy state is provided to guide planners and policy makers. The target audience for this work includes utility executives, staff, analysts, policy makers, consultants, regulators, environmentalists, and academics interested in how we can reach 100% clean energy targets.

CHAPTER 1

Introduction to electric utilities and how they plan for the future

Introduction

Affordable and reliable electricity is a fundamental building block of modern society. Electricity provides clean lighting in our homes, at our workplaces, on the streets, with no smoke or fumes from open flames. We use it to cool our homes in the summer and heat them in the winter. It breathes life into industrial facilities. Silent and unseen, its unceasing flow allows us to tap into the digital world with our televisions, computers, and smartphones [1].

Billions of people depend on the electrical grid every day without thinking of where the electricity comes from. At most they might think of it in passing when the electricity bill arrives from the local utility. There is, however, a growing consensus, from everyday people through the highest political bodies, to divest from fossil fuel use due to environmental concerns related to CO_2 emissions, which are believed to drive climate change. Greater numbers of people are pressuring their governments and utilities to strive toward the use of carbon-free, renewable resources, with some demanding that 100% of our electricity comes from renewables such as wind and solar.

Most people are not aware of the complex industrial, engineering, and economic hurdles that had to be overcome to get to where we are today, let alone what it will take to get where they want to go. Understanding the history of the utility industry, combined with the emergence of new forms of energy production and storage and the analytics required to stitch all the pieces together, is critical for modernizing and advancing toward a world with 100% affordable renewable energy. We must understand fundamental questions and how to answer them—where does electricity come from, and what does it cost?

While there are countless opinions and ideas around the production and consumption of electricity, to understand the issues, we require a common understanding of how electric utilities operate and plan for the

Electric Utility Resource Planning
DOI: https://doi.org/10.1016/B978-0-12-819873-5.00001-0

future. Long-range plans (LRPs), also referred to in the industry as integrated resource plans (IRPs), are planning documents used by utilities to characterize their best view of the coming years; 5, 10, or more years into the future, and to determine the optimal mix of resources they must maintain to satisfy customer loads and maintain reliability. The plan typically accounts for changing load profiles, variations in expected fuel prices, existing power plants, and potential retirement of the same as well as the need for new resources, what they could potentially be, and their costs. Once these factors are accounted for, they must be analyzed to answer the following question: What mix of resources for some future date provides maximum reliability at lowest cost? As we will see, using the same assumptions for a given utility, one can get dramatically different answers depending on the analytical approach used to address the question.

Many utility systems today still use approaches that were modern 50 years ago, however, more rigorous approaches to planning provide a more accurate picture in a world with high-renewable penetration. Simple approaches that worked in the past do not strictly apply to modern power systems because renewable sources such as wind and solar do not behave at all like traditional fossil-fueled generation. This chapter addresses the history of the electric utility industry and introduces the thought processes and challenges utility planners, policymakers, regulators, researchers, and politicians have faced in the past. It discusses how that institutional momentum is driving some of the outcomes we see today and influencing our plans for tomorrow.

Electric utilities: the basics

There are thousands of electric utilities across the planet, each with its own technology mix in its power generation portfolio, from hydropower to nuclear, from coal to natural gas, from biofuels to renewables. They each have different localized idiosyncrasies to deal with and varying regulatory pressures. Depending on the utility, they can even have different mission statements. For example, a municipal electric utility exists to provide reliable low-cost electricity to the residents of that city, and decisions are made, to a large extent, by elected city councils and/or mayors who must answer to voters. At a broader scale, some government-owned utilities provide similar services to entire nations, with decisions made again by elected officials. Electric cooperatives, member-owned utilities, tasked with providing reliable electricity to residents within their footprint also strive to minimize costs for customers, and decisions are made by their board of directors. Then there are investor-owned utilities (IOUs). These can be large or small. They are required to maintain reliability and competitive pricing, which is generally capped or subject to market rates set by regulatory bodies but are profit-making businesses. Across this, spectrum of utility types is an overlay of government regulations and governing bodies whose purpose is to ensure compliance with laws such as air emission standards or renewable portfolio standards.

One common factor cuts across all utility types. They plan in a way that minimizes costs, which is challenging as there are numerous costs to consider; operational costs such as fuel, staffing, and maintenance; capital costs such as new power plants or major overhauls; compliance costs such as addition of complicated and expensive emission controls on an older plant. Lower costs mean lower customer pricing or, for IOUs, greater profit.

If the utilities are focused on reducing cost, it would be natural to ask how "cost" is defined and/or calculated. This seems like a simple question, until you dig into the details. Several factors were mentioned above such as fuel, capital cost, compliance costs, etc. These are each complicated, interrelated, and often time-dependent. For a utility to prove they are minimizing cost, either to themselves, to regulators, or to customers or voters, there must be some common basis, or so one would think. In reality, the concept of quantifying costs is an evolving discipline. There are countless peer-reviewed articles in engineering and economics journals over the course of decades dedicated to questions related to how costs are calculated for utilities. And there are a host of approaches used in practice that can vary dramatically from one utility to the next. Given greater resource choices, ever greater regulatory and societal pressures, and evolving technologies, the complexity of the question has only increased over time.

All utilities are at some stage on the "evolutionary scale" of cost calculations that started with the simplistic approaches of the first utilities and progressed through ever-more complex methodologies to what is considered the state-of-the-art today. The complexity of the cost question increased as the number of power plants grew to keep pace with the dramatic explosion of electricity consumers across broader geographic expanses. New technologies emerged with varying costs and reliant on a wider array of fuels, in addition to having widely disparate technical features such as start times, start costs, minimum up and downtimes, minimum stable loads, varying needs for emission controls, and water use. Approaches that worked well for the early utilities are not applicable for the large modern utility. There are, however, legacy issues. Utility staff and management may be comfortable with a certain methodology and apprehensive of investing in the training and software necessary to apply more complex approaches. The trend toward modern cost optimization approaches is happening, but not everyone is at the same place on the evolutionary scale.

To understand how and why this range of cost-economic calculations even exists requires understanding a bit about the early history of electric utilities and the evolution of the approaches in time. This first chapter of the book is dedicated to an exploration of the early history of electric utilities through the modern day and an introduction to basic planning approaches. This information will form a building block for the following chapters.

The early history of the electric utility

The first examples of electric utilities emerged in the 1870s with the world's first generating stations, facilities that used something, be it water/hydropower, or combustion of fossil fuels, to generate electricity. The initial driver was to take advantage of the newly invented light bulb as an alternative to gas/kerosene lamps and/or candles. One of the first generating stations was installed by Lord Armstrong to power his house in 1878. Lord Armstrong built an estate called Cragside, located in Northumberland, England, in which he integrated a hydroelectric generator to produce electricity to power everything from electric lights to a dishwasher [2]. The nearby city of Godalming, in 1881, built the first street lamps that took advantage of electricity from hydropower [3].

In 1882, Thomas Edison's Edison Illuminating Company built the first coal-fired generating station in Manhattan, United States. This facility was called the Pearl Street Station and initially served fewer than 100 customers, including street lighting and building lighting. Within 2 years, the number of customers had increased to 500. The concept of a generating station within a municipality spread rapidly. For example, the Borough of Chambersburg, PA, less than 300 miles from Manhattan, started official discussions of what it would take to build a power plant in their town in August of 1888. By September 1889, the residents of Chambersburg voted on a bond resolution to fund the plant, and by February 1890, the "lights went on," powering a total of 40 street lamps. The Borough of Chambersburg is still in the utility business and is one of the oldest municipal utilities in the United States [4]. The emergence of municipal utilities quickly spreads across North America. For example, while Chambersburg, Pennsylvania was considering a power plant, the city of Albuquerque opened its first electric light utility in 1883, almost 30 years before the state of New Mexico was admitted to the United States as its 47th state [5]. In 1886, Japanese immigrant Hutchlon Ohnick was granted a franchise for gas and electric service by the City Council of Phoenix, Arizona, giving rise to the Phoenix Electric Light Company (Fig. 1.1). The first power plant they built was a "fifty horsepower" unit that could power 45 lights at 1500 candlepower each, by burning mesquite wood collected in the surrounding desert and hauled to the site by mules [6]. The Phoenix Electric Light Company was the foundation of what would later become Arizona Public Service, a regulated IOU now serving

Figure 1.1 Display in lobby of Arizona Public Service headquarters (Phoenix, AZ, United States) commemorating the beginnings of the utility.

2.7 million customers [7]. Emergence of utilities and expansion of electrical power was mirrored across the globe in quick succession. For example, Tokyo Electric Lighting commenced operation in Japan in 1886 [8]. The Municipal Council of Sydney (Australia) first powered electric lights in 1904 [9]. Practically all of these first electric utilities started with a single generating plant primarily dedicated to street lighting.

The commercial success of these small generating stations was not guaranteed, as street lighting was traditionally provided by gas companies. Fierce competition arose between the newly founded electric utilities and gas suppliers particularly for lighting of public spaces such as streets [10]. As generation and distribution of electricity became more cost-effective, it was natural for municipalities to consider electric lighting as a cost-effective alternative to traditional sources. The invention of electric street cars in the 1880s greatly expanded the potential need for electricity from a strictly night-time service to something that was needed to some extent all day, every day [11]. This, in turn, drove up demand, which led to competition and technological advances, which in turn led to rapidly growing economies of scale and reduction of electricity price.

In the United States, by 1900 electricity sales exceeded 100 million US dollars [12], and the service was expanding beyond a few simple light poles directly connected to a generating station. It became quickly apparent that the industry had to provide infrastructure to serve the demand based on three central pillars that are still the backbone of every electric power system in existence today;

Generation: The sources that generate MW for delivery across transmission and distribution systems.

Transmission: The infrastructure needed to move large volumes of high-voltage electricity from generators to the distribution system(s) to serve load. Volumes of electricity are moved at high voltage because it is more efficient and cost-effective to do so in this manner.

Distribution: The infrastructure needed to step-down high-voltage electricity to lower voltages that can be used directly by the end user(s).

Early on the electric needs of consumers were met by a mix of small private enterprises, such as the Pearl Street Station, or municipals, such as the Borough of Chambersburg. Municipals dominated in the United States with more than 3000 municipally owned power companies in the early 1920s. However, private utility holding companies were formed and in the business of buying and consolidating to take advantage of economies of scale. So much so that by the early 1930s more than

1200 municipal electric utilities had gone out of business or been sold [11,13]. By 1932 in the United States privately held IOUs generated and received revenues for more than 95% of all MWh sold in the United States and provided electricity to more than 90% of all customers [10,11,14]. Some or all of the transmission and distribution services were retained by municipal or state agencies and have since been overtaken by the same consolidation, so that today's transmission and distribution are often held by large IOUs as well. In 2019, the electricity generated by IOUs in the United States served more than two-thirds of the US population, with the remainder being provided by a mix of municipal utilities, member-owned electric cooperatives, and a small number of federally chartered, government-run utilities.

The early stages of the evolution of cost approaches

Regardless of the organization of an electric utility, public or private, economic planning for a small station in the early 1900s was rather straightforward. The decision variables included at a minimum, and not taking consideration of transmission or distribution, the following;

- *Capacity (MW)*: an estimate of capacity needs, how many kW or MW the plant could be expected to serve at any one instant in time, typically sized for the maximum or peak load.
- *Energy (MWh)*: an estimate of the energy that would be generated, in terms of MW need times the time needed to provide for that load, often expressed as MWh.
- *Owners' cost ($ per kW of capacity)*: cost to build the power plant, including the cost of the equipment, cost to install the equipment, land purchase, any infrastructure improvements such as roads, and the cost to connect the plant to transmission or distribution networks as well as permitting and legal costs.
- *Fuel*: type of fuel used and cost of the fuel.
- *Efficiency*: efficiency of the power plant determines the amount and subsequent cost of fuel needed to generate MWh.
- *Operational cost*: annual costs to run and maintain the facility, from the cost of payroll and benefits to property taxes and/or utilities such as sewer or water.

Putting all of these factors together allows one, via a number of simple algebraic approaches, to estimate the total cost of providing power to customers. This allows the plant owner to determine what they must charge per MWh of electricity generated, also allowing for any profit margins or required return on investment. If the cost per MWh to provide for street lighting, for example, is less than the alternative gas-fired lamps then electric lighting is competitive.

In the early stages of utility development, the investment decisions were rather straightforward as there were only a handful of companies that made equipment that could generate electricity. The equipment was based on a very narrow pool of technology choices and fuel options were limited. As time went on, a host of changes happened across the electric utility space, including the consolidation of smaller utilities into larger ones and covering broader geographic ranges. Now cities became loads, and the generators were not always near the load, requiring transmission lines to move energy from where it was produced to step-down stations that energize distribution systems. A utility could no longer simply say they had 100 customers being served by 1 plant, they could have tens of thousands of customers across broad expanses being served by 10, 20, 50, or more generators. Power delivery increasingly became a network problem, with the loads considered as nodes or sinks (of MWh), the generators being sources (of MWh) and the transmission system being the network of physical cables moving MWh from sources to sinks. While complexities related to network systems are relevant, the idea of how changing technology and fuel types complicate cost decisions was, and still is, a fundamental issue in utility planning, so let us look at some of the technologies that emerged during the early years, up to the 1960s and 1970s.

Varying technology types that made up (and still make up) the generation mix of most utilities

Historically power generation relied on fuel combustion. Fuels such as coal to oils of various types, to wood or other forms of biomass, to gaseous fuels (natural gas). In general, fuel is burned to provide a driving force for a shaft that in turn spins a generator that generates electricity. The same is true for hydroelectric and wind turbines, which simply use water and wind for the same purpose. Regardless, power plants that burn fuel are generally referred to as thermal plants.

In thermal plants, fuel is burned in a combustion chamber. The combustion chamber admits air and fuel. Carbon in the fuel reacts with oxygen in the air to provide heat and pressure, which are converted to mechanical power that drives a shaft connected to the generator. In some cases, as with combustion turbines (CTs), the products of combustion drive turbine blades connected to the shaft. In others, such as reciprocating engines, combustion moves pistons that are connected to the shaft. Boiler plants have a combustion chamber connected to heat exchangers that convert water to steam, which is then used to spin a steam turbine connected to a shaft (that turns a generator). In all cases, the heat of combustion is converted to mechanical energy and then to electricity. The combustion gases cool in the process, so that what comes out as exhaust is very hot, but considerably cooler than the temperature in the combustion chamber.

Coal boiler plants

Across the entire history of coal-fired power generation, one thing has remained constant. In all cases, the coal is burned in a boiler that extracts heat from the coal combustion and uses the heat to convert water to steam. This boiler is often referred to as a heat recovery steam generator (HRSG). The steam is then used to turn a steam turbine which is connected to a generator, which makes electricity.

Coal-fired power plants are similar to most thermal technologies in that bigger is better. The larger the plant, the greater the economy of scale, and the lower the investment cost on a per kW basis simultaneous with maximizing fuel efficiency. A 1000 MW coal plant will have lower cost ($/kW owners' cost, and higher efficiency) than a 10 MW coal plant.

A coal-fired boiler plant in the early 1900s might be in the 1−10 MW size range [15] with an efficiency of 10%−15%. By 1930s, coal-fired plants in the 300 MW range were available with higher efficiencies. By 1970s, unit ratings in excess of 1000 MW were the norm, with net efficiencies greater than 30%. Net efficiency refers to the fuel needed per MWh of energy delivered to the transmission system and is different than gross efficiency. Gross efficiency refers to the amount of fuel needed per MWh as measured at the generator itself. Net efficiency accounts for parasitic loads, losses across the step-up transformer, and any loads within the plant itself, such as lighting. Net efficiency is the metric of meaning for utility planners as it measures the fuel needed to provide useable energy, while gross efficiency is often used by equipment OEMs as that is the efficiency they can measure and test in manufacturing facilities.

The prevalence of coal as an abundant and low-cost fuel is why coal has been, and in some places is still, the dominant fuel source for electricity. As of 2019, countries such as India and China produce most of their electricity with coal, although the share of coal generation is expected to fall with time. In the United States, from 1950 to 2000, coal provided between 45% and 60% of all US power needs, dropping sharply after 2000 as aggressive environmental regulations limiting coal combustion were put in place. However, the bigger factor leading to coals reduced dominance in the United States was the emergence of hydraulic fracturing (fracking) for natural gas, which provided a lower cost fuel and lower subsequent power prices, putting coal generation at a competitive disadvantage.

Coal plants are a subset of a broader class of generation technologies referred to as boiler plants. Alternate fuels can be burned, such as biomass or natural gas. Given the large investment utilities have made into coal-fired boiler plants, in some cases, it is advantageous to convert them to burn natural gas as opposed to retiring them This allows them to leverage the lower fuel prices, higher efficiencies, and lower emission profile of natural gas combustion. [16].

Combustion turbines

The CT is the workhorse of most modern utilities, able to burn several fuels from liquid/oils to natural gas. The first patent for the technology was filed by John Barber in the United Kingdom in 1790s. It was not until 1939 that the first working example of anything resembling a modern CT was installed, a 4 MW unit at a municipal power station in Neuchatel, Switzerland, with an efficiency of 17%[17]. In post-World War II, there was a race to develop CTs for aircraft propulsion and stationary use. In 1949 the first CT to generate power in the United States was installed at the Belle Isle facility in Oklahoma, by Oklahoma Gas & Electric Company [18]. The 3.5 MW turbine was added to an existing coal-fired power plant. Since that time, the basic inner workings of CTs have remained virtually unchanged, with better efficiencies and economies of scale mostly a product of advances in materials science that allows for higher operating temperatures. At present, a wide range of manufacturers provides CTs in sizes ranging from 1 MW to more than 500 MW per unit. Efficiencies for modern units range from 30% to 40%, depending on the type and size of the CT, and they can burn a number of fuels, from kerosene to oil to natural gas.

In general, CTs fall into two groups, referred to as "Frame" and "Aero," short for aeroderivative. Frame CTs are generally large, many greater than 100 MW, and designed for industrial or electric utility use. They are typically low cost (on a $/kW basis) and have lower efficiencies than Aero CTs, in the 30%−35% range. Frame CTs are typically used for peaking services with low run hours per year and are generally not considered for long-run hours or for frequent starts. Aero CTs are derived from aerospace propulsion designs and are more compact and more efficient than Frame CTs, around 40%. They are generally smaller in output, with the largest units reaching 100 MW, and are used for applications ranging from intermediate (a few thousand hours per year) to peaking (a few hundred hours per year).

CTs are sensitive to altitude and ambient temperature, with output and efficiency falling at higher elevations and higher temperatures, mainly due to decreased air density related to each. To compensate some CT installations use intercoolers, which remove heat from inlet air and increase air density entering the combustion chamber, allowing the CTs to maintain output and efficiency at higher temperatures. Other approaches use direct water injection to increase output and boost efficiency. Intercooling and water injection are typically found on more advanced Aero CTs.

Combined-cycle combustion turbines

A jet engine for aircraft propulsion uses the exhaust energy to move the plane forward. When a generator is added to a CT for land-based power generation, much of that exhaust energy is used to turn the rotors that turn the generator, but a good amount of fuel energy leaves the unit as hot exhaust gas. That is, if a CT takes 100 units of fuel in and generates 30 units of electricity, the remaining 70 units of fuel energy is sent out the stack as hot exhaust. Starting in the 1940s, engineers leveraged decades of experience in boiler plants to leverage the heat from CT exhaust. The first use of CT heat recovery occurred in 1949, when General Electric (GE) used the exhaust heat from a CT to perform feedwater heating of a 35 MW conventional boiler plant [19]. While an example of heat recovery from CTs, boiler preheating is not strictly a combined cycle. The first combined-cycle CT (CCCT), taking hot exhaust gas to make steam to power a steam turbine, was installed by an Austrian utility at Korneuburg in 1960 with an efficiency of 32.5% [20].

The allure of combining the CT with an HRSG/steam turbine is that you do not have to burn any more fuel, rather you are simply getting more power out. Thus, a 100 MW CT with a 35% efficiency can be linked with an HRSG and a steam turbine to generate approximately 30 MW more power without burning any additional fuel. While modern CT efficiency tops off at approximately 40%, the same unit in combined-cycle configuration can achieve efficiencies of 50%–55%, and in some cases, even higher. Like coal power plants, combined-cycle plants become less expensive ($/kW) the larger the plant. Fully predesigned and preengineered combined-cycle facilities were made available to the utility industry by GE and Westinghouse in the early 1960s.

Frame CTs are typically paired with HRSGs and steam turbines due to their low $/kW cost and lower simple cycle (CT only) efficiency. A CT with lower efficiency rejects greater amounts of high temperature exhaust gas than a more efficient Aero CT. This larger stream of higher temperature gas from Frame CTs is better suited for maximizing the efficiency of the HRSG and steam turbine, such that the overall efficiency of a frame CT-based CCCT is higher than that from a CCCT using a more efficient (and more expensive, on a $/kW basis) Aero CT.

Reciprocating engines (Recips)

In 1794, Thomas Mead and Robert Street each obtained patents in England for what can be considered the first spark-ignited internal combustion engines. In the late 1850s and early 1860s, Belgian engineer Jean J. Lenoir made advances in spark-ignition Recip technology, leading to the first mass-produced Recip engines in France, then later in England, for use in horseless carriages. This advance was noted by the magazine "Scientific American" in 1860 claiming "the age of steam is ended" by Lenoirs engine, in reference to Recip engines envisioned as replacing steam engines for locomotive and propulsion purposes [21]. Further advancements were made, including George Braytons patents in the 1870s for multipiston spark-ignited internal combustion engines. The first gasoline-type engine that resembles what we now call a "gasoline engine" for cars and trucks was invented by Nikolaus Otto in 1876, using a means to compress the fuel-air mixture which in turn increased efficiency. In the 1890s Rudolf Diesel filed a blitzkrieg of patents in several European countries and in the United States for varying design stages of internal combustion reciprocating engines that relied on compression ignition. Unlike spark-ignited engines, high compression ratios in diesel engines auto-ignite the fuel mixture. Most early applications of Recips were for automotive and marine propulsion.

Most people know of "engines" as something found in cars, trucks, and diesel locomotives. They all have a series of cylinders that combust fuel to move a piston, which in turn rotates a shaft. That shaft can be used to propel a vehicle through a drive-shaft, to propel a boat via a propeller, or to turn a generator to make electricity. The majority of large transport and cruise ships on the high seas use massive reciprocating engines for propulsion, with some units being close to 100 MW in size. While smaller power generating units are typically and historically used for emergency power at hospitals or other critical infrastructure, they have been used for primary power generation by utilities for decades. Installed globally for smaller applications (sub 10−20 MW), it was not until the 1970s that some of the first large-scale (100, 200 + MW) reciprocating engine power stations were built in Latin America to power economies that did not have access to coal or natural gas but did have access to low-cost liquid fuels that cannot be burned in CTs. These oil-fired Recip plants used compression ignition engines. More recently spark-ignited natural gas-fired Recip machines have entered utility service in markets with access to natural gas.

There are three different categories of Recip technologies based on rotational speed: high (1000 + rpm), medium (500−900 rpm), and slow (sub 150 rpm) speed. Any of these can be compression ignited (diesel), spark ignited (gaseous fuels), or dual fuel (capable of burning liquid or gaseous fuels, dependent on compression ignition of a liquid pilot fuel). The size and efficiency increase with slower speeds. High-speed machines are low efficiency but small and compact, ideal for backup/standby or peaking power generation, generally under 5 MW in size. Slow-speed machines are generally compression ignited, running on liquid fuels, with very high efficiency, but are large (50 + MW per unit), and most often used for ship propulsion. There are some stationary power plants using slow-speed Recips, but their large size makes delivery to inland sites difficult and expensive. The majority of stationary Recip power plants use medium-speed machines, typically 5−20 MW per unit, which boast high efficiency, are robust across a wide array of operational profiles and can be transported to remote sites with commercially available equipment such as barge, rail, or trailer.

The allure of reciprocating engines is their high efficiency and flexibility. While a boiler plant can burn oil or gas, its efficiency maxes out at around 30%. Reciprocating engines burning the same fuel can exceed 40%−45% efficiency. Due to their success, further evolutions in the technology resulted in reduced start times, making them ideal for renewable integration. Unit size for power generation ranges from 5−20 MW, and a power station typically consists of multiple units for plant sizes of 100, 200, or more MW. The largest reciprocating plant to date was built in the country of Jordan in 2014, a 600 MW multifuel (gas and liquid) plant comprised of 38 Wärtsilä Recip engines.

Hydro

Hydro has long been a staple of power systems. Long before hydropower was used to generate electricity, it had been used to provide mechanical power and was instrumental in the industrial revolution. The first hydroelectric power plant in the United States was a 12.5 kW unit installed in Appleton, Wisconsin in 1882. Within 7 years, more than 200 hydroelectric plants were in operation in the United States. Most of the hydropower is provided by reservoirs, where a river is dammed, and water released from the base of the dam spins turbines that generate electricity. In 1936, the Hoover Dam, which captured the flow of the Colorado River, was opened and generated 1345 MW of electricity. More recently, the Three Gorges Dam in China was built to generate 22,500 MW. Some countries including Brazil, Canada, Norway, and Venezuala generate more than 50% of their electricity using hydro. Paraguay is entirely powered by hydro.

While hydro facilities offer renewable energy, they can be quite expensive and are themselves massive civil engineering projects that can take decades to complete. More recently, concerns over the ecological impacts of dams on aquatic life, river health, and biodiversity have narrowed the number of potentially new hydro generators to a small number, particularly in developed countries.

Nuclear

And finally, nuclear power. The first nuclear power plant installed in the United States was a 60 MW facility in 1957 at the Shippingport Atomic Power Station, located on the Ohio River and operated by Duquesne Light Company. Energy from this plant primarily served the city of

Pittsburgh, Pennsylvania, for 25 years. This plant was retired in 1982, but it provided some of the earliest real-world knowledge on the safe operation of nuclear power facilities and led to an expansion of nuclear power in the United States. By 1989, 109 nuclear reactors were in operation in the United States serving close to 20% of all electric load, second only to coal generation.

As of 2019, the World Nuclear Association reported that 450 power reactors produced 11% of the worlds' electricity [22]. In 2017 there were 13 countries that produced at least 25% of their electricity from nuclear power reactors. In general, due to economies of scale, larger is better, with many more recent units exceeding 1000 MW. These large facilities are expensive to build and take decades to develop and bring online. The dramatic failures at Chernobyl and Fukushima led many countries to question, if not halt or even reverse, the pace of nuclear development.

Many policymakers and utilities are concerned with maintaining nuclear assets already in service, as they are large and critical pieces of their energy supply portfolio. They are also carbon-free generation sources, leading some environmental interests to promote their use over fossil fuel sources. A large concern has arisen in recent years given the fact that nuclear reactors are not flexible. They are designed to run at full load for thousands of hours in a row, they are not designed to start/stop or cycle from low to high loads on a regular basis. This can cause challenges for high-renewable systems, particularly when wind and solar are providing all or close to all of the MW needs for a given hour. What does the utility then do with its nuclear generation? They cannot cycle the nuclear unit downward in output, so low-cost wind and solar generation must be rejected from the system in preference for higher cost nuclear. This is always a possibility, but it is not sustainable in the long run.

To this end, a new wave of nuclear facilities is under development, called small modular reactors (SMRs). While a traditional nuclear plant has one large reactor producing hundreds to more than a thousand MWs, SMR plants make use of numerous smaller reactors, each less than 300 MW in size. Smaller in size and based on standardized designs, SMRs can be installed in small increments to satisfy specific capacity needs, with cost benefits over large custom-designed central station facilities. SMR design and implementation are still in its infancy but are gaining increasing support from several governments, including the US Department of Energy [23].

Other

Throughout the past century, there were other forms of electrical generation being developed and installed globally. These include biofuels, trash-to-steam, geothermal, wind, and solar power. However, the super-majority of generation globally has been provided by the major technologies listed above. Utilities with a relatively large share of renewables in their fleet of assets still have a tremendous amount of generating capacity based on the technologies listed above.

How and why utilities have chosen to install various mixes of technologies in the past has been based on economic and regulatory environments, which vary regionally. Also, the types of generating capacity utilities could consider were quite narrow. Initially, the investment decisions were rather localized and straightforward, but as nations became electrified and utility loads grew and became more diverse, the age of long-range planning came into being.

Long-range planning (also referred to as long-term planning or integrated resource planning)

Insofar as utilities are expected to serve instantaneous demand at any moment, without exception, planning today for expectations years from now can have a dramatic impact on what is installed to meet future loads. And planning must occur years before any action is taken given their historical size (hundreds of MW) and the time required to complete the siting, environmental permitting, financing, interconnection studies, fuel supply agreements, construction, and physical interconnection with the grid. While utilities may be shifting toward more renewables, or a wider array of smaller distributed generating sources, the process can take just as long. Practically every electric utility has some working process for long-range planning.

Long-range, long-term, or integrated resource planning all refer to a similar process by which a utility formalizes long-term plans for maintaining reliability. In the United States, regulatory pressures reaching back to the 1970s [24] led to formal requirements for utilities to file IRPs. State and federal agencies were placing greater emphasis on ensuring utilities were producing strategies that delivered lowest costs for ratepayers, driven by concerns that this may not actually be happening. Several states enacted legislation requiring IOUs to file regular IRPs with state regulatory agencies called Public Utility Commissions (PUCs). The IRP generally contains a full assessment of the utility's current capabilities to meet load as well as a 20- to 30-year forward projection of plans to address forecasted power demand and changes in fuel availability and price. In other words, the purpose of the IRP is to provide a long-term plan that ensures reliability, compliance with state and federal regulations, and adherence to principles of least-cost planning.

A 20- to 30-year planning horizon is used because development, permitting, and construction of a large central power plant can often take 10 or more years. When a utility breaks ground for construction of a new power plant, it has already spent considerable time and money rationalizing the need for the investment and completing financial and regulatory reviews. Most IRPs also include 3- or 5-year plans indicating next steps. For example, if the utility forecasts a need for an additional 5000 MW of capacity over the next 20 years, with 300 MW being built in the next 5 years, the IRP will provide greater detail on how it plans to meet that shorter term 300 MW need, and place less emphasis on what might happen 20 years in the future. In the United States, as of the writing of this work, more than 30 states require periodic filing of IRPs by IOUs, many of which are made available to the public. Municipal utilities and electric cooperatives are generally not required to file IRPs with PUCs, even if they are quite large, however, most recognize their value and engage in some form of the IRP process. These plans are not necessarily made public but are presented to the CEO, Board of Directors, and Management to inform the direction of their business moving forward.

This planning process is followed globally and is referred to at times as LRP [25]. While not necessarily a legal requirement, the electricity sector in China generally follows the basics of least-cost planning. South Africa is one of the few countries that legally requires IRPs for the electricity sector at the national level. European Union member states are required to follow "rational planning techniques" that mirror the concepts in an IRP. Hydro-dominated countries like Brazil may not formally require utilities to draft IRPs, but they do require planning methodologies to address societal needs during drought years when hydroelectric production is curtailed. While formal requirements mandating development of IRPs is most pronounced in the United States [25], the elements of IRP planning are used globally by government agencies and academia to assess policy implications or potential trajectory changes due to societal needs and technical advances. For example, in 2015, Pagnarith and Limmeechokchai

[26] applied a systematic IRP approach to evaluate optimal power generation investment decisions throughout Cambodia, Laos, Thailand, and VietNam. In 2017, Meza et al. [27] used IRP planning approaches to assess the feasibility of a 100% renewable power system in Nicaragua.

Basics of utility long-range planning

LRPs generally have the following three features:
— load forecasting
— capacity expansion/portfolio analysis
— risk/uncertainty assessment

Over the course of decades utility staff and consulting agencies, academic researchers, and regulatory bodies have continuously refined business models and mathematical approaches to quantify each of these three factors.

Load forecasting

Planning for future capacity needs implies a knowledge of load, which is then met by capacity providing energy to meet that load. The utility must understand how much energy to provide (MWh) as well as the expected peak loads (MW) and plan accordingly. A century ago, utilities had small loads and could estimate by hand what future loads may look like, but even then, they could not anticipate technological, social, and economic trends that may affect load growth 5 or 10 years into the future. For example, when utilities were first planning to meet street lighting needs, they did not anticipate the magnitude of energy needed to provide for the emergence of electric street cars or mass adoption of indoor lighting, let alone the difference in energy needs depending on the type of light bulbs used. Fast forward to today, we have far more of our everyday lives connected to the grid, from air conditioning to televisions, from heating to electric car charging, our entire connection to the digital world is dependent on it. Then we have the added complexity of demand-side management, working with customers to determine what loads could be economically shed (or manipulated) during specific times to reduce loads, offsetting (potentially) the need for new generation.

Predicting future electricity demand requires consideration of weather changes, population growth/loss, technology adoption (both new energy-consuming devices and those which provide the same service but use less energy), consumer behavior, prevalence and effectiveness of demand-side management, local and global economic trends. Predicting any of these individual aspects accurately is extremely difficult. Predicting all of them simultaneously to arrive at a robust and accurate portrayal of energy needs and peak loads decades into the future is nearly impossible [28]. As a consequence, utility estimates of future energy and peak load needs are typically not very accurate, with deference given to overestimating loads [29]. This overestimation is a conservative approach to ensure reliability. That is, if a utility underestimates peak load, one particular hot day could lead to blackouts and potentially heat-related deaths due to lack of air conditioning. Alternatively, utilities may be forced to buy emergency power on the spot market during periods of high market stress and high prices. Insofar as utilities are tasked with supplying energy at lowest cost, reliance on volatile markets during times of emergency could violate that premise. Many utilities must also provide for their own reserve margins, excess capacity to account for unforeseen circumstances such as units being unavailable.

While load forecasting is an inexact science, some have observed utilities with heavy reliance on large industrial loads tend to have the largest discrepancies between estimated and observed loads [29]. The reason is suspected to be due to the lumpy nature of large industrial loads and the difficulty inherent in predicting entry, exit, or changing use patterns of industrial loads within a utility service area. Regardless, there are several increasingly complex load forecasting approaches [30,31], yet their accuracy is dependent on several independent factors which all have inherent uncertainty, including the potential impacts of climate change on utility loads [32,33]. Even for small utility systems, the number of complex mathematical approaches for load forecast can give a range of results. For example, in 2014 Idoniboyeobu and Ekanem [34] provided load forecasts for the Akwa Ibom State of Nigeria with a peak load of 130 MW in 2011 and estimated a peak load in 2020 of 248 MW, with two different approaches yielding 5% and 10% growth rates (the larger was chosen as the preferred route as it most accurately captured 2011 peak loads in a calibration).

While electricity load forecasting is pivotal to the planning process, most utilities (and regulatory bodies) recognize the uncertainty inherent in such a difficult task. At some point, without full transparency into the future, they need to make their best attempt at the forecast and plan accordingly. LRPs are typically performed every 1−3 years, so the load forecasts are continuously updated to account for new information.

Capacity expansion planning

This aspect of long-range planning is often referred to simply as "portfolio planning," but whether or not the utility is adding or retiring capacity they generally rely on approaches referred to as "capacity expansion models." If any assets are to be retired, they are simply considered a negative expansion. The question of whether new resources are needed, or older units retired, depends on the load forecast. Once the utility has the load forecast, it can then quickly determine any shortfalls. Are the average and peak loads in excess of what the utility has available in its portfolio of assets? If the answer is no, this does not mean the utility should do nothing. Older assets may be considered for retirement, but often the older capacity is supplanted (if not in whole, then in part) by new, more efficient and cost-effective facilities. In other scenarios, the load could be falling due to efficiency measures on the consumer end, but increasing in a specific transmission constrained load pocket, perhaps due to the construction of new data centers, necessitating new generating capacity locally. Of course, if load growth is occurring and despite active demand-side management, the utility sees a shortfall in capacity, then they will have to add new resources (Fig. 1.2).

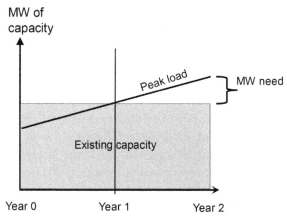

Figure 1.2 Simplified schematic of capacity expansion. At year 0, there is enough capacity to meet peak load requirements. Starting at the beginning of year 1 and to the beginning of year 2, peak load exceeds existing capacity indicating a MW need. If the MW need is served by a new asset that takes 3 years to permit, 1 year for a competitive bidding process, and 2 years to build and be ready to provide electricity, then formal investment in the process of providing for this new MW need has to start 6 years prior to year 1.

Today utilities face greater regulatory burdens with laws aimed at minimizing emissions, maximizing renewable penetration, mandating adoption of specific technologies, etc. In some cases, utilities are obligated to demonstrate to the public that their decisions adhere to least-cost principles [35], which are provided for using capacity expansion planning. Greater detail will be provided later in this chapter on basic ways utilities can demonstrate least cost.

Risk/uncertainty assessment

Once a utility has prepared load forecasts and has methodology in place for capacity expansion/portfolio planning simulations, it must assess the information in the context of risk and uncertainty. It should be noted here that across the utility industry, the terms "risk assessment" and "uncertainty analysis" are often used interchangeably. A negative outcome from uncertainty in assumptions is a risk that utilities must consider. This is not the equivalent of a risk of a physical or cyber–attack. Risks include potential threats from the following:

- Cyber threats that could negatively impact the utilities ability to control assets.
- Physical threats (sabotage) that could impact system or power plant control systems.
- Extreme weather or natural disasters that can damage or destroy power generation and transmission assets.
- Loss of load-serving capabilities due to unplanned outages of individual power plants.
- Variance in outcomes due to uncertainty in the assumptions used for planning purposes.

For cyber threats or to counter physical espionage, utilities take various measures to harden key infrastructure. These can include physical and/or cyber barriers and security systems. Decisions on security measures are typically made by the electric utility independent of the planning process. Natural disasters are by definition "disasters" and it is not possible for an electric utility to have redundancy and backup plans to account for every possible contingency. For example, Hurricane Sandy hits the east coast of the United States in 2012, with high winds toppling down power lines, rising water levels flooding electric substations. Eight million utility customers (across several states) lost electrical power [36]. Hurricane Sandy was just one example out of countless that electric utilities have and will continue to face globally. While utilities may not simulate every potential catastrophe in the planning process, they do attend to these issues with foresight by requiring power plants and associated equipment be built to certain design criteria (e.g., built to withstand certain wind speeds, designed for specific seismic events, flood protection such as levees), based on the best engineering practices applied to local conditions. Estimates of potential new-build pricing used in capacity expansion analysis will generally account for cost impacts related to building to more robust design criteria.

A more immediate risk (from a day-to-day perspective) is related to blackouts caused by mechanical failures. Every power plant is a mechanical system, some more complex than others. Any mechanical system is prone to failure, even when proactive maintenance activities are implemented. Utilities rely on their own experience, information from original equipment manufacturers (OEMs), and/or third parties for data on forced outage rate (FOR). FOR is expressed as percent of hours each year the unit will be down for unplanned maintenance (outages). They also assign values for mean time to repair (MTTR). FOR and MTTR are the basic pieces of information utilities need to calculate loss of load probability (LOLP), which is an estimate of the probability that the utility will not be able to serve load. LOLP is calculated by assessing the utility portfolio in an iterative process where every unit in every power plant is randomly taken out of their total capacity based on FOR estimates. The results can be presented as loss of load expectation (LOLE) as well, the accumulated amount of time (annually) power shortages will occur [37]. Several utility systems use a criterion that LOLE not exceed 0.1 days per year, often expressed as 1 day in 10 years ([1]).

Utilities can manage or understand LOLP/LOLE in the capacity expansion phase by considering value of lost load (VOLL). VOLL assigns a monetary value to reflect economic ramifications of a temporary inability to serve load, such as a blackout, expressed as $/MWh. Economic ramifications of load loss are difficult to quantify, and many approaches are in use today to quantify VOLL [38]. One thing a utility can do is use VOLL estimates to assign a cost to each MWh not served. If the VOLL level is sufficiently high, the model will build capacity or purchase electricity (at lower cost) rather than pay high VOLL penalties. As the model builds additional capacity to reduce or eliminate VOLL costs, it is indirectly improving LOLP and/or LOLE expectations. The interplay between VOLL, LOLE, and LOLP may be an iterative process, as many capacity expansion software products do not calculate LOLE or LOLP, so each simulation to solve for capacity expansion must be postprocessed for LOLE/LOLP.

Closely linked to LOLP/LOLE and VOLL estimations is the concept of a capacity reserve margin. A capacity reserve margin simply means the utility maintains a certain percentage of capacity above and beyond their annual peak load. In the United States, utilities often maintain a capacity reserve margin at a minimum 15%, and similar levels are often required in lieu of more complicated LOLE, LOLP, and VOLL estimates, which can be time-consuming and costly to generate. Internationally, national-level reserve margins of 50% or higher have been observed [39]. Here it should be noted that capacity reserve margins a utility set for itself are not the equivalent of system-wide reserve margins in decentralized energy markets. Utilities may be required by regulatory mechanisms to maintain a specified capacity reserve margin or may opt to do so adhering to "best practices." System loads (at the national, market, or regional level), however, may be served by merchant operators or independent power producers, and the system operators have no mechanism for forcing additional capacity into the market. In general, as electricity markets become decentralized (at a broad regional or national level), capacity reserve margins fall and shortage pricing, or additional mechanisms (e.g., capacity markets), may be required to incentivize new capacity to maintain reserve margins at adequate levels.

Uncertainty analysis is an additional consideration and addresses other forms of potential risk that could lead to suboptimal investments. Utilities do not solve just for capacity expansion for a fixed load forecast and a single trajectory for fuel pricing. They will consider multiple load forecasts (low, medium, and high growth scenarios), which may be impacted by various adoption rates for electric vehicles, multiple weather estimates (comparing long periods of high rain vs drought periods for hydro), potential ranges in fuel pricing across the planning horizon, regulatory uncertainty related to potential carbon taxes and rates. Capacity expansion modeling approaches are mostly deterministic, they yield a specific "answer" given fixed input data, where "answer" equates to a series of investments over time that yields the lowest cost according to the simulation. One way to estimate the range of potential outcomes is to simply run the deterministic model against every convolution of high/medium/low estimates (of load, fuel price, etc.). By analyzing a range of potential outcomes, a utility can then choose the optimal scenario using a variety of metrics and also a bit of expert judgment on the part of utility management. This process is often called scenario analysis.

Reliance on deterministic outcomes alone is often insufficient given the uncertainties not captured by the scenario analysis. Newer elements of modern utility planning do not fit neatly into the scenario analysis approach. Demand-side management participation rates and efficacy can be highly uncertain [40] not just in their adoption rate, but in their efficacy through time. Higher penetrations of variable renewable energy (VREs), such as wind and solar, require that utilities invest in forecasting methodologies to better estimate day-to-day variations between forecast and actual VRE output [41]. However, VREs exhibit seasonal trends and uncertainty related to weather events that are not easy to model or characterize decades into the future. Long-term capacity expansion models typically use annual shape profiles of VRE production that capture their bulk expected contribution to energy production but cannot inform "worst-case" scenarios. VREs and hydro are necessary elements of power systems seeking decarbonization, but they are climate dependent and their output is not strictly correlated with demand. Use of annual shape profiles (typically hourly generation estimates based on historical data) is useful but not necessarily sufficient. If solar profiles are used based on prior years information, they do not necessarily represent future performance. For example, Trainer [42] observed solar irradiation across a number of sites in Australia across a 3-month period in 2010 and found 12 periods of 3 or more consecutive days where solar output was effectively 0. Even if an Australian utility was to capture this using annual solar shape profiles based on 2010 data, future years can and most likely will have similar multiday periods with no solar output but at different times of the year. Northern climates may experience snowfall that covers solar panels completely for days to weeks, and it is not unheard of for wind to fall to nothing for multiday periods. A robust LRP should account for atypical conditions that are extreme, yet credible, based on historical data, and projections of future climate conditions: the conditions must be assessed for each type of VRE (as well as hydro) in isolation, and in concert [43]. For example, a utility with heavy reliance on hydro, wind, and solar may face weather events yielding little to no wind and solar generation during a drought year where hydro resources are already stressed. While plausible, this scenario may not be captured by annual VRE profiles used for capacity decisions. Utilities can address this concern using Monte Carlo analysis, where future portfolios are run against randomly drawn climate (e.g., rainfall) and VRE expectations based on historical (or future anticipated) data. By performing hundreds to thousands of such simulations, the utility can determine "worst-case" planning scenarios which are then used to inform reliability indices and other factors related to uncertainty.

Major approaches to capacity expansion planning

There are numerous texts available that address load forecasting and uncertainty/risk assessment. Brief descriptions were provided above with references to allow the reader to begin exploring these topics, which are evolving rapidly with new approaches under constant development. They are critical to successful resource planning. In this work, focus is primarily on the capacity expansion planning aspect. For the remainder of this work, the phrase "capacity expansion" will be used while understanding a utility may be reducing capacity or changing its mix of resources (through time).

Capacity expansion planning can take several forms depending on how a utility expects to make decisions, understanding in all cases, the utility is trying to minimize cost. At the simplest level, a very small utility may need 100 MW of capacity and just based on experience they probably know how the asset will be dispatched. For example, they might need 100 MW for 30% of the hours in each year. How do they decide what is "lowest cost"? It is a simple question, but there are several ways to find the answer and they do not all give the same results!

Approach 1—capital cost

Capital cost approach is most appropriate if a utility knows the MW of capacity needed and knows the type of capacity is from a very small pool of choices. In 1919 it might have been a coal plant. In 2019 it might be wind. If the technology is known, and regardless of manufacturer, performance and maintenance costs, land requirements, and interconnection costs are basically the same across manufacturers, then the only real differentiator is installed cost. For a small utility detailed capacity expansion planning may be considered unnecessary, they simply quantify a MW need, based on a specific technology, and issue request for proposals (RFPs). The lowest cost bid wins. This approach also holds if a utility is mandated to install a specific technology, like energy storage or renewables, where the major differentiator between bids is often the capital cost.

Approach 2—annual cost

A utility may know the MW capacity need, but is unclear regarding the overall cost of one technology versus another. What's more, for a given technology, different manufacturers can have varying installed costs as well as performance and maintenance costs. In this instance, a utility can solicit bids or they can assemble their own internal database of representative costs and performance and other requirements (staffing levels, water consumption costs if needed, etc.). This information can be obtained from any number of publicly available sources, from their own experience base, and/or from third parties. They can then very quickly calculate the annual cost as the cost of capital/financing + fuel (if needed) + maintenance + staffing + taxes + any other costs. Typically, capital/financing costs include costs related to plant construction as well as land, interconnection permitting, engineering, etc. An easy way to think of annual capital/financing costs is to compare it to a mortgage payment for a new house. When you buy a new house, the cost includes everything (land, water/sewer/electrical connections, permitting, construction, etc.). When you finance it through a bank, you must then pay an annual mortgage payment (including interest) for 20–30 years, until it is paid off. Similarly, a newly built power plant will have annual capital/financing costs. In the utility industry, the annualized capital cost is often referred to as Capex, operating costs such as fuel are referred to as Opex, and other costs such as taxes and staffing are referred to as fixed costs. The total cost per year (Capex + Opex + fixed costs.) across technologies is presented as an annual cost. The technology with the lowest annual cost is chosen, then RFPs are issued to vendors of that technology.

Approach 3—levelized cost of energy

Levelized cost of energy (LCOE) includes all the factors discussed for annual cost but is calculated across a multiyear time horizon (20 years is typical, or the commercial life of the technology being considered). Levelized cost essentially calculates individual annual costs across the planning horizon and applies discount rates, to account for the time value of money, to determine the net present value (NPV). The NPV is divided by the MWh the plant is expected to generate across the horizon, such that results are presented in units of $/MWh. Because the calculation is performed across multiple years, it can account for changing fuel prices through time. LCOE can also account for varying capacity factors across time, where, for example, a plant may be expected to run 50% of the time in year 1 falling to 10% in year 20, although it is rarely used in this way. Some utilities simply calculate LCOE for all technology types using a common capacity factor. Utilities often lump technologies into bins of baseload, intermediate, and peaking and assigned common capacity factors for each grouping. For example, a large nuclear plant would be considered baseload, running 95% or more hours per year at full load. Smaller units only needed a few hundred hours per year or less to meet peaking needs would be assigned a low capacity factor, 5%−10%. Intermediate units are those that run somewhere "in between" and assigned capacity factors in the 30%−70% range. The exact determination is dependent on the utility.

A common way to assign capacity factors is through use of the load duration curve (LDC) (Fig. 1.3). It is also not uncommon for utilities to assess numerous potential technologies and assign LCOE values to them, and use this information as a prescreening step, choosing only those options with favorable LCOE for further analysis (e.g., Energie NB Power, 2017 IRP [44]).

Approach 4—load duration curve-screening curve approach

With the load duration curve-screening curve approach (LDC-SCA) approach utilities assess the LDC for shortfalls to identify capacity needs in the peaking, intermediate, and baseload categories. They then rely on annual cost or LCOE curves to identify the lowest cost technology in the respective category. Screening criteria may include other factors such as "commercial maturity" or "public sentiment" in addition to cost considerations. An example of this process can be found in the 2010 draft Integrated Resource Plan of Oklahoma Gas & Electric Company [45], a regulated electric utility serving 750,000 customers in the states of Oklahoma and Arkansas in the United States.

Approach 5—all source-load duration curve approach

Some utilities use LDCs to determine capacity shortfalls then simply issue RFPs for that amount of capacity. "All Source" means they do not specify what technology should be entertained, but the utility may broadly specify what technology type—for example, "renewable," which would allow bids for wind, solar, hydro, geothermal, etc. Bidders offer whatever technology they want including multiple technologies on the same site

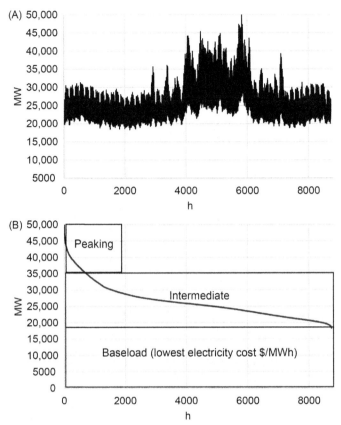

Figure 1.3 (A) Annual 2017 load curve for the California-Independent System Operator (CAISO) and (B) the resultant load duration curve (LDC). Baseload refers to those units that will run almost all hours of the year. Intermediate refers to units that may run anywhere from 1000 h to baseload. Peaking refers to units only expected to run less than 2000 h. Definitions (based on hours) can vary from utility to utility.

(e.g., hybrid solar + storage). Bidders may also offer capacity that is short of the total need. The utility then assesses each offer (and/or combination of offers) to find that provides the least lifetime cost for the utility. With the prevalence of commercial software platforms for least-cost-dispatch optimization, it is becoming increasingly common for utilities to simulate the proposed solutions at hourly (or even sub-hourly) time steps against load. Least-cost dispatch simulation tools are designed to optimize dispatch of all assets in a portfolio such that the total Opex is minimized for each time interval (typically hourly) and across the modeling horizon. The offered solution (or combination of solutions) with the lowest NPV of Capex + Opex + fixed costs is chosen. Modern least-cost dispatch software did not become commercially available until the early 2000s and did not obtain widespread use until the late 2000s. Although this approach is straightforward, it can be laborious for utilities to evaluate potentially hundreds of bids. Utilities may use some form of screening methods, such as LCOE, to narrow the pool of choices assessed by detailed Opex calculations.

An example of this type of approach includes the 2016 Electric Resource Plan [46] filed by Public Service of Colorado (PSCO). PSCO is one of four operating subsidiaries of Xcel Energy, which together serve more than 3 million electric customers. The 2016 PSCO resource plan identified potential capacity needs. In 2017, PSCO issued four RFPs simultaneously [47]. The RFPs were issued for different blocks of capacity types (e.g., one RFP for dispatchable resources, another RFP for renewable resources, etc.).

Approach 6—load duration curve-based capacity expansion models

Smaller utilities with few generators and infrequent new-build capacity decisions can often use annual cost or LCOE approaches directly, or even an LDC-SCA approach. They can be done by hand or with simple spreadsheets, but the approach becomes messy and quickly impossible to solve as the number of generators increases, especially when the operation of one unit can affect other units in the portfolio. With the LDC-capacity expansion model (CEM) approach, LDCs are created for each year across a planning horizon, taking account of any load growth. The integral of the area under the LDC curve represents the total sum of MWh (energy) a utility must generate each year to satisfy load. Then two questions must be answered each year and across the entire planning horizon:

1. Is there enough capacity to meet peak MW and energy MWh needs, and if not, how much capacity must be added?
2. What is the optimal type of capacity to add (if any) so that total NPV across the planning horizon is minimized?

The answer to the second question is not as simple as just adding the lowest cost option to meet peak, as changes in the LDC could indicate a need for more baseload or intermediate as well. That is, adding more baseload or intermediate increases the utility capacity and could allow the new portfolio to satisfy the peak requirement as well. The trick is determining the lowest cost option at the portfolio level achieved by specialized software performing portfolio simulations to determine the lowest cost annual dispatch of all assets in the portfolio simultaneously. Each power plant will be dispatched differently depending on what else is in the portfolio, so new capacity can impact the dispatch of everything else in the system. For example, VREs such as wind and solar will be expected to inject all of their MWh into the system when generated, which means other units will run fewer hours per year. An LDC-CEM performs an NPV calculation across the planning horizon minimizing the total NPV of capital and operating costs of the entire portfolio of assets.

LDC-CEMs were first brought to market in the 1990s and were designed to work on computers available at that time. Simplifying assumptions were inherent in the solution. For example, hourly chronological least-cost-dispatch models were not commercially available, so the Opex calculations were relatively crude and reliant on 4, 12, or even 24 hour time "blocks." Annual simulations (of all days in a year) are not done, instead representative days or weeks from each of two to four seasons were evaluated. Physical factor grid operators must respect such as start costs or minimum run times were ignored completely. These simplifying assumptions were considered valid at the time as the approach was designed for large utilities (GW of capacity) reliant on large central station power plants, where fuel prices were well known and relatively stable, load shapes did not vary significantly day to day or year to year, variable sources (wind, solar) were not prevalent, and where the number of capacity choices was rather limited.

Many utilities have resource planning departments well versed in LDC-CEM approaches, and their computational speed makes them well suited for running the model hundreds to thousands of times for sensitivity analyses. Examples of utilities using LDC-CEM approaches are given below, although this is only a subset of all utilities using this approach.

- The 2013 Integrated Resource Plan, filed by BC Hydro [48]. BC Hydro is a Crown Corporation, meaning it is owned by the government and people of British Columbia, Canada [49], serving more than 4 million customers.
- The 2016 Appalachian Power Company Integrated Resource Plan, filed with the State of West Virginia [50]. Appalachian Power Company serves approximately 1 million customers across the states of West Virginia, Virginia, and Tennessee and is part of the American Electric Power system, one of the largest utilities in the United States [51].

- The 2018—2032 Integrated Resource Plan of Great River Energy [52], a nonprofit wholesale electric power cooperative that provides electricity to 28-member-owned distribution cooperatives that together serve 700,000 families, farms, and businesses in Minnesota [53].
- The 2017 Integrated Resource Plan filed by Pacificorp [54], which provides energy to nearly 2 million people in the northwestern United States [55].

The long-term IRPs for 43 IOUs were reviewed by the author in 2018 for methodologies, 39 of them used LDC-CEMs. The same simplifications that make this approach so speedy are also not well suited for high-renewable power systems. As the proportion of VREs increases in a system, the balance of the fleet is tasked with more frequent starts and may only be needed 1—2 hours at a time, while the assets in the fleet may have physical limitations making it impossible for them to service this sort of intermittent dispatch. A growing number of utilities are moving to a modified approach to more correctly account for Opex in high-renewable environments.

Approach 7—modified load duration curve-based capacity expansion models

Modified LDC-CEMs use the new-build capacity determined from a standard LDC-CEM model and takes only the capital expenditures (Capex) and new-build capacity decisions from the model. Opex costs from the LDC-CEM are discarded. The annual capacity mix across the planning horizon is instead simulated against hourly loads and VRE output to more accurately determine Opex. The Opex determination makes use of complex least-cost-dispatch software described earlier. An example of this process can be found in the 2017 Integrated Resource Plan of Public Service Company of New Mexico [56].

The modified approach is becoming more popular as utilities realize the shortfalls of simplified Opex estimates in legacy CEMs. Recall that the LDC-CEM approach attempts to minimize the NPV of Capex + Opex across the planning horizon. The modified approach assumes Capex is already minimized by the capacity choices from the LDC-CEM model and attempts to use independent detailed dispatch simulations to obtain more realistic estimates of Opex, based on capacity choices already made. The modified approach then calculates the NPV of the Capex + Opex as determined from detailed dispatch simulations. The modified approach has the risk of choosing inflexible assets ill-suited for high VRE systems as the initial capacity optimization was based on incorrect Opex estimates.

Approach 8—chronological capacity expansion models

Chronological CEMs do not use the LDC at all. They take the raw load and variable wind and solar data at hourly granularity and simultaneously calculate that mix of new-build capacity (by technology type and MW amounts) that minimized the NPV of Capex + Opex across the planning horizon. Depending on the application (and commercially available software used), a utility may use the full hourly chronology over the planning horizon or decide to use 2- or 4-hour time blocks. The blocks can be evenly distributed or fitted in such a way that more attention is focused on periods of sharp load or VRE output changes, while "smooth" periods are represented with less detail. The computational cost of such high granularity is steep. To reduce computational cost, some approaches advocate using representative days or weeks [57], but retain hourly or subhourly time blocks for dispatch simulations.

C-CEM approaches make use of mixed-integer programming where some variables are binary while others are continuous. This is necessary for the simulation to know a unit can either be on or off (1 or 0) while its output can vary between min load and full load, which are continuous values. The mathematical optimization algorithms inherent in C-CEM approaches are complex and computationally intensive. One of the first applications of this approach was performed for the South Australian power system in 2012 [58]. Chronological CEMs are considered the most appropriate and yield the most accurate solutions for utilities with heavy penetration of VREs [57]. C-CEMs also attend to concerns of regulatory bodies, who advocate that utilities must attend to fine-scale, hourly or subhourly modeling in their long-term plans to fully quantify the value of flexible capacity (e.g., National Association of Regulated Utility Commissioner [NARUC] [59]), and in particular to quantify the value of flexible capacity in support of heavy VRE penetration.

At present few utilities have long-range or IRPs publicly available that are based on C-CEMs, although a growing number of utilities are moving in this direction. The computational cost of C-CEMs is quite high relative to LDC-based approaches, and the data needs are substantially greater. However, the difference in outcomes of a C-CEM approach can be quite dramatic relative to LDC-based approaches. LDC-based approaches underestimate actual system costs for high VRE penetration (more than 15%–20% of annual GWh from VREs). C-CEMs account for the volatility and complexity of high VRE penetration and tend to suggest new-build capacity additions that best support renewables, minimize CO_2 generation, and minimize ratepayer costs at the same time [60].

Summary and timeline of capacity expansion planning approaches

Global reliance on affordable electricity is a rather "new" occurrence in the course of humanity, only taking hold in the past century or so. The history of this development is one of continuous growth and evolutions of utility types and business models, regulatory and policy approaches, and technological advances. Parallel with this background of constant change has been the evolution of analytics and costing approaches to optimize decision-making processes and ensure the lowest cost for utility customers.

Simple capital cost and annual cost approaches were the mainstay of generating capacity additions through 1960s [61]. These simple cost approaches were (and still remain) appropriate for small, relatively simple utilities with a small number of generators in their portfolio. Even today a small municipal utility with only one power plant may comfortably use simple approaches such as these—particularly if the generating station in question is isolated from the grid and not expected to participate in decentralized markets. If a generating station is expected to participate in a market environment, especially a market with increasing renewable penetrations, more advanced and sophisticated approaches are needed.

With greater utility consolidation and regulation, the emergence of integrated resource planning requirements and larger pools of potential capacity choices LCOE, LDC/screening curve, All Source LDC came into use commensurate with advances in computing power and are still used by utilities today. The appeal of these approaches is their simplicity, which comes at a cost. For example, simple LCOE and SCAs imply that capacity additions are evaluated in a vacuum, where costs and performance are known in advance independent of anything else in the utility portfolio. This is a gross simplification as the addition of a new resource often impacts everything else in the portfolio, so the full range of costs (or revenues) associated with an asset is not accounted for. For example, a new-build coal power plant may have an excellent, very low-cost LCOE and fit within the decision-process of an LDC/screening curve approach and appear on paper as the lowest cost new-build option. But what if this new coal plant is being installed in a portfolio that is experiencing rapid buildout of wind and solar? The VREs will cause volatility in energy supply that will require flexibility, generators able to start/stop often and ramp between minimum stable loads and full loads. Large coal boiler plants are not designed to support VREs in such a manner: they are designed to produce low-cost baseload power. LCOE and LDC/screening curve approaches are not capable of taking flexibility concerns into account and could very well lead to suboptimal investments. Investing in a new inflexible coal plant parallel with expanding wind and solar could lead to energy imbalance, requiring even more investment in additional capacity once it is determined that the new coal cannot balance wind and solar. The major issue with using LCOE or even simpler approaches (cost, annual cost) is they include no information on externalities that can and do impact the investment.

Advances in methods and computing power gave rise to LDC-CEMs in the 1970s and later modified LDC approaches. As noted, utilities today are still using modified LDC-CEM approaches. The advantage of LDC-based approaches is they do not use all the data on chronological load but only crude representations. More recently, starting in the 2012 timeframe, true chronological CEMs emerged.

The evolution of approaches has ramifications for power systems of today and into the future. In large part because simpler legacy approaches in use by utilities and regulatory agencies literally give entirely different answers than more advanced approaches [60] (what technology to build and when, Capex and Opex). Older methods tend to pick new capacity in a binary fashion—any non-VRE capacity is either the lowest capital cost or the most efficient, because the approaches have no mechanism to quantify the value of flexibility (or the costs of not having enough flexibility). The older approaches are also unable to truly value the contribution of energy storage, for which the business case is dependent on hourly or subhourly energy shifting that is impossible to analyze using LDC approaches or simple LCOE. But we should not be too hard in terms of criticism of past approaches—the simple approaches were entirely appropriate for their time, but new regulatory pressures, societal demands for CO_2 minimization, new advances in VREs, and various forms of energy storage all contribute to an ever-more complex power system requiring more sophisticated approaches. To truly understand what and how these technologies influence planning and necessitate the need for more detailed chronological modeling through the entire planning process, it is necessary to present and discuss the attributes and features of both renewable energies, including VREs such as wind and solar, and also explore the exciting world of energy storage.

References

[1] S. Biewald, B. Bernow, Electric utility system reliability analysis: determining the need for generating capacity. Synapse, Energy Econ. (1988). Available from: https://www.synapse-energy.com/sites/default/files/SynapsePaper.1988-09.0.Reliability-Analysis.A0033.pdf.

[2] Hydro-electricity restored to historic Northumberland home, BBC News. <https://www.bbc.com/news/uk-england-tyne-21586177>, 2013 (accessed 19.04.19).

[3] Godalming Museum: Godalming and Electricity. http://www.godalmingmuseum.org.uk/index.php?page = 1881-godalming-and-electricity>, (accessed 19.03.19).

[4] M. Marotte, Chambersburg Electric Dept.: lights on since 1890, USA Today. <https://www.publicopiniononline.com/story/life/2015/11/25/chambersburg-electric-dept-lights-since-1890/76364956/>, 2015.

[5] A brief history of Albuquerque. <https://albuqhistsoc.org/SecondSite/pkfiles/pk47cityhistory.htm>, (accessed 20.03.19).

[6] The history of Arizona Public Service. <https://www.aps.com/library/communications1/HistoryofAPS.pdf>.

[7] Arizona Public Service. <https://www.aps.com/en/ourcompany/Pages/home.aspx>, (accessed 19.02.19).

[8] History of Japan's Electric Power Industry. <https://www.fepc.or.jp/english/energy_electricity/history/>, (accessed 19.05.19).

[9] A brief history of electrical utilities in NSW. <http://www.ewh.ieee.org/r10/nsw/subpages/history/history_electricity_syd_county_council.pdf>, (accessed 19.01.15).

[10] R. Bradley, The origins of political electricity: market failure or political opportunism? Energy Law J. 17 (1996).

[11] R. Pomp, A brief history of the electric utility industry, in: Impacts of Electric Utility Deregulation on Property Taxation, Lincoln Institute of Land Policy, 2000.

[12] H. Passer, The Electric Manufacturers: 1875-1900, Arno Press, New York, NY, 1972.

[13] D. Schap, Municipal ownership in the electric utility industry, United States, 1986.

[14] B. Behling, Competition and monopoly in public utility industries, 1938.

[15] S. Harvey, A. Larson, A. Patel, History of power: the evolution of the electric generation industry. (2017). Available from: https://www.powermag.com/history-of-power-the-evolution-of-the-electric-generation-industry/?lc = 1.

[16] S. Gossard, Coal-to-gas plant conversions in the U.S, Power Eng. 119 (2015).

[17] V. Smil, Gas turbines have become by far the best choice for add-on generating power, IEEE Spectrum, 2019. Available from: https://spectrum.ieee.org/energy/fossil-fuels/gas-turbines-have-become-by-far-the-best-choice-for-addon-generating-power.

[18] A. DeFrance, Belle Isle faces lights out power plant once height of technology, Oklahoman, 1999. Available from: https://oklahoman.com/article/2639809/belle-isle-faces-lights-out-power-plant-once-height-of-technology.

[19] Combined cycles: looking back, looking ahead—I, Turbomachinery. <https://www.turbomachinerymag.com/combined-cycles-looking-back-looking-ahead-i/>, 2014.

[20] S. Patel, A brief history of GE gas turbines, Power. <https://www.powermag.com/a-brief-history-of-ge-gas-turbines-2/>, 2019.

[21] Improved Gyrascope Steam Engine Governor, Scientific American 3:13. <https://archive.org/details/scientific-american-1860-09-22>, 1860.

[22] Nuclear Power in the World Today. World Nuclear Association. <https://www.world-nuclear.org/information-library/current-and-future-generation/nuclear-power-in-the-world-today.aspx>, 2019 (accessed 04.04.19).

[23] Advanced small modular reactors (SMRs), <https://www.energy.gov/ne/nuclear-reactor-technologies/small-modular-nuclear-reactors>, (accessed 19.05.19).

[24] A. Kahrl, F. Mills, A. Lavin, L. Ryan, N. Olsen, The future of electricity resource planning. Lawrence Berkeley National Laboratory 1006269, Report No. 6. <https://emp.lbl.gov/sites/all/files/lbnl-1006269.pdf>, 2016.

[25] A. D'sa, Integrated resource planning (IRP) and power sector reform in developing countries, Energy Policy 33 (2005) 1271−1285.

[26] B. Pagnarith, K. Limmeechokchai, Integrated resource planning for long-term electricity supply in selected GMS countries, part 1, Energ Sources Part B Econ. Plan. Policy 10 (2015) 167−175.

[27] I. Meza, C.G. Amado, N.B. Sauer, Transforming the Nicaraguan energy mix towards 100% renewable, Energy Procedia 138 (2017) 494−499.

[28] G. Wilkerson, J. Larsen, P. Barbose, Survey of Western US electric utility resource plans, Energy Policy 66 (2014) 90−103.

[29] C. Corvallo, J. Larsen, P. Sanstad, A. Goldman, Load forecasting in electric utility integrated resource planning. US Department of Energy, Lawrence Berkeley National Laboratory report LBNL-1006395. <https://emp.lbl.gov/sites/default/files/lbnl-1006395.pdf>, 2016.

[30] I. Bobmann, T. Staffell, The shape of future electricity demand: exploring load curves in 2050s Germany and Britain, Energy 90 (2015) 1317−1333.

[31] W. Phuangpornpitak, N. Prommee, A study of load demand forecasting models in electric power system operation and planning, GMSARN, Int. J. 10 (2016) 19−24.

[32] G. Parkpoom, S. Harrison, Analyzing the impact of climate change on future electricity demand in Thailand, IEEE Trans. Power Syst. 23 (2008) 1441−1448.

[33] E. Sullivan, P. Colman, J. Kalendra, Predicting the response of electricity load to climate change. NREL Technical Report NREL/TP-6A20-64297. <https://www.nrel.gov/docs/fy15osti/64297.pdf>, 2015.

[34] M. Idoniboyeobu, D.C. Ekanem, Assessment of electric load demand and prediction of future load demand: a case study of Akwa Ibom State of Nigeria, Asian J. Sci. Res. 7 (2014) 525−535.

[35] J. Eto, ed., Least-Cost Utility Planning: A Handbook for Public Utility Commissioners, vol. 1. National Association of Regulated Utility Commissioners, 1988. <http://eta-publications.lbl.gov/sites/default/files/least_cost_utility_handbook_vol_1.pdf>.

[36] D. Sandalow, Hurricane sandy and our energy infrastructure. U.S. Department of Energy. <https://www.energy.gov/articles/hurricane-sandy-and-our-energy-infrastructure>, 2012 (accessed 19.02.17).

[37] P. Vijayamohanan, Loss of load probability of a power system, J. Fundam. Renew. Energy Appl. 5 (2015) 1.

[38] W. Schroder, T. Kuckshinrichs, Value of lost load: an efficient economic indicator for power supply security? A literature review, Front. Energy Res. 24 (2015) 55.

[39] J. Rosellon, Different approaches to supply adequacy in electricity markets, Energy Stud. Rev. 14 (2006) 101–130.

[40] R. Hildebrandt, E.W. Wirtshafter, Incorporating DSM uncertainty and flexibility into integrated resource planning, 1994 ACEEE Proceedings, vol. 7, 1994. Available from: https://aceee.org/files/proceedings/1994/data/papers/SS94_Panel7_Paper10.pdf#page = 1.

[41] M. Orwig, K.D. Ahlstom, M.L. Banunarayanan, V. Sharp, J. Wilczak, J.M. Freedman, et al., Recent trends in variable generation forecasting and its value to the power system, IEEE Trans. Sustain. Energy 6 (2015) 924–933.

[42] T. Trainer, Limits to solar thermal energy set by intermittency and low DNI: implications from meteorological data, Energy Policy 63 (2013) 910–917.

[43] C. Heard, B.P. Brook, B.W. Wigley, T.M.L. Bradshaw, Burden of proof: a comprehensive review of the feasibility of 100% renewable-electricity systems, Renew. Sustain. Energy Rev. 76 (2017) 1122–1133.

[44] Energie NB power, Integrated resource plan. <https://www.nbpower.com/media/772015/nb-power-2017-irp-public-english.pdf>, 2017.

[45] Oklahoma Gas & Electric Company, Integrated resource plan. <http://www.apsc-services.info/pdf/12/12-067-U_28_3.pdf>, 2010.

[46] Public Service Company of Colorado, 2016 electric resource plan. <https://www.xcelenergy.com/company/rates_and_regulations/resource_plans/2016_psco_electric_resource_plan>, 2016.

[47] Colorado 2017 All-Source Solicitation. Public Service Company of Colorado. <https://www.xcelenergy.com/company/rates_and_regulations/resource_plans/psco_2017_all_source_solicitation>, 2017 (accessed 17.03.19).

[48] BC Hydro November 2013 Integrated resource plan. <https://www.bchydro.com/toolbar/about/planning-for-our-future/irp/current-plan/document-centre/reports/november-2013-irp.html>, 2013.

[49] BC Hydro, About us. <https://www.bchydro.com/toolbar/about.html>, (accessed 19.03.19).

[50] AEP Appalachian Power Integrated Resource Plan to the Public Service Commission of West Virginia. <https://www.appalachianpower.com/global/utilities/lib/docs/info/projects/APCOIntegratedResourcePlans/2015APCOWVIRP_Final_12232015.pdf>, 2016.

[51] Appalachian Power Facts, Figures & Bios. <https://www.appalachianpower.com/info/facts/>, (accessed 19.03.19).

[52] Great River Energy, 2018-2032 integrated resource plan. <https://greatriverenergy.com/wp-content/uploads/2017/04/GRE-2017-IRP-Final.pdf>, 2017.

[53] Great River Energy. <https://greatriverenergy.com/>, (accessed 14.02.19).

[54] Pacificorp, Integrated resource plan, vol. 1. <https://www.pacificorp.com/content/dam/pcorp/documents/en/pacificorp/energy/integrated-resource-plan/2017-irp/2017_IRP_VolumeI_IRP_Final.pdf>, 2017.

[55] About Pacificorp, <https://www.pacificorp.com/about.html>, (accessed 03.01.19).

[56] Public Service of New Mexico. Integrated resource plan, 2017-2036. <https://www.pnm.com/documents/396023/396193/PNM + 2017 + IRP + Final.pdf/eae4efd7-3de5-47b4-b686-1ab37641b4ed>, 2017.

[57] M. Fripp, Making an optimal plan for 100% renewable power in Hawaii — preliminary results from the SWITCH power system planning model. University of Hawaii Economic Research Organization, Working Paper 2016-1. <https://www.uhero.hawaii.edu/assets/WP_2016-1.pdf>, 2016.

[58] M. Nweke, C. Leanez, F. Drayton, G. Kolhe, Benefits of chronological optimization in capacity planning for electricity markets, in: 2012 IEEE International Conference on Power System Technology (POWERCON), Auckland, 2012, pp. 1–6.

[59] National Association of Regulated Utility Commissioners, NARUC (2018) Resolution on modeling energy storage and other flexible resources. <https://www.naruc.org/resolutions-index/2018-annual-meeting-resolutions/>, 2018.

[60] J. Ferrari, Incorporating flexibility in utility resource planning. <https://cdn.wartsila.com/docs/default-source/power-plants-documents/downloads/white-papers/americas/wartsila-bwp---incorporating-flexibility-in-utility-resource-planning.pdf?sfvrsn = 63b6f145_8>, 2014.

[61] Expansion planning for electrical generating systems: a guidebook. International Atomic Energy Association Technical Reports Series No. 241. Vienna, 1984.

CHAPTER 2

Influx of variable renewable energy sources, the way things are going

Introduction

Renewable energy. The idea that we can harvest energy from the environment directly, energy that will continuously be renewed from some endless source. This dream is not new. Enterprising individuals have been using water to drive mechanical power for centuries, to grind wheat and power sawmills. Wind has been used to propel ships for thousands of years, and for hundreds of years before anyone heard of electricity wind was used to move water for irrigation. More recently renewable power sources are being used to generate electricity. The drivers for adoption range from concerns over energy security and overreliance on foreign fuel sources to the need for carbon-free energy to offset climate change concerns.

There are entire books written about every aspect of renewable energy for electricity generation such as hydropower, geothermal, and biofuels. These forms of renewable energy have some limitations and some specific niches. For example, large-scale hydropower requires significant investment and has impacts on the environment that society is finding harder to accept. While hydropower is a significant factor in many countries, it is unlikely, specifically for developed nations, to provide significantly more to power our electric grids. Geothermal and biofuels have promise but are limited to geographic regions where conditions are right for their use and adoption. What separates these forms of renewable energy from solar and wind is that they are dispatchable. That is, an operator can modulate water release from a dam to control the power flow from the turbines. Geothermal can regulate heat transfer to control output. Biofuels can be used in thermal power plants to generate on demand. The main point is that geothermal, hydro, and biofuels may be considered renewable but planning for them is not so different from planning for a thermal power plant. Wind and solar are different, their energy throughput is dependent on weather, and they are not strictly dispatchable—they are variable renewable energy sources (VREs).

Electric Utility Resource Planning
DOI: https://doi.org/10.1016/B978-0-12-819873-5.00002-2
39

The physical potential needed to make electricity from solar and wind is ubiquitous. Just about every place on Earth can generate energy from either or both. Solar (Fig. 2.1) and wind (Fig. 2.2) potential maps are maintained by multiple international agencies to provide a guidance on locations that are most suitable to capitalize on either. For example, in Latin America solar potential is generally good, but is maximized in the higher altitude regions of countries such as Chile, which has some of the most favorable solar conditions on the planet. Europe and the United States have solar potential throughout their whole range, with better conditions occurring (as would be expected) closer to the equator. Wind potential (Fig. 2.2) is geographically diverse and at times complements solar potential. For example, in Scandinavian countries solar potential is dismal, while wind potential is quite high. In the United States solar potential is highest in the West and Southwest, while wind potential is highest mid-continent in a region known as the "Wind Corridor." Northern Africa and parts of Asia have both favorable wind and solar conditions.

Not surprisingly, the largest proportions of renewable energy being installed today are wind and solar. These forms of energy have enormous potential but also have some idiosyncrasies that present challenges for utility planners and dispatchers, as well as for policy makers. The main challenges stem from the fact that they only produce energy when their

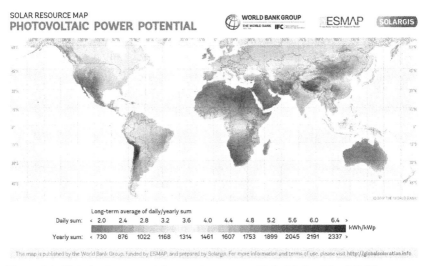

Figure 2.1 Global solar potential map, data source Global Solar Atlas 2.0 [1].

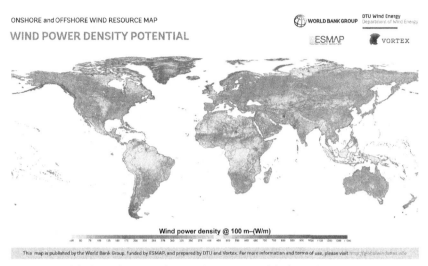

Figure 2.2 Global wind potential map, data source Global Wind Atlas 2.0 [2].

"fuel" (sunlight, wind) is active. Solar panels produce zero power in the middle of the night. Wind turbines do not produce power if there is no wind. And when they are producing power, their output is variable. A utility-scale solar facility might generate near its maximum capacity at noon, then drop off suddenly with the appearance of clouds. What's more, both wind and solar exhibit seasonal trends. Solar plants produce more energy in the summer when days are longest. Wind also often has seasonal shifts, with higher capacity factors in some months than others. These trends are seasonal, meaning they repeat themselves year after year, and offer some intriguing questions for utility planners to address.

Policy and incentives driving change

Numerous policies and incentives have accelerated adoption of VREs in utility portfolios. One set of policies are considered mandates, another set are considered incentives. Sometimes they are adopted or implemented simultaneously. The most popular form of mandate is a Renewable Portfolio Standard, or RPS for short.

RPS mandates can be imposed at the federal, state/province, county, or city level. They require utilities to source a certain amount of capacity or percentage of the energy they deliver to consumers from renewable or otherwise "clean" sources. The definition of what qualifies as clean may include nuclear energy as it is carbon-free. In most cases targets are set for a future year, allowing utilities time to plan for compliance. RPS standards are imposed for reasons ranging from fuel security to climate change concerns so they are not necessarily economic and are in fact contrary to least-cost planning principles. Therefore RPS legislation may include clauses allowing for nonconformance if costs of meeting the requirements exceed thresholds identified in the RPS legislation. This provides an escape valve for politicians if the implementation of the RPS program causes electricity prices to increase considerably, which is generally not viewed favorably by the voting public.

RPS standards also evolve with time, sometimes quite rapidly (Table 2.1). This evolution of standards within a region is to be expected as new technologies emerge, as public acceptance increases, and as costs for the various technologies come down, making the process adaptive and iterative. The major aim of most mandates is decarbonization and one can imagine any number of ways to achieve this goal. Language in RPS policies can vary accordingly, at times mandating capacity or energy amounts from specific technologies, to requiring the targets (Table 2.1) be met by any arrangement or amount of certain technologies and/or require progress on metrics such as average CO_2 intensity, measured as grams of CO_2/MWh.

Until recently wind and solar were simply too expensive to be placed economically within a utility fleet to any great extent. To overcome this issue, various subsidy programs can incentivize investments. Subsidies for

Table 2.1 Evolution of RPS standards in California (United States) [3,4], the European Union [5], and China [6,7] as of 2019.

Region	Year	Target (%)	By year
California	2002	20	2017
	2011	20	2013
		25	2016
		33	2020
	2015	50	2030
	2018	100	2045
European Union	2014	27	2030
	2018	32	2030
China	2016	15	2020
	2020	20	2030

Target (%) refers to the proportion of electricity sold or provided by utilities that must come from renewable or otherwise designated "clean" energy sources.

renewable energy projects come in the form of investment tax credits, production tax credits (PTCs), or feed-in tariffs. The government can directly subsidize some of the capital cost of the renewable plant with investment tax credits, though concerns arise when taxpayer money is used to subsidize a state-of-the-art facility that may experience problems and not actually generate as much renewable energy as expected. An alternative form of subsidy, PTCs, are also popular. With PTCs taxpayers pay the renewable plant a fixed payment per MWh generated, thus giving greater rewards to renewable facilities that generate the most energy. PTCs are valid for as long as legislation continues to support them, with no guarantee that the PTC will be available for the life of the plant. This mechanism is similar in principle to a feed-in tariff, except feed-in tariffs are contracts with set terms, giving greater security to investors. PTCs have been used in the United States. Feed-in tariffs are popular in Europe.

The combination of legislation mandating that utilities adopt renewables, government-funded research into the fundamental science of renewables, subsidies to help investors take the leap toward renewables, forward thinking and investment by major energy companies, and public opinion demanding greater amounts of clean energy, has promoted massive economies of scale that make renewables increasingly affordable. Below are brief histories of solar and wind technologies, along with their respective price trajectories through time.

Brief history of solar power

Any child who has ever held a magnifying glass outside on a sunny day trying to ignite a leaf pile knows the power of sunlight can be manipulated. But it was not until the past 200 years or so that we learned how to harness it. French physicist Alexandre-Edmond Becquerel discovered the photovoltaic effect in 1839, the process by which electric voltage, which induces current, is produced using light as the energy source. Several physicists in Europe and the United States in the following decades made advances along this line of thought. In 1873 English inventor Willoughby Smith first demonstrated the photoconductivity of Selenium. Three years later it was demonstrated that Selenium could produce electricity when exposed to light. In 1883 New York inventor Charles Fritts created the first solar panels by covering Selenium with a thin layer of gold. In 1941 American engineer Russell Shoemaker Ohl filed US patent 2402662

"Light Sensitive Device," a Selenium photovoltaic device used to make electricity. Later advances in material science and physics demonstrated in the 1950s that silicon could be used instead of Selenium, raising the efficiency of photovoltaic power from around 1% to 6%. For comparison today's solar panels have efficiencies of 15%−20%.

From the 1950s onward photovoltaic power devices (solar panels) were extremely expensive and not very efficient, but they held great promise, especially for space exploration. The Vanguard 1 satellite was launched by NASA in 1958 as the first satellite to be powered by solar panels, which could produce 1 W at an efficiency of approximately 10%. Interestingly (as a side note) the advance of spacecraft with solar panels led to problems with panel efficiency and output decaying over time due to random impact from space debris punching holes through the panels. Scientists enlisted something called percolation theory [8] to estimate the decay rate due to impacts. Percolation theory was later cross-applied to the field of landscape ecology [9], which explores (among other things) how habitat fragmentation impacts biodiversity and how wildfires spread across the landscape.

It was not until the oil crisis in the 1970s that research into photovoltaics was accelerated by commercial and societal concerns related to energy security. Some of the early investors in commercialization of solar energy were oil companies. Exxon was one of the largest investors into fundamental research, providing the means for Dr. Elliott Berman to design a solar cell that could be manufactured for 20 $/W, significantly less than 100 $/W pricing effective at the time [10]. In 1983 the Atlantic Richfield Oil Company (ARCO) installed one of the first commercial, utility-scale solar plants with a peak output of 5.2 MW [11]. ARCO manufactured the solar panels themselves due to a scarcity of large-scale solar panel manufacturers. While most solar applications at the time were not large, they did begin to power remote navigation warning lights, railroad crossings, and other applications where it was not economical to extend grid-connected electricity.

There were many other advances, including harvesting of solar energy with other means. Parabolic mirrors or arrays of black tubing were constructed to generate hot water directly. Concentrated solar arrays were invented that consisted of large mirror systems concentrating sunlight onto a form of boiler that generated steam to power a steam turbine, or some other thermal process. While all of these advances are interesting in their own right, the majority of utility-scale investment for power

Figure 2.3 Utility-scale solar farm.

generation is simple panel-based [12]. Solar panels are simple and easy to install and their cost continues to fall. Any size solar farm can be built by simply adding more solar panels. There are no complicated pieces of machinery and little to no specialized labor needed to install them (Fig. 2.3).

As noted previously, a great deal of investment in research and development was initiated in the 1970s in response to the oil crisis, as nations searched for alternate energy sources. So much so that median photovoltaic solar pricing in the United States in 2017 was pushing 2 $/W, a 10-fold decrease in pricing relative to the 1970s [12]. This same storm of events applies equally to wind power as it does to solar.

Brief history of wind power

Wind turbines provided mechanical power for grinding wheat to irrigation for several hundred years before humans started to harness electricity. One of the earliest pioneers of using wind energy for electricity generation was the Danish scientist Poul la Cour. In 1891 la Cour created an experimental wind turbine that converted wind power to electricity. Once his experimental work was completed, he offered the wind turbine to the town of Askov as a source of electricity for the town. La Cour was a fairly accomplished aerodynamicist for his time, with pioneering work on blade design to maximize power output from wind turbines. By 1908 there were more than 70 wind turbines across Denmark with outputs ranging from 5 to 25 kW.

Across the ocean in the United States, in 1920 brothers Marcellus and Joe Jacobs lived on a ranch in Montana with an old gasoline-fired generator they used to power an electric iron, some lights and a radio. Traveling back and forth to town for gasoline was a multiday trip with a horse-drawn wagon, so the brothers tried using an old water-pump windmill to turn a generator as an alternate electricity source. The brothers quickly found out the slow speeds of the existing turbine were insufficient to power their generator. They decided to replace the original turbine blade system with a World War I surplus airplane propeller. The propeller-based rotational speed varied so dramatically that it could not provide reliable electricity. The brothers invented a governor that maintained constant rotor speed independent of wind speed, allowing for more reliable power generation.

The success of the Jacobs brothers' modified wind-turbine design led to local fame. They quickly found themselves being asked to build wind-power plants for neighbors, which were originally designed to charge batteries. Demand for their invention increased to the point where they were devoting more time to wind power projects than to ranching, so they incorporated the Jacobs Wind Electric Company in 1928. They moved to Minnesota to be closer to part suppliers and opened a factory in 1932. By the 1940s Jacobs Wind Electric Company had sold hundreds of wind turbines ranging in size from 2.5 to 10 kW.

Leading up to the 1940s other inventors were hard at work on increasing turbine size and power output. In 1941 the first MW-class wind turbine (1.25 MW) was connected to supply energy to Central Vermont Public Service Corporation. It was called the Smith—Putnam turbine after the manufacturer, S. Morgan Smith Company and the designer, Palmer Cosslett Putnam. It had two blades and was over 50 m (175 ft.) in diameter. The center of the turbine was attached to a 36 m (120 ft.) steel tower. In 1945 the privately funded Smith—Putnam venture proposed an additional six units with a combined output of 9 MW for a price of 190 $/W [13], but this was considered too expensive by the utility.

If this project in 1945 with Central Vermont Public Service Corporation had happened, it would have been the world's first wind farm. Instead that distinction goes to US WindPower, opened in 1979 as the first modern wind turbine manufacturer in the United States, located in Burlington, Massachusetts. They installed the first wind farm at Crotched Mountain in New Hampshire, consisting of 20 wind turbines rated at 30 kW each. These turbines were still rather small compared to today's standards for utility-scale wind generation. The trend toward mass production of large turbines was accelerated when NASA started a wind-turbine research and development program in the mid-1970s. This was also a by-product of the 1970s oil crisis when president Richard Nixon set up a federal task force to explore renewable energy sources, such as solar and wind. From 1974 to 1981 NASA's Glenn Research Center in Ohio led the Wind Energy Program for advanced research on horizontal axis wind turbines. Throughout the program NASA developed 13 experimental wind turbines, exploring variations including the use of steel tube towers (instead of steel lattice structures), blade manufacturing, aerodynamics, composite materials, and partial span pitch control, with the intent to lead to more robust and cost-effective designs and then transfer them to industry. Wind turbines developed under this program broke multiple world records for both physical size and power output.

The trend toward larger and more powerful wind turbines led to favorable economies of scale. While earlier applications from the 1970s into the mid-2000s used large numbers of small, sub 1 MW turbines, in the United States, the average size of utility-scale wind turbines has broken the 1 MW mark and increased substantially. Just in the 10-year period from 2007 to 2017 average turbine output increased from 1.65 to 2.32 MW. Tower heights are stable at 80−90 m, while rotor diameters grew from approximately 80 to 113 m (Figs. 2.4 and 2.5).

Trends in installed solar and wind capacity and pricing

The investments and commitments made regarding solar and wind as viable sources of renewable energy have stimulated massive growth in the industry. Globally the installed base of wind and solar (Fig. 2.6) increased 880% from 2007 (103 GW) to 2017 (905 GW). Offshore wind offers great promise, especially for developed countries with restrictions on land use; however, it is more difficult and expensive to build than onshore wind. As of 2017 514,000 MW of wind capacity had been installed globally, of which only 19,360 MW, or 3.8% of the total, were installed offshore [15]. Similarly, the majority of installations are photovoltaic panels.

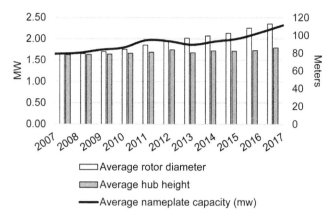

Figure 2.4 Average installed US land-based wind turbine nameplate capacity, rotor diameter, and rotor height [14].

Figure 2.5 Wind turbines in Texas (author photo).

As of 2017 there were 391,000 MW of total solar installations globally, of which only approximately 5000 MW, or 1.3% of the total, consisted of concentrated solar. Given their dominance, in the following discussion attention is given to solar panels and onshore wind.

Subsidies and national or state policies helped stimulate the growth and sparked the consequent economies of scale and competition. While a number of price points can be explored, such as $/kW for the equipment (wind turbines, solar panels), these typically refer to the cost without installation. Installation costs can vary widely and are difficult to compare

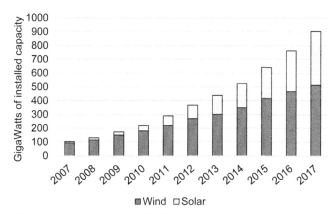

Figure 2.6 Global installed capacity of solar and wind [15,16].

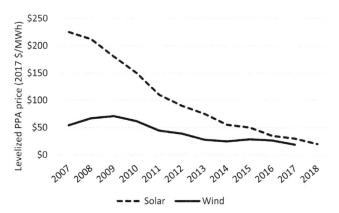

Figure 2.7 Average power purchase agreement (PPA) pricing 2007–18 for solar (292 contracts, 14.5 GW AC) and wind farms (Wind [14], solar [12]).

across technologies. A simpler way to evaluate trends in solar and wind costs is to look at power purchase agreement (PPA) prices.

Utilities may build and own renewable facilities, or they can enter into PPAs. Under a PPA construct some third party, a developer or independent power producer (IPP), builds and operates a renewable plant and delivers clean energy to the utility for an agreed upon price, with contract terms of 10, 20, or more years. PPA prices reflect the total cost of producing energy, inclusive of all equipment, design, land, installation, interconnection to the grid, permitting, maintenance, and so forth. While statistics are difficult to obtain globally, data for hundreds of power plants are recorded and tabulated for projects in the United States (Fig. 2.7).

On average, solar and wind PPAs as of 2017−18 had fallen to the range of 20−30 $/MWh. These prices are now equivalent to or below the cost of generation from coal and natural gas in the United States, which generally enjoys low fossil-fuel prices.

How solar and wind impact dispatch and pricing

So far, we have covered an elementary history of solar and wind energy, government policies that have stimulated growth and investment, and pricing trends. These all lead to the increase in globally installed renewable energy. What we have not covered is the impact solar and wind have on utilities, what challenges they bring, and how these elements affect utility resource planning. To understand these impacts at a high level, let us first look at how renewable energy is used within a utility to supply energy to customers.

Electric utilities aim to deliver electricity at lowest cost. On a day-to-day basis they achieve this using the principle of least-cost economic dispatch. Let us assume a hypothetical utility has predicted with reasonable accuracy what the hourly loads will be for a given day, and that they have three power plants (Table 2.2A). Now let us assume at a certain hour their load is 900 MW. The cost to serve all 900 MW is determined from the operational cost of the units tasked with meeting load. Operational costs do not include capital recovery or fixed costs related to owning or running the plant. They typically include a fuel cost, calculated from heat rate in MBtu/MWh or kJ/kWh times fuel cost $/MBtu. Variable operations and maintenance (VOM) includes day-to-day costs beyond fuel just to keep the plant running. From Table 2.2A we see the utility has exactly 900 MW of capacity to meet its 900 MW load. The operational cost of the system is the sum of total operational cost ($/MWh) times the MW

Table 2.2A Hypothetical utility fleet with only thermal.

Power plant	Type	Size (MW)	Heat rate (MBtu/ MWh)	Fuel cost ($/MBtu)	Fuel ($/MWh)	VOM ($/MWh)	Total operational cost ($/MWh)
1	Coal boiler	500	10	2	20	4	24
2	Combined cycle	300	7.5	3	22.5	3	25.5
3	Peaker	100	9	3	27	3	30

Table 2.2B Hypothetical utility fleet with thermal and renewable assets generating 100 MW.

Power plant	Type	Size (MW)	Heat rate (MBtu/ MWh)	Fuel cost ($/MBtu)	Fuel ($/MWh)	VOM ($/MWh)	Total operational cost ($/MWh)
1	Coal boiler	500	10	2	20	4	24
2	Combined cycle	300	7.5	3	22.5	3	25.5
3	Peaker	100	9	3	27	3	30
4	Renewable	100	NA	0	0	1	1

NA, Not applicable

output per unit for each hour, which for the example in Table 2.2A equates to $22,650. This is the operational cost the utility must bear to serve 900 MW of load for this 1 hour.

Now imagine the utility has a new 100 MW solar park or wind farm that is generating at full capacity. The renewable plant has no fuel expenses and minimal VOM (Table 2.2B). Here the most economic dispatch would be to run power plants 1, 2, and 4. The consequent cost of serving load for that hour is now $19,750, or 87% of the operational cost if the load was served wholly by thermal as in Table 2.2A. The example shows a reduction in generation cost as VREs are added to the system, and the concept of lowered prices is considered a benefit for utility customers, as they reap the rewards of less expensive clean energy. This is only part of the story.

The other part of the story is related to marginal cost. In an organized market, every plant running to meet load is paid the marginal cost, defined as the cost of the most expensive unit for the hour. Energy revenues are the difference between operating cost and marginal price, and the difference is what pays off debt and allows for profits. The power plant that sets the margin collects only enough revenue to pay its operating costs, with nothing left over. As greater amounts of VREs are added to the system marginal costs go down, meaning every plant in the system is paid less per MWh generated.

If load was met entirely with renewables the marginal cost would be close to zero and revenues for most of the capacity, including VREs, would be close to zero as well. Additional capacity is required for reliability, and some of these reliability assets may only run a few hours per year. This poses a "missing money" problem. If market revenues do not support maintenance of critical infrastructure, the missing money can be recovered in several ways, including fixed fees that allow utilities to charge their customers a variable charge for energy (MWh) and a fixed charge for capacity (MW). The collection of fixed-fee revenues is then used to cover fixed costs and debt paydown. In the case of a utility outside of a market, they are still operating on least-cost dispatch principles and ratepayers would pay a smaller variable fee on a $/kWh basis but be assessed larger capacity charges to cover costs.

Some markets attend to the missing money problem with capacity markets. Capacity markets award each generator a fixed monthly or annual fee for their contribution to system reliability. The mechanics of fixed fees and payments is beyond the scope of this work. The point of mentioning them here is that when a utility increases its share of VREs, it has legacy investments in assets it may still owe money on, that have operational lives of 20–40 years. It is not free to simply jump to serving all load with solar and wind without having a means to attend to debt and costs of existing assets. It will also need to invest in new flexible capacity to support renewables, such as storage, which all must be paid for as well.

While the cost of new solar or wind is dropping the land, interconnection, supporting technologies, and stranded asset costs assigned to ratepayers are not. And these factors tend to grow as more VREs are added. There appears to be quite a debate in the literature over the impact of VREs on customer electricity pricing. Some argue that the cost of serving energy with renewables can be higher than from traditional sources, inclusive of all associated costs [17] and some empirical data suggest utility systems with higher VRE penetrations have higher ratepayer costs than states with lower penetrations [18]. Other studies have found the opposite that it would be less expensive to install clean energy, mostly VREs supported by storage and energy efficiency measures [19]. It must be noted that many analyses showing renewables are less expensive than traditional generation do so by comparing simple metrics such as levelized cost of electricity (LCOE) and assuming VREs generate at their maximum rated capacity factor. These types of assessments do not compare total system costs, which are the domain of the utility resource planner. An integrated resource plan must determine the total costs to serve load and maintain reliability. Reliability attributes of a system required to maintain high VRE penetrations are directly linked to the variability and volatility of solar and wind.

Variability of solar and wind

VREs such as solar and wind cannot be relied upon to the same extent as dispatchable thermal units. If a solar park or wind farm has a nameplate capacity of 100 MW, that is the maximum output it can achieve at peak sun or peak wind conditions. These peak conditions do not happen at the same time every day nor do they produce similar outputs month to month, due to seasonal variations. Fig. 2.8 provides one example of this variability, though the principles apply globally.

Annual and monthly regional or national summaries of VRE behavior are informative but paint a rather tame picture of realities electric utilities must face locally. An example can best illustrate this point. Historical output data at 5-minute time resolution was obtained from the National Renewable Energy Laboratory (NREL) for a wind [21] and a solar [22] site in the vicinity of Albuquerque, New Mexico, located in the southwest of the United States. On a representative April day (Fig. 2.9A) wind capacity factor was 12.2%, while solar capacity factor was 24.6%. For comparison, a representative June day yielded a 22% capacity factor for wind and 26.1% for solar (Fig. 2.9B).

We can quickly see the following from Fig. 2.9;

1. Solar tends to follow repeatable trends, peaking in the afternoons.
2. Wind does not necessarily follow a clear trend, at least from comparison of these two representative days.

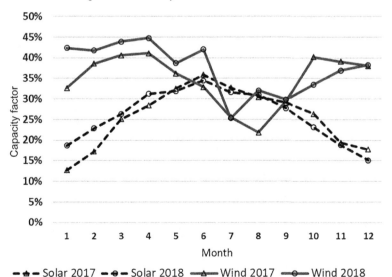

Figure 2.8 Average monthly solar and wind capacity factors for the United States for 2017 and 2018 [20].

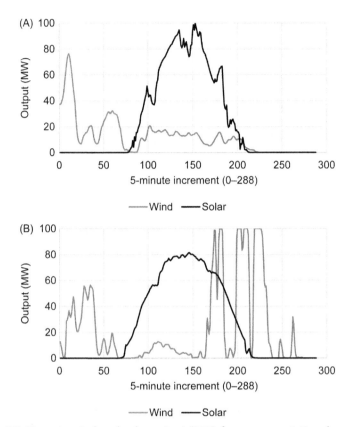

Figure 2.9 Five-min wind and solar output (MW) from representative days in April (A) and June (B), near Albuquerque, New Mexico (United States). Time = 0 at midnight at beginning of day, and ends at increment 288, at midnight at end of day.

3. Both wind and solar can experience dramatic ramps up and down; these can be due to cloud cover or wind gusts, but both are outside the control of the utility or grid operator.
4. Wind and solar output for both days is essentially zero at the same time, right at sunrise

The data shown here for New Mexico underscore important points that are true globally. Solar is more predictable with a peak at mid-day, assuming no cloud cover, heavy rain, or deep snowdrifts covering the panels. Wind output is far more variable. There is no common rule of thumb for determining what time of day or season of the year wind output will be at a maximum. It is apparent from Fig. 2.9 that trying to power a utility system 100% with wind and solar would be extremely difficult without some other form of capacity to supply MWh when VREs cannot. How a utility attends to the challenges is understood through utilization of net load.

Net load versus load

The first MWs of utility load is served by the lowest cost generators. Wind and solar have close to zero operational cost. They burn no fuel and only have minor maintenance expenses. If load is first served by VREs their contribution can be considered a negative load from the perspective of the balance of fleet. For example, in Table 2.2B we see a hypothetical utility with 100 MW of renewable energy available and 900 MW of thermal capacity. The load may be 900 MW, but 100 MW of the load is served by renewables. Conceptually the remaining assets are not being dispatched to meet a 900 MW load, they are dispatching to meet the net load of 800 MW.

Net load (MW) = load (MW) − renewable generation (MW).

Let us look at a hypothetical utility in New Mexico with a shoulder, low-load representative day in April and a peak load of 900 MW on a representative June day (Fig. 2.10A and B, respectively).

These load profiles (Fig. 2.10A and B) have typical utility load shapes and are here used for demonstration purposes only. In the absence of wind and solar capacity, the traditional utility fleet consisting of thermal units, hydro and nuclear power would be called to respond, in real time, to these load forms that are quite tame. On the peak day (Fig. 2.10B) there is a load ramp from $t = 50$ to $t = 200$, which represents a 12.5-hour time frame, during which utility assets must move from generating 550 to 900 MW. Most utilities, globally, can easily manage this. The thermal technologies installed over the years were chosen to attend to this sort of operational profile from day to day and season to season.

Now imagine that the utility installed 100 MW each of wind and solar capacity with profiles as shown in Fig. 2.9. The net load (Fig. 2.11A and B) is not dramatically different from the load. On the April day (Fig. 2.11A), there appears to be some erosion of net load as solar contributes mid-day. On the peak day (Fig. 2.11B) the net load trend is similar to the load, though more erratic near the peak. In this example, wind generation peaks around the same time as the load peak, but wind is also showing erratic swings from low generation all the way to maximum output of 100 MW over time spans as short as 10 minutes.

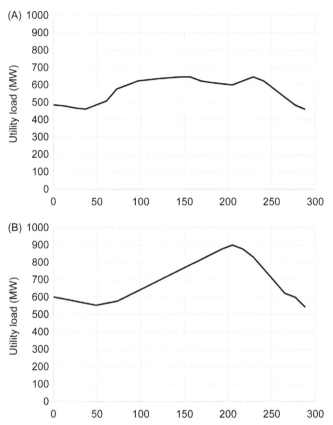

Figure 2.10 Representative load for hypothetical 900 MW peak utility on (A) April day and (B) June day, which is also the peak day. Horizontal axis ranges from 0 (midnight, beginning of day) to 288 (midnight, end of day) in 288 5-min increments.

This means that other elements of the portfolio must be able to ramp up and down almost 100 MW multiple times across the same time spans. This challenge is currently most often met either by fast start peaking units or by having a large generator run at part loads, holding its output back so that it can ramp up when needed. Energy storage is an alternate solution, which will be discussed later in the text.

Looking at this simple example in which renewables only serve a small percentage of the load, it is already evident that net load differs from load. The disparity grows with increasing renewable penetration. Assume that instead of 100 MW each of wind and solar, the utility had 225 MW each, for a total of 450 MW of renewable capacity (Fig. 2.12). The load profiles remain those shown in Fig. 2.10.

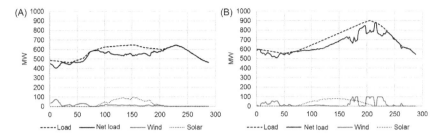

Figure 2.11 Load and net load on April (A) and June (B) days assuming 100 MW each of wind and solar capacity. Renewable energy serves 6.4% (A) and 6.9% (B) of daily load MWh, respectively.

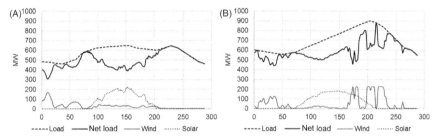

Figure 2.12 Load and net load on April (A) and June (B) days assuming 225 MW each of wind and solar. Renewable energy serves 14.4% (A) and 15.6% (B) of daily load MWh, respectively.

As the utility absorbs more renewable energy we see that on shoulder month days a more pronounced "double hump" appears in the net load (Fig. 2.12A), which occurs because mid-day solar generation is at its peak output and net load drops accordingly. On the peak day (Fig. 2.12B) the late afternoon/evening peak output from wind is causing the net load to be quite erratic, with net load ramps of more than 200 MW and a number of smaller ramp events as well. This is happening on days where solar and wind are only producing approximately 15% of the MWh, which is not very aggressive. Note that the installed nameplate VRE capacity of 450 MW is 50% of peak load, yet only contributes approximately 200 MW during the peak hour.

If the utility were to then again double its renewable capacity, now with 450 MW each of wind and solar, having the exact match of renewable capacity relative to its peak load, the net load starts to look quite frightening to your average grid dispatcher (Fig. 2.13). On the shoulder

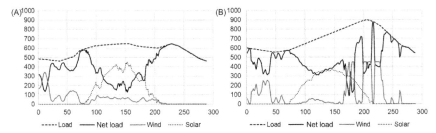

Figure 2.13 Load and net load on April (A) and June (B) days assuming 450 MW each of wind and solar. Renewable energy serves 28.8% (A) and 31.2% (B) of daily load MWh, respectively.

month day (Fig. 2.13A) the "double-hump" effect is more pronounced, with clear peaks in the morning and evening and a large drop in net load down to 100−200 MW mid-day as solar peaks. On the peak day (Fig. 2.13B) the net load looks nothing at all like the load profile. As the sun sets, net load swings wildly with wind output. Net load ramps of more than 400 MW up and down occur across time periods as short as 10 minutes. Recall that utilities have traditionally built large baseload units to serve the minimum load on the shoulder month day, about 500 MW for our hypothetical utility. Under traditional planning approaches a utility such as the one considered here would have invested in a 500 MW baseload unit years before they started to invest in solar and wind. But a 500 MW baseload unit would rarely run at full load attending to net load and, designed to start in 3 hours, could not be dispatched up/down on/off as quickly as needed for more erratic renewable behavior. Even so, this example utility is only generating 30% of its energy from solar and wind power.

What if our hypothetical utility, for any number of reasons from regulatory pressure to public demands to simply wanting to take advantage of very low-cost energy, decided to install even more renewables? Suppose the utility builds or purchases 900 MW each from solar and wind, installing twice as much renewable capacity as their peak load MW (Fig. 2.14). With such large amounts of renewables there are times, particularly in low-load shoulder month days, when renewable output exceeds load, at which point net load becomes negative. Negative net load implies an overabundance of renewable energy which can be:

• *Sold* to neighboring utilities, assuming they are short on energy and not experiencing similar overgeneration.

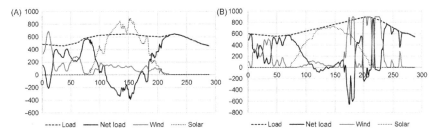

Figure 2.14 Load and net load on April (A) and June (B) days assuming 900 MW each of wind and solar. If all renewable energy was utilized, including the excess stored, renewables would serve 58% (A) and 62% (B) of daily load MWh, respectively. If excess renewable energy was shed or dumped, renewables would serve approximately 50% of load for each day (A and B).

- *Curtailed*. The renewables are directed to stop generating when the net load approaches zero.
- *Stored* in some form of energy storage.

Any attempt to meet the majority if not the entire load of a utility with wind and solar *will necessarily manifest in large overbuilds of renewable capacity to meet peak needs, which in turn means in off-peak times renewable generation will far exceed demand*. If storage capacity is unavailable to absorb excess generation renewables will be curtailed, else the excess must be sold.

Selling excess generation could be a viable way to dispose of this energy and is the basis of the energy imbalance market (EIM) in the western United States [23]. The State of California and the California Independent System Operator (CAISO) have arranged with investor-owned utilities in neighboring states to open a real-time energy market, the EIM. CAISO manages economic dispatch of the states three large investor-owned utilities as well as any IPPs operating within CAISOs footprint. It is one of the world's largest systems with a peak load in 2018 of 46,427 MW [24]. Prior to the EIM and due to a number of reasons, the state of California, and the CAISO system as a whole, experienced shortages of flexible capacity needed to manage net load ramps, necessitating curtailment, particularly of solar. By opening a broader regional market, the EIM allows neighboring utilities to purchase low-price energy when renewables are overgenerating relative to the load experienced by CAISO. CAISO also benefits by taking advantage of capacity in neighboring utilities to attend to net load ramping events in California. This arrangement has value for as long as the neighboring utilities have substantially less renewable capacity and energy production in their portfolios relative to CA. Many of the states neighboring California have their own RPS mandating installation of more wind and solar. In time they will also be meeting 50%–100% of their energy needs with renewables, at which point they will be overgenerating when California is overgenerating, and the ability of the EIM to act as a balancing mechanism will diminish.

Curtailment of renewables is a revenue loss since utilities get paid for generating MWh, and in some cases get subsidies for generation in the form of PTCs. However, curtailment may be necessary if available thermal capacity is unable to ramp quickly enough to respond to sudden fluctuations in renewable power production. In other words, curtailment is the product of lack of flexibility in the system. The majority of installed thermal capacity consists of older plants that simply cannot start/stop within the time frames of net load ramp events. The only way operators can meet the net load challenges is to operate several thermal plants at part load, reserving the ability to quickly ramp to full load, which takes substantially less time than it would take to start the unit. This imposes a minimum net load bound on the system, which is completely dependent on the technical features of the power plants that make up the remainder of the utility's capacity, other than solar and wind. That is, a utility with primarily large thermal generators may need to curtail renewable energy just to maintain reliability. They need to keep the thermal units running because the portfolio is inflexible and unable to cope with net load ramps, and this lack of flexibility increases the carbon footprint while diminishing the value of VREs.

For the hypothetical 900 MW peak load utility in the southwestern United States, a 30% renewable penetration may be an upper bound on the fraction of renewables they could absorb without requiring dramatic changes to their thermal fleet. With 450 MW each of solar and wind, on its peak day the minimum net load is 100 MW, and it experiences net load ramps of 200 + MW shortly after the minimum is reached (Fig. 2.13B). This could be met, theoretically, by a 300 MW combined cycle combustion turbine (CCCT) running at minimum stable load of 33% (100 MW), which has the capability of ramping up to full output in a short amount of time. If the CCCT is unable to ramp quickly enough the utility will have to rely on fast-start thermal, such as reciprocating engines, or have an even larger pool of units on-line with a greater ramp capacity, which in turn increases the minimum net load bound and limits the amount of renewable MWh the utility can leverage. If the utility wanted to install more wind or solar, the minimum load of the CCCT would be the limiting factor because the minimum load on the CCCT sets the lower bound of net load. The minimum net load bound is a limiting factor for many utilities and will remain so until there is a major turnover of their portfolio of assets. Nuclear plants and large coal facilities are perhaps the least flexible assets in a portfolio and can set this lower bound.

Challenges renewables impose on baseload generators

The challenges our hypothetical utility faces are common across the utility industry globally. The specifics differ depending on whether the utility is more wind-dominated or more solar-dominated, but minimum net load bounds are real. Existing thermal units will be forced to start, stop, and ramp up/down more often attending to net load than if they were running to serve load without renewables. The fuel savings associated with higher renewable penetration can be substantial leading to dramatic reductions in CO_2 emissions, but the volatility of VREs places mechanical and financial stresses on the balance of the fleet. For example, the New England Independent System Operator (ISO-NE) is tasked with dispatch of generation assets across six states in the northeastern United States. In 2011 ISO-NE issued a report [25] exploring the impact of 20% of the regions' energy needs supplied by wind power. They found the combined cycle fleet in ISO-NE (GWs of capacity) would have its capacity factor cut in half. Our simple example from earlier in this chapter showing how renewables reduce the marginal cost and experience from actual markets indicating the same (e.g., ref. [26]), suggests thermal units responding to net load will not only run fewer hours, but they will get paid less per hour of generation. Many of the existing thermal units were built years prior under anticipation of very different market conditions, and the reduced revenues as VRE adoption increases calls into question whether they can remain viable in a competitive market. In at least one case in 2019 California, a 750 MW CCCT was shut down only a few years after being built *"because the plant is no longer economically viable in a state where wind and solar supply a growing share of inexpensive electricity"* [27]. Similarly, in Germany 2015 a new 1400 MW CCCT was forced into early retirement *"... as competition from renewable energy pushes conventional stations out of business"* [28].

Early retirement of thermal units is a positive thing for those wanting rapid decarbonization but should be a warning sign for utilities. When investors and utilities made the choice to build these thermal plants, they used traditional planning approaches that indicated these were optimal investments. If the same approaches are used today, there is a good chance what appear to be optimal choices may fall flat once they are operational. The reason is that traditional LCOE, screening curve and load duration curve (LDC)-based capacity expansion tools are not capable of accurately modeling high renewable environments. They cannot account for the variability or volatility of VREs and make suboptimal investment choices.

Effect of geographic diversity

In the previous discussion of a hypothetical utility installing 100−900 MW each of wind and solar, the wind and solar profiles were based on the 5-minute data from an individual station for each type of renewable. This could be accurate for a small utility installing wind and solar facilities locally to serve load. When solar and wind sites are concentrated the individual panels or wind turbines have highly correlated behavior. But this is not typically how larger utilities or national systems experience the impact of higher renewable penetrations. Rather, they take advantage of the output from multiple wind and solar sites scattered across the landscape. They may own the assets, or they might sign PPAs with owners of renewable facilities that are located some distance away. With this "geographic diversity" the system operator sees the combined contribution from all of the sites in aggregate. So how does blending VREs from numerous sites impact the behavior of the whole of their collective output? For argument's sake, let us use the state of New Mexico in the United States as an example and make use of NREL data for solar [22] and wind [21] to look at ensemble data from 30 randomly drawn sites for each.

The average output per solar site varies throughout the day (Fig. 2.15), but follows some generic trends, namely that they produce nothing at night and generally peak in mid-day. Individual variations from site to site can be explained by varying cloud cover and other atmospheric conditions. The average conditions are smoothed out collectively such that net load ramping would be damped relative to the output of a single solar plant. However, the collective output of 30 solar sites never reaches nameplate output since individual sites will not reach nameplate at the

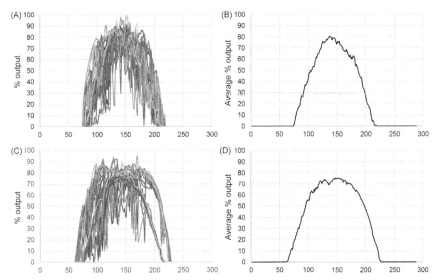

Figure 2.15 Five-min ($n = 288$) solar output (expressed as %) from $N = 30$ sites in New Mexico for an April (A) and June (C) day, and the average output (B and D), respectively.

same time, if at all, on a given day. For the 2 days selected here, the collective output of all 30 sites never exceeds 80% of the nameplate capacity (Fig. 2.15B and D).

Wind is harder to characterize in that it is far more variable at any given site (Fig. 2.16). The sites in New Mexico had varying peak wind periods, with some sites peaking in the evening and others in the afternoon. The trends are not necessarily repeatable day to day. That is, one can assume without too much generalization that solar will peak every day, year-round, at mid-day. Unlike solar, one cannot assume that wind will peak at any particular time day to day. Similar to solar, the ensemble output across sites rarely, if ever, matches their aggregate nameplate capacity (Fig. 2.16B and D).

Time scale is important

Whether they make their information publicly accessible or not, every utility and system operator has access to real-time VRE data as shown in the previous figures. They have this information not just for renewables, but also for every power plant in their system as well as the loads. Often

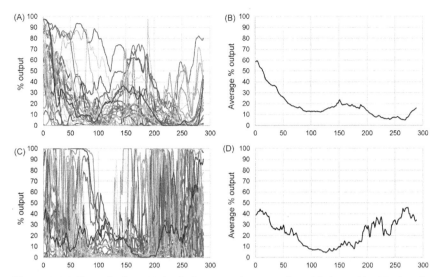

Figure 2.16 Five-min ($n = 288$) wind output (expressed as %) from $N = 30$ sites in New Mexico form an April (A) and June (C) day, and the average output (B and D), respectively.

this data is collapsed into hourly average data for the purpose of graphical representation and even for modeling. Using hourly average data has advantages. Hourly information for 1 year requires 8760 data points. The same data in 5-minute time resolution requires 105,210 data points. If 1-minute resolution were used there would be more than 500,000 data points, for each plant and load, for each year.

More often than not, the data are averaged to hourly. The impact of hourly averaging is to lose information. For example, the average wind data for the June day (Fig. 2.16B) are plotted next to the hourly average (Fig. 2.17). The major trends are retained, wind output decreased from midnight toward mid-day, then climbs again toward the evening. The hourly plot (Fig. 2.17B) does show wind output dropping 10%, from hours 19 to 20, across the 5-minute intervals ranging from 225 to 250. What the hourly average misses are the more erratic ramps in real time, and most real-time dispatch commitments are done at 5-minute increments. Resource planners and policy makers must understand that real-time ramp events are not trivial. Independent of broad trends keeping the lights on reliably requires that there be something besides VREs that can ramp up and down as wind and solar MW go down and up, respectively.

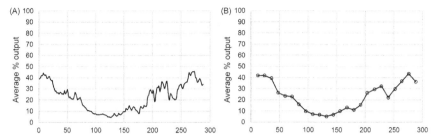

Figure 2.17 Average (*N* = 30) wind output in New Mexico, expressed as % of name-plate, in 5-min (*n* = 288) time resolution (A), as well as the same information expressed as hourly average (B).

These data shown in this chapter from sites in New Mexico are idio-syncratic and not representative of all regions of the Earth. However, they do illustrate generic trends resource planners must account for.

1. Output from VREs follows seasonal variations.
2. VRE output can be quite variable from site to site and volatile throughout the day for a given site.
3. Geographic diversity smooths out but does not eliminate some of the volatility.
4. Solar patterns are easier to predict and incorporate into planning than wind.
5. Numerous VRE sites rarely reach nameplate capacity at the same time; therefore the aggregate output of VREs for a given hour is almost always lower than the aggregate nameplate capacity.
6. VRE peak output is out of phase with peak load hours.
7. Hourly averaging of wind and solar data retains the major trends in energy production but loses information on real-time ramping.

Solar and wind degradation rates

Every generation technology experiences some form of degradation. Solar panels are electro-mechanical devices that convert solar energy into MWh. With no moving parts the panel systems are robust and can last 25−40 years. However, the panels themselves experience degradations in efficiency over time [29], ranging from 1% to 3% in the first year, and slower rates (0.4%−1%) subsequently [30,31]. Degradation translates to a reduction in the peak MW the facility can produce and the volume of MWh the panels produce relative to their nameplate conditions.

Degradation rates are a function of the chemistry in panel manufacturing as well as exposure to extreme weather and damage from tree limbs or other sources. In high dust environments fouling can occur due to film build-up, leading to reduced output. Resource planners should account for panel degradation in capacity expansion simulations. A 1000 MW solar park in year 1 could degrade to 800 MW in year 20. If degradation is not accounted for in the planning, the system could be short on capacity in future years.

Wind turbines are mechanical devices that convert wind energy into MWh. Degradation on wind turbines is attributable to mechanical wear and reduced aerodynamic performance of the blades over time, which can vary based on manufacturer, design, and location. For example, airfoil performance (either wings on an airplane or blades on a wind turbine) is seriously impacted by the crust of dead insects that builds up over time as they impact the airfoil. This is a big reason airplanes are washed periodically, removing the film buildup maximizes their fuel efficiency. Dusty or sandy environments can also yield accelerated degradation of airfoil performance [32]. One study that reviewed operations of close to 300 wind farms in Europe over a 10-year period found annual degradation rates on the order of 1.4%–1.8% [33]. Like solar, mis-accounting (or not accounting at all) for wind-turbine degradation can lead to overestimates of available capacity in future years, and/or overvaluation of the asset. The LCOE ($/MWh) of both wind and solar have denominators of MWh, and both are typically presented as functions of known or estimated capacity factors and assumed nameplate output. Degradation reduces the total MWh generated over 20 years, a typical time span of LCOE calculations, which leads to a higher LCOE in reality than the optimistic value based on nameplate conditions. Degradation on wind farms can increase LCOE for wind projects by 10% [33].

Solar and wind are not alone in having degraded performance over time. Thermal plants also have degradation rates, but they are typically not a constant rate across the life of the project. Large boiler plants can have an initial degradation of 1%–3% from fouling, coating of the combustion, and working/heat transfer surfaces with a film of combustion byproducts. All thermal plants have derating over time, a loss in output or decreased efficiency as various components wear with use. Major overhauls typically return the plants to close to new and clean performance, but some degradation is irreversible. Energy storage, depending on the type, can experience performance degradation with time. Resource planners at utilities should account for performance degradation of all technologies in short-term assessments, production costing, and in long-term planning models.

Baseload is going away, enter residual loads

Utility systems globally are installing greater amounts of renewable energy. Part of this trend is due to legislation and mandates requiring decarbonization, while more recently the trend is accelerated by the falling cost of these energy sources. Adding renewables is a sensible choice at a global level, but questions remain on how utilities plan for the balance of their fleet of assets. Net load volatility imposes stress on the remainder of the portfolio that translates to cost and economic impacts that are not necessarily intuitive or easy to quantify. This is especially true for utilities relying on LDC constructs for long-term capacity expansion planning. This is perhaps best exemplified with an example. In 2017 the CAISO, which manages the load and assets of the three large investor-owned utilities in California, had a peak load of close to 50 GW (Fig. 2.18A). Twenty-four percent of the MWh was provided by renewables, which include dispatchable resources such as geothermal and biofuels. VREs (wind, solar) accounted for 17% of the MWh serving load for CAISO. Subtracting VRE MWh from load for each hour and creating an LDC for the net load (Fig. 2.18B) yield a curve that looks similar to load-based LDC but is significantly different.

The LDC based on load indicates a baseload need of 18,300 MW. Once VREs are netted from load, the baseload need is only 9300 MW, or approximately half that if looking only at load. That is, the need for

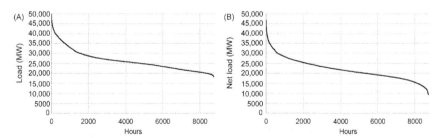

Figure 2.18 Load duration curves for CAISO for 2017 for total system load (A) and net load after wind and solar generation accounted for (B). *Data from California ISO Markets & Operations. <http://www.caiso.com/market/Pages/default.aspx>, 2019 (accessed 18.02.19) [34].*

baseload in the CAISO system is roughly cut in half as the system approaches 20% VRE penetration. This empirical data from the CAISO system mirrors the expectations from a report published by the New England Independent System Operator (ISO-NE) in 2011 [25]. The ISO-NE study asked what would happen if 20% of the energy in the northeastern United States, referred to as New England, was supplied by wind? The report [25] found one impact would be that the baseloaded CCCT fleet could expect its capacity factor to be cut in half.

CAISO data (Fig. 2.18) indicate there are no hours where load is smaller than 18,300 MW, and no hours where net load is less than 9300 MW. Since the baseloads are constant, we can remove them from the load and net load entirely and look only at the residuals.

Residual weekly loads for CAISO are plotted for a low load week in a shoulder month and for a peak season week (Fig. 2.19).

The weekly residual net load minima occur at or near intervals 12, 36, 48, 60, etc., corresponding to mid-day, which is when solar output is maximized. This is true for both off-peak (April week) and on-peak weeks. Residual load is more erratic in the off-peak week because load is low, while renewable output is relatively high, with wind and solar providing 18.9% of the MWh for this week. Residual net load is less erratic during the on-peak week in part because wind and solar are only serving 11.6% of the load.

Residual net load is always higher than residual load. *This means the CAISO system needs more intermediate and peaking resources than if they simply served load with no wind or solar at all.* In addition, while on-peak residual load and net load appear to follow similar trends, there are intermediate peaks and ramps in residual net load that are not there for the residual

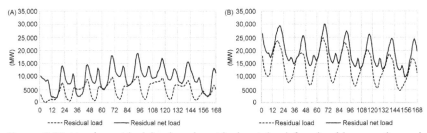

Figure 2.19 Hourly residual load and residual net load for shoulder month week (April 2−8, 2017) (A) and for peak season week (September 3−9) (B). *Data from California ISO Markets & Operations. <http://www.caiso.com/market/Pages/default. aspx>, 2019 (accessed 18.02.19) [34].*

load. This becomes far more pronounced in off-peak time periods, when renewable energy tends to provide a larger share of the energy needs. The balance of fleet will have more frequent and more dramatic ramps than the system with no renewables at all. The trends are here evident for a system with a modest 17% of annual MWh from wind and solar.

Ramifications for resource planning

Net load residuals indicate a need for flexible assets. The LDC has no information to inform what type of capacity would serve this need best. Often utilities look at high-efficiency CCCTs, which have 1—3-hour start times, or inefficient peaking CTs, which are low cost, to fill the intermediate and peaking needs, respectively. These types of technologies have been used for decades and were never designed to start/stop on a regular basis, potentially multiple times per day. Yet LDC-based approaches may select them solely because the approach cannot account for seasonal variability, impact of falling marginal costs, or net load volatility. The same is true for LCOE approaches, which calculate discounted annualized $/MWh costs based on a prescribed run-hour assumption with plants running at full load independent of starts. LCOE will give a low $/MWh cost for certain units that, when they are subjected to frequent ramping and start/stop sequences, will have a far higher annualized $/MWh cost than suggested by LCOE. Similarly a utility planning for large amounts of VRE might assume average annual capacity factors, but if VREs end up being curtailed 50% because the rest of the portfolio is inflexible, the real LCOE will in effect double. There is no way to know the impact of starts and curtailment without leveraging accurate least-cost dispatch simulations.

A utility with access to least-cost dispatch planning software can run various portfolios against VRE contributions to determine the cost impacts of seasonality, volatility, etc. Historically these dispatch approaches reduced the data to representative weeks, which use simplistic representations of wind and solar outputs. They may use 4, 8, or 12-hour time blocks to speed up calculations, although more recently utilities have started to at least go down to 1-hour time resolution. In the past, when utilities were only concerned with serving load with traditional thermal and small amounts of VREs these simplifications were defendable and often rather accurate. However, with increasing solar and wind penetration, reliance on these approaches is less than ideal. What if a utility made purchasing decisions using data from 1 week per month for simulations and missed other weeks in the month when VRE output was close to zero? The analysis and may suggest investments that will leave the utility short on capacity in low VRE periods that were not accounted for in the modeling.

Whether levelized cost or basic least-cost dispatch, most utilities retain certain simplifications that make the outcomes less than ideal for a system hoping to reach or exceed 15%–20% of their energy from VREs. These simplifications fail to account for the cost or reliability impacts of dynamic features for technologies other than VREs, which include:

- Start time (hours or minutes to go from start command to full load),
- Minimum run time,
- Minimum downtime,
- Minimum stable load,
- Full efficiency curve (from minimum stable load to maximum output), and
- Temperature effects (most thermal units have degraded performance with hotter temperatures).

Start times for many gas turbines exceed 10 minutes, some in excess of 30 minutes. Many CCCTs have start times of one or more hours. Minimum run and down of 2–4 hours are typical for many thermal plants. Units may be required to run for hours at their minimum load or tasked with starting multiple times per day.

Why are we talking about thermal units in a chapter dedicated to renewables? Because adding renewables to a portfolio impacts the dispatch of everything else on the system and will influence the choice of new-build technologies for years to come, including energy storage. If resource planning fails to account for the vagaries of VREs and ignores dynamic features of nonrenewable technologies, there is a very real risk the recommended future portfolio will overvalue solar and wind, be unable to quantify the value of storage, and instead build inflexible thermal. The build-out will be suboptimal; costs will be higher than expected and CO_2 reductions will not be as great as expected. Therefore getting the most out of renewables in the planning phase requires state-of-the-art capacity expansion simulations that leverage and account for all dynamic features via chronological dispatch modeling. When overgeneration of renewables leads to curtailment, it would be advantageous for planners to have super-dynamic capacity to choose from that could absorb overgeneration and reduce curtailment. Such a resource does exist—it is called energy storage.

References

[1] Global Solar Atlas 2.0, a free, web-based application developed and operated by the company Solargis s.r.o. on behalf of the World Bank Group, utilizing Solargis data, with funding provided by the Energy Sector Management Assistance Program (ESMAP). <https://globalsolaratlas.info>, 2019.

[2] Global Wind Atlas 3.0, a free, web-based application developed, owned and operated by the Technical University of Denmark (DTU). The Global Wind Atlas 3.0 is released in partnership with the World Bank Group, utilizing data provided by Vortex, with funding provided by the Energy Sector Management Assistance Program (ESMAP). <https://globalwindatlas.info>, 2019.

[3] History of California's renewable energy programs. <https://ww2.energy.ca.gov/renewables/history.html>, 2019 (accessed 19.04.19).

[4] L. Dillon, California to rely on 100% clean electricity by 2045 under bill signed by Gov. Jerry Brown, Los Angeles Times, 2018.

[5] European Commission, Renewable energy. <https://ec.europa.eu/energy/en/topics/renewable-energy>, (accessed 19.05.14).

[6] S. Patel, China Sets a New Renewable Portfolio Standard, Power. <https://www.powermag.com/china-sets-a-new-renewable-portfolio-standard/>, 2018.

[7] China Sets New Renewable Portfolio Standard, Asian-Power. <https://asian-power.com/regulation/news/china-sets-new-renewable-portfolio-standard>, 2019.

[8] A. Stauffer, D. Aharony, Introduction to Percolation Theory, second ed., Taylor & Francis, Philadelphia, PA, 1994.

[9] R. Gardner, R.H. Turner, M.G. Dale, V. O'Neill, A percolation model of ecological flows, in: F. Hansen, A.J. DiCastri (Eds.), Landscape Boundaries: Ecological Studies (Analysis and Synthesis), vol. 92, Springer, New York, NY, 1992, pp. 259–269.

[10] History of Solar, <https://www1.eere.energy.gov/solar/pdfs/solar_timeline.pdf>.

[11] Abandoned Solar Power Plant, California. The Center for Land Use Interpretation, Land Use Database. <http://clui.org/ludb/site/abandoned-solar-power-plant>, 2019 (accessed 21.01.19).

[12] J. Bolinger, M. Seel, Utility-Scale Solar, Empirical Trends in Project Technology, Cost, Performance and PPA Pricing in the United States — 2018 Edition. <https://emp.lbl.gov/sites/default/files/lbnl_utility_scale_solar_2018_edition_report.pdf>, 2018.

[13] E. Hau, Wind Turbines, Fundamentals, Technologies, Applications, Economics, Springer-Verlag, Berlin, 2006.

[14] M. Wiser, R., Bolinger, U.S. Department of Energy 2017 Wind Technologies Market Report. <http://eta-publications.lbl.gov/sites/default/files/2017_wind_technologies_market_report.pdf>, 2017.

[15] Renewable Capacity Statistics 2018. International Renewable Energy Agency (IRENA), Abu Dhabi. <https://www.irena.org/-/media/Files/IRENA/Agency/Publication/2018/Mar/IRENA_RE_Capacity_Statistics_2018.pdf>, 2018.

[16] Renewable Capacity Statistics 2017. International Renewable Energy Agency (IRENA), Abu Dhabi. <https://www.irena.org/publications/2017/Mar/Renewable-Capacity-Statistics-2017>, 2017.

[17] C.R. Frank, The net benefits of low and no-carbon electricity technologies. Working Paper No. 73. <https://www.brookings.edu/wp-content/uploads/2016/06/Net-Benefits-Final.pdf>, 2014.

[18] I. Greenstone, M. Nath, Do renewable portfolio standards deliver? Working Paper No. 2019-62, Chicago. <https://bfi.uchicago.edu/wp-content/uploads/BFIEPIC_WP_201962_v4.pdf>, 2019.

[19] G. Teplin, C. Dyson, M. Engel, A. Glazer, The growing market for clean energy portfolios: economic opportunities for a shift from new gas-fired generation to clean energy across the United States electricity industry. <https://rmi.org/cep-reports>, 2019.

[20] Electric Power Monthly. U.S. Energy Information Agency. <https://www.eia.gov/electricity/monthly/epm_table_grapher.php?t = epmt_6_07_b>, (accessed 19.06.01).

[21] Wind Prospector, U.S. National Renewable Energy Laboratory, <https://maps.nrel.gov/wind-prospector/>, 2019 (accessed 07.01.19).

[22] Solar Power Data for Integration Studies. U.S. National Renewable Energy Laboratory. <https://www.nrel.gov/grid/solar-power-data.html>, 2019 (accessed 21.01.19).

[23] A. Larson, How does the western energy imbalance market work? Power (2018). Available from: https://www.powermag.com/how-does-the-western-energy-imbalance-market-work/.

[24] California ISO Peak Load History 1998 Through 2018. California Independent System Operator. <https://www.caiso.com/Documents/CaliforniaISOPeakLoadHistory.pdf>, 2018 (accessed 23.05.19).

[25] New England Wind Integration Study. ISO-New England. <https://www.iso-ne.com/static-assets/documents/committees/comm_wkgrps/prtcpnts_comm/pac/reports/2010/newis_report.pdf>, 2011.

[26] K. Bushnell, J. Novan, Setting With the Sun: The Impacts of Renewable Energy on Wholesale Power Markets. Energy Institute WP-292. <https://ei.haas.berkeley.edu/research/papers/WP292.pdf>, 2018.

[27] A. Scott, General Electric to Scrap California Power Plant 20 Years Early, Reuters Business News. <https://www.reuters.com/article/us-ge-power/general-electric-to-scrap-california-power-plant-20-years-early-idUSKCN1TM2MV>, 2019.

[28] C. Steitz, UPDATE 2-Germany's Irsching Gas-Fired Power Plant Set to Close, Reuters. <https://www.reuters.com/article/e-on-irsching/update-2-germanys-irsching-gas-fired-power-plant-set-to-close-idUSL6N0WW1NB20150330>, 2015.

[29] K. Pickerel, What causes solar panel degradation? Sol. Power World (2017). Available from: https://www.solarpowerworldonline.com/2017/06/causes-solar-panel-degradation/>.

[30] Best Practices in Photovoltaic System Operations and Maintenance, second ed., NREL Technical Report NREL/TP-7A40-67553. <https://www.nrel.gov/docs/fy17osti/67553.pdf>, 2016.

[31] J. Jordan, D.C. Kurtz, S.R. VanSant, K. Newmiller, Compendium of photovoltaic degradation rates, Prog. Photovolt. 24 (2016) 978−989.

[32] Z. Biab, A. Alaa, M. El-Din, A.H. Salem, H. Ghoneim, Performance degradation of wind turbine airfoils due to dust contamination: a comparative numerical study, in: ASME Turbo Expo: Power for Land, Sea and Air, vol. 9. <https://asmedigitalcollection.asme.org/GT/GT2015/volume/56802>, 2015.

[33] R. Staffell, I. Green, How does wind farm performance decline with age? Renew. Energy 66 (2014) 775−786.

[34] California ISO Markets & Operations. <http://www.caiso.com/market/Pages/default.aspx>, 2019 (accessed 18.02.19).

CHAPTER 3

Energy storage and conversion

Energy storage (ES) is a rather new and exciting space in the utility and energy planning world. The single largest motivator for increased interest in storage is the acceleration of renewable deployments. Any system with large provision of energy from variable renewable energy sources (VREs) will have periods of overgeneration, or excess energy. This happens when, for example, solar is peaking mid-day and generating more MW than the system load. Without a means to absorb this excess, renewable resources are ordered to disconnect or reduce generation of MWh, a process called curtailment. Storage allows utilities to store this excess for later use, in effect time-shifting the MWh. Time-shifting excess renewable energy has the potential to offset thermal resources in other parts of the day or week, further reducing carbon footprints. Utilities have been slow to effectively include ES in integrated resource plans for a number of reasons, including lack of familiarity with storage options, their characteristics, performance and pricing, and inability to capture the full value of storage in valuation [1].

There are two ways to take advantage of storage: arbitrage and time-shifting of energy. Arbitrage refers to buying energy when it is cheap, storing that energy, then discharging it when prices are higher. If the economics show storage can net a profit from arbitrage, then the system makes economic sense. This sort of economic decision drove the installation of the first "grid-scale" ES, pumped hydro (PH), long before anyone believed wind and solar would provide any great amount of energy. Time-shifting is a more fundamental consideration, trying to find a place to store overgeneration from massive wind and solar deployments that would otherwise be curtailed, so that energy can be released back into the system at a later time. Overgeneration storage provides system-wide benefits and value, increasing the capacity factor of renewables and reducing their average $/MWh costs. Storage capacity makes use of low-cost MWh from renewables, offsetting the need to install thermal or other types of capacity that may be higher cost. Regardless, it is often the case that arbitrage makes the most sense in systems with overgeneration, where excess MWh from renewables drive market prices for energy ($/MWh)

Electric Utility Resource Planning
DOI: https://doi.org/10.1016/B978-0-12-819873-5.00003-4

toward zero, in which case arbitrage is implicit even if it is not the driving force promoting ES. It is imperative for resource planners and regulators to understand that the full benefit and value chain of ES, or any flexible capacity, cannot be viewed at the project level. The benefits are at the system, or portfolio level.

While thermal and renewable technologies are mature, well understood, and easy to describe, ES is a bit more difficult to characterize, as there are numerous approaches which are dramatically different from each other in a technical and commercial sense. Storage technologies are evolving, some faster than others, making them almost impossible to describe without resorting to an entire treatise on each type of ES system, which is beyond the scope of this work. Given the pace of development, any such treatise would be out of date by the time the work was published. The goal here is to provide a survey of storage technologies and their general features and to provide guidance on how utility planners should characterize these systems in their long-term plans.

Basic principles of energy storage

Every ES system is designed to take MWh during charging, and store them for future use. In this sense ES is a device for time-shifting MWh, which is rather revolutionary as for more than a century electricity was considered a commodity that had to be consumed as soon as it was produced. A simplistic representation of ES time-shifting of renewable overgeneration is shown in Fig. 3.1. An attentive reader will notice that the

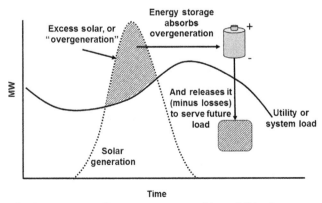

Figure 3.1 Basic premise of energy storage "time-shifting" excess renewable generation (MWh).

shaded area representing "overgeneration" is larger than the MWh released at a later time in Fig. 3.1. All ES approaches have inefficiencies such that amount of energy available for discharge is less than the energy used to charge. A common metric used in ES discussions is "round-trip efficiency," which describes the amount of useable energy output relative to the energy input. Round-trip efficiencies vary between 50% and 95 + % depending on the type of storage.

All forms of ES absorb MWh and store them as some form of potential (Fig. 3.2), which in physics refers to an ability to do work, like release useful forms of energy. This potential can be in the form of volts, heat or pressure, gravity, or chemical bonds. In a battery, electrochemical reactions drive a voltage difference which in turn drives current (electricity). In a compressed air system, high-pressure air is released to spin a turbine connected to a generator, which delivers MWh. Similarly, a PH system releases water from an elevation, which makes use of gravity as it falls to spin a turbine. Other forms of potential (e.g., heat, chemical, or kinetic energy) are also used for ES. Regardless, they all operate on the same principle of stored potential but can be completely different in terms of their inner workings. Likewise, they all have different costs to build and install, they have different maintenance requirements and component lifetimes, and different round-trip efficiencies.

Size and duration

Any ES device can be characterized by two metrics: size and duration. Size refers to its capacity at peak output, measured in MW. Discharge duration refers to the amount of time a storage device can deliver peak MW, measured in minutes, hours, or days. The most common duration metric is "hours," so that storage systems are characterized by their available energy, in MWh. Different ES and conversion technologies are applicable to varying needs in terms of size and duration (Fig. 3.3).

Size, or peak MW capacity of a storage device is part of the core structure of any ES technology but means nothing without some duration for which that energy is available. The duration is generally a function of the size of the system. For example, a 1 MW water turbine at the bottom of a PH reservoir will have a duration commensurate with the size of the reservoir. A small reservoir might have enough water to power the turbine for 4 hours. Tripling the size of the reservoir will change the duration to 12 hours. For a battery-storage system an inverter takes the place of the

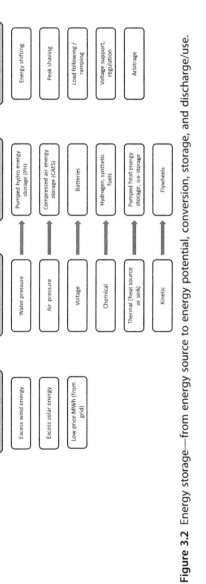

Figure 3.2 Energy storage—from energy source to energy potential, conversion, storage, and discharge/use.

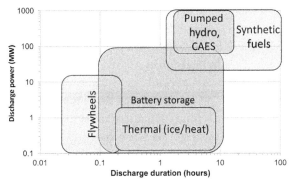

Figure 3.3 Schematic representation of utility-scale storage types, discharge power (MW), and discharge duration (hours).

turbine in the PH system. Inverters convert DC electricity into AC and typically at a higher voltage. The inverter sets the peak MW output of a battery ES system, and, for a lithium-ion (Li-ion) system, the duration is controlled by the number of cells installed. For a fixed inverter size, to get twice the duration you install twice as many cells.

The main time domains of ES are as follows:
- minutes (frequency regulation, voltage support);
- hours (capacity resource, energy shifting, typically 4−12 hours);
- days (seasonal shifting).

The majority of ES assets and applications rely on technologies with durations less than 24 hours and can be characterized as "power" or "energy" devices. *Power devices* are short-duration and designed to provide fast ramping up and down to manage grid voltage, regulation services, and real-time energy. For these applications the units are not expected to maintain long-duration discharge and are often rated at 15, 30, or 60 minutes. *Energy devices* are longer-term storage, more appropriate for energy shifting or load following, though they may also provide shorter bursts to serve as power devices. Energy devices have durations of multiple hours, often in the 4−8 + hour range.

Seasonal shifting can be provided by storage technologies with much longer durations, typically on the order of days. This is important if, for example, a utility system has ample sun and wind part of the year, and a noticeably smaller amount of the same in other parts of the year. One solution would be to simply overinstall wind and/or solar capacity so that even in the worst possible week of low seasonal wind and sun, there would still be enough capacity installed to serve all load with minimal to no reliance on storage, which is a path suggested by some (e.g., [2−4]). However, the amount of land required and the total system cost make this option prohibitive for most utilities to consider, in which case ES is needed. But even if traditional forms of ES are included, such as PH and batteries, renewable capacity needed for decarbonization can range from three to eight times the peak load of a utility system [5]. Short term ES on the order of minutes to hours can attend to system stability and energy shifting, but longer-term storage may be needed. This is less of a concern for small utilities with access to competitive markets, as they often assume enough energy will always be available for purchase if needed. Larger utilities or state or national systems may need to provide long-term reliability in the form of seasonal storage. PH may be able to attend to seasonal shifting concerns, but the majority of PH installed globally has a duration (at rated output) of 24 hours or less. Compressed air energy storage (CAES) is similar, with few existing applications globally, but capable of durations greater than 24 hours. Renewable synthetic fuel production allows for very long-term ES and has such a dramatically different business case that it is reserved for the following chapter.

Types of energy storage

There are numerous types of ES available on the market, including PH, flywheels, thermal, batteries, compressed, and liquefied air systems. Each are discussed below.

Pumped hydro

Many forms of ES have great potential and fascinating technological developments, with legions of graduate students and professionals shaping their careers around advancing these forms of energy conversion. Rightly so, these other forms of ES tend to get more attention in the media and academia, and puzzle policymakers challenged with incorporating their unique features into market designs, as well as confound utility planners trying to simulate them correctly in dispatch and long-range planning exercises. Meanwhile a mature and simple approach has been deployed at GW scale across the globe for almost a century: PH.

PH is extremely simple in concept. Use a turbine attached to a motor to pump water from one reservoir to a second reservoir at higher elevation through one or more large pipes, thus converting electrical energy to potential energy. When electricity is needed, water is discharged from

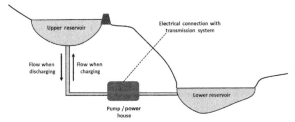

Figure 3.4 Schematic of a pumped hydro storage facility.

higher elevation through the same pipes to turn the same rotors, connected to a generator, in the opposite direction, and the potential is converted back to electrical energy. Upper and lower reservoirs (Fig. 3.4) can be closed loop (not connected to other water bodies) or open loop, where one or both reservoirs are connected to a river or lake.

PH is often referred to as a "water battery." The first PH project in the United States was installed by Connecticut Electric Light and Power Company in 1930, near New Milford, Connecticut (United States). The magazine Popular Science (July 1930 edition, page 60) ran an article about the facility titled "A Ten-Mile Storage Battery," in which they referred to the project as "a sort of gigantic electric storage battery." In the same article they even report the efficiency as... "So efficient is this great "storage battery" that it delivers sixty-one horsepower for every hundred horsepower that is used to pump water." The plant was reported in the article as having a 44,000 horsepower generator, which is equivalent to 33 MW.

At present, PH storage represents more than 95% of all stationary utility-scale ES systems deployed globally. PH facilities exist with capacities on the order of multiple GW. The Bath County Pumped Storage Station in Virginia (United States), which came on-line in 1985, is described as the largest battery in the world with a maximum output of 3000 MW which can be sustained for 8 hours. More recently China has installed pumped storage stations of 2400 MW capacity (Guangdong Pumped Storage Power Station and Huizhou Pumped Storage Power Station).

Flywheels

The concept of using kinetic energy in a spinning mass to do work has been used by people as far back as 6000 BC, with spindle devices found in China and Mesopotamia for the production of thread, and potters-wheel devices dating back to 4000 BC. Flywheels for propulsion were first introduced by Lieutenant Commander John Howell of the US Navy, who designed a flywheel-powered torpedo in his spare time, which he patented in 1871. In the 1950s the Swiss company Oerlikon developed the first flywheel-powered passenger bus [6]. Flywheel development for utility-scale ES was developed and brought to market in the 1990s.

Flywheel ES systems use electric energy to turn a spinning mass (a rotor) in a close-to-frictionless enclosure. The spinning mass then has potentially stored as kinetic energy. When energy is needed, the spinning mass engages with and turns a generator, which produces electricity. High rotational speeds of 10,000 to 100,000 rpm are required to get the most potential from the flywheel. Flywheel ES systems have a high energy density, very low environmental impact, and can be cycled thousands to several hundred thousand times, depending on manufacturer and materials, before major maintenance is required. Flywheel systems are used for short-duration discharge and are capable of almost instantaneous response and very fast ramp rates. Flywheel systems can go from full discharge to full charge in a matter of seconds and are most often used to manage power quality, frequency response, and regulation within a power system. Unlike battery systems, flywheels can charge/discharge and ramp over thousands of cycles with practically no performance degradation and are expected to have long lifetimes (decades). Early flywheel systems could lose up to 50% of their energy within 2 hours from rotational/mechanical drag. More advanced systems using magnetic bearings and high vacuum containers can achieve round-trip efficiencies as high as 90%−95% [7].

One of the first grid-scale applications was supplied by Beacon Power, a 20 MW project in Stephentown, New York, in 2011. The Stephentown project includes 200 flywheels that perform 3000−5000 full discharge cycles per year [8]. A project of similar size was installed in 2014 in Hazle Township, Pennsylvania [9]. These flywheel projects provided 15-minute duration and are used primarily for fast-response frequency regulation services. Amber Kinetics was awarded a contract to build a 20 MW flywheel system for the California utility Pacific Gas & Electric in 2015 [10], and in 2018 was selected for a longer duration 8 kW, 32 kWh pilot project on the island of Oahu, Hawaii [11].

Most flywheel systems are small and designed for short (sub 1 hour) duration, although some systems are attempting the 4-hour mark. Most analyses looking at high renewable penetration where massive amounts of storage (hundreds to thousands of MW) and long durations (4−8 hours or more) are needed, consider ES systems other than flywheels. However, their fast response, low environmental impact, and durability provide a solution for frequency regulation services, which typically only require fast-acting capacity on the order of a few % of load.

Thermal storage

While the topic of ES has become very popular in recent years, energy shifting thermal storage has provided tremendous benefit in terms of energy conservation for several decades. This conservation in turn requires less generation and reduces system CO_2 emissions. Stored ice or chilled water is used as a heat sink to offset the considerable air conditioning load of large commercial buildings or campuses. Electricity is purchased during off-peak hours, when electricity price is low, to chill water or make ice. Low night-time ambient temperatures also improve the efficiency of both energy production and ice production. The building owner enjoys reduced cooling costs and the building's contribution to daytime peak loads is significantly reduced. If adopted by enough industrial/commercial customers, load shifting reduces peak load and ultimately the amount of capacity a utility needs to install.

Installation of ice-storage in a building, campus, or commercial district is outside the sphere of influence of most utility planners, but it is within the realm of policymakers and the government to impose standards mandating and/or subsidizing its use. For example, in China approximately 50% of the energy used by commercial/industrial buildings is related to air conditioning, with peak energy use during the day while energy use is peaking for every other need as well. Cities in China have had to increase investments in generation capacity just to attend to air conditioning loads. The Chinese State Council in 2011 prepared the Energy-Saving and Pollution Reduction Comprehensive Action Plan, which identified thermal ice-storage as a key measure for reducing peak loads and emissions from its power system. Various incentives exist or are under development to further stimulate adoption of ice-storage systems throughout China [12].

Other forms of thermal energy storage

A great deal of work has been put into various means by which electrical energy is stored as heat. Practically all concentrated solar facilities use a molten salt system to absorb solar radiation as heat, then release it to the grid as power. Outside of concentrated solar facilities, which make up only a small fraction of solar installations, molten salt technologies are rarely used. However, there is some discussion recently about Pumped Heat Electrical Storage (PHES) devices. PHES operates analogous to PH storage. With PH, energy is used to pump water uphill to a higher elevation where it is stored until discharge is needed, and the water goes back downhill to generate electricity with a turbine and generator. With PHES, instead of pumping water, heat is pumped from a cold temperature reservoir to a high-temperature reservoir, and the temperature difference between the two provides a potential which can be exploited to generate electricity. When pumping heat from cold to hot the PHES uses energy to power a reversible heat pump/heat engine. Reversing the process drives the heat engine and generates electricity. Typically, a closed circuit connects the cold and hot reservoirs and is filled with an inert gas such as argon, which can cool down and heat up much more than air. The gas is then used to heat or cool containers filled with crushed rock or ceramic material. Round-trip efficiencies of 65%–75% are expected. PHES promises to be a relatively cost-effective means of ES for utility or grid-scale applications, is easily scalable, has low environmental impact, and can cycle thousands of times without impact on performance. At present PHES is still in development. A small pilot project (150 kW, 600 kWh, or 4-hour duration) is installed at the Sir Joseph Swan Centre for Energy Research, Newcastle University in the United Kingdom, which claims it is the first grid-scale deployment of this technology [13].

Battery energy storage

Battery ES is ubiquitous, used to provide energy for everything from cellular phones, watches, laptop computers, and tablets to aircraft, automobiles, and satellites. Batteries provide critical backup power for uninterruptable power supplies (UPS) in hospitals, data centers and a broad range of commercial, industrial, and military applications. More recently, batteries provide bulk ES for utility-scale applications.

Battery ES has several features of interest to utility planners:

- zero emissions and little to no sound, can be sited within or near residential areas, including inside residential and commercial buildings;
- not dependent on specific geographic or geological requirements;
- modular, scalable, good for applications ranging from kWh to MWh; and
- very fast response times (milliseconds).

While most people understand the concept of a battery, the field of battery ES is comprised of numerous chemistries and technologies, all of which have different features that influence their cost, power density (size), longevity/degradation, and risks. The following discussion is provided for high-level guidance purposes. The reader is encouraged to explore any number of specialized texts or papers on a specific form of battery for further details. The major forms of battery storage are shown in Fig. 3.5.

Lead-acid

Lead-acid batteries are some of the oldest and most widely used rechargeable battery technologies available, invented in 1859 by French physicist Gaston Plante. In the 1890s the Japanese inventor Genzou Shimadzu patented a method for manufacturing lead powder, which was instrumental in mass-manufacture of lead-acid storage batteries, originally made in Japan. Billions of units have been sold for starting engines and powering electronics in cars, trucks, and boats. Advantages of lead-acid batteries include low cost, good performance across a range of ambient temperatures, and high voltage per cell. They are not commonly used for large-scale utility applications because of their low power density, weight, and poor low temperature performance (as many of us have experienced starting our cars in cold weather). However, lead-acid systems have been deployed in recent years, typically under 5 MW and for several hours duration. One example is a 1 MW × 3-hour duration system on the Shetland Isles in Scotland, installed in 2013 and used for peak shaving and renewable integration [14]. Lead-acid batteries are considered by some to be more sustainable than other battery technologies since they are made almost entirely from recycled materials [15].

Nickel cadmium and nickel—metal hydride

Nickel cadmium (Ni-Cd) batteries were invented in 1899 by Swedish engineer Ernst Waldemar Junger as an alternative to lead-acid batteries. Ni-Cd batteries can be charged faster and cycle more deeply and repeatedly than lead-acid batteries. Ni-Cd uses nickel oxide hydroxide and cadmium as positive and negative electrodes, respectively. They have found extensive use for portable power tools, flashlights, and other devices, providing good performance at low temperatures, and can deliver close to their full power at high discharge rates. In the 1990s superior performing, and lower cost Li-ion batteries took market share from Ni-Cd in the

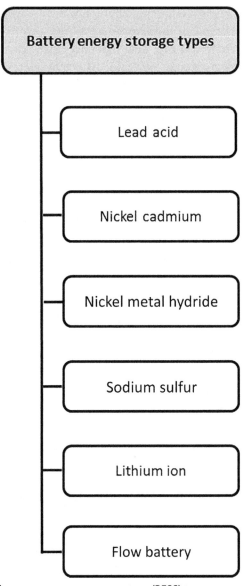

Figure 3.5 Major battery energy storage system (BESS) types.

commercial/retail world, leading to less of a presence today than in the past. Several storage projects are in existence using Ni-Cd, with one of the first being a 27 MW system with 15-minute duration installed in 2003 by Golden Valley Electric Association in Alaska.

Difficulties related to the disposal of toxic cadmium have led to the development of nickel—metal hydride storage technologies. Research on nickel—metal hydride (Ni-MH) batteries began in the 1960s and, after various improvements related to chemistry and construction, came into broad-scale market use in the 1990s. They are similar to nickel cadmium in that they both use nickel oxide hydroxide as the positive electrode; however at the negative electrodes, the Ni-MH systems use a hydrogen absorbing alloy instead of cadmium. Both Ni-Cd and Ni-MH are special cases of a broader class of technologies referred to as "alkaline" batteries [16] which use an alkaline-based electrolyte as opposed to acid based as in lead-acid batteries. Practically all alkaline electrolyte batteries use nickel electrodes (Ni-Cd, Ni-MH, as well as nickel-iron [NiFe]), nickel-zinc (NiZn), and nickel-hydrogen (NiH). The advantages in moving from Ni-Cd to Ni-MH and other types include higher power density and lower costs.

Sodium-sulfur

Lead-acid and alkaline batteries were developed for mass deployment at the smaller scale. Sodium-sulfur (NaS) batteries are much larger and made specifically for power systems, with applications consisting of thousands to tens of thousands of cells packaged together for large MW-scale systems. They were originally developed by Ford Motor Company in the United States in the 1960s, with later development and deployment for power systems by the Japanese company NGK Insulators in the 1980s. Sodium-sulfur batteries must be kept in a heated state, as the positive electrode is molten sulfur and the negative electrode is molten sodium. The electrodes are separated by ceramic materials that only allow positively charged sodium ions to pass through. Even though these batteries require heaters to maintain the system at greater than 300°C, the round-trip efficiency of NaS batteries is quite high, approaching 90%. Because NaS systems are made from low-cost materials they enjoy economies of scale, with lower prices for larger systems.

While Li-ion batteries are more common in power systems, NaS systems show great potential. One of the largest projects to date is installed in Abu Dhabi, United Arab Emirates, 108 MW of capacity with 6-hour duration (648 MWh). The UAE system consists of 10 NaS batteries linked through a common control system so that they collectively operate as one large battery [17].

Lithium-ion

Lithium-Ion batteries represent the predominant type of utility-scale storage deployment globally. The first Li-ion batteries were invented by American physicist John Goodenough and commercialized in the 1990s, competing with other battery chemistries for powering computers, power tools, and other devices. The growth of electric vehicle and stationary storage applications has fueled development and driven costs down dramatically, such that Li-ion technology supplanted advanced lead-acid and alkaline batteries for most applications.

Li-ion batteries consist of an anode material, a cathode material, a separator, electrolyte, and current collector. As the name implies, Li-ion batteries use lithium salts for the anode and cathode. Most often lithium is intercalated (bound) within a compound such as lithium cobalt oxide or lithium-ion manganese oxide, and this is where Li-ion batteries expand into numerous types. The most common chemistries found in utility-scale storage applications are Li-ion phosphate (LFP), lithium-manganese oxide (LMO), lithium-nickel-manganese oxide (LNMC), and lithium-titanate oxide (LTO). The first three (LFP, LMO, and LNMC) are typically matched with graphite anodes, while LTO refers to anodes that are often matched with LMO or LNMC cathodes. While LTO chemistries are more efficient than others, they have lower nominal voltages, which adds size, weight, and cost to achieve an installation with the same characteristics (MW and MWh). Each of the combinations of Li-ion chemistries offers advantages and disadvantages and is in continuous states of development (including development of additional chemistries beyond those listed here).

Li-ion battery installations are built by packaging thousands to hundreds of thousands of battery cells together. Manufacturers provide cells in the traditional cylindrical shape as well as other form factors [18]. Prismatic form factor batteries are rectangular or box-shaped, allowing them to be packaged neatly together, eliminating void spaces. Both cylindrical and prismatic Li-ion batteries have a metal outer structure for strength. A third form factor, called pouch, are typically wrapped in a thin metal film, reducing weight while maintaining the same packing-economy as prismatic cells.

Flow batteries

Flow batteries rely on chemical reduction-oxidation (redox) processes to generate electricity. Two chemical solutions, the anolyte and the catholyte, are stored in tanks separated by a membrane. Redox refers to the differential charge states on either side of the membrane that are used as potential. When the liquids are pumped past the membrane, ion exchange induces electric current, with charge added or removed through two electrodes. The energy capacity is purely a function of tank size, and the power is a function of the anode surface area. Vanadium and iron solutions are the most common electrolytes. If the anolyte and the catholyte are different forms of the same metal, there is no possibility for cross-contamination (Fig. 3.6).

Other types of flow batteries include hybrid systems. Unlike vanadium or iron flow batteries, with similar electrolytes on either side of the membrane, hybrid systems use two different electrolytes. In the case of zinc-bromine, much of the energy is stored by plating zinc metal onto the anode plates during charging. While a vanadium flow battery energy is a function of tank size, and output (MW) a function of anode area, each independent of the other, with the hybrid zinc-bromine battery these are interrelated. Benefits of the hybrid approach include

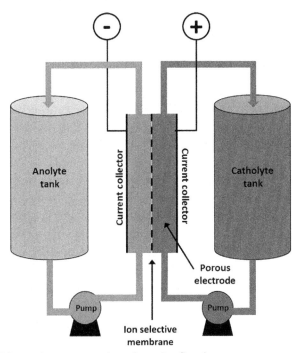

Figure 3.6 Schematic representation of a redox flow battery.

a higher power density than nonhybrid flow batteries. Round-trip efficiency is in the 65%−75% range. Risks are associated with bromine, which is highly toxic.

Maria Skyllas-Kazacos, an Australian chemical engineer, developed the first flow battery, the vanadium redox battery, at the University of New South Wales in the 1980s [19], which led to the first patent for an all-vanadium redox battery in 1986. There are few installations to date, however in December 2018, San Diego Gas & Electric (California, USA) launched a 2 MW/8 MWh system for participation in the California Independent System Operator (CAISO) wholesale market [20]. Exploration into advanced materials and alternate flow battery chemistries is ongoing and the technology may gain traction in utility markets.

Compressed air energy storage

CAES is what its name implies, a device that compresses air and stores it in a chamber. When needed, use the compressed air to do work. The concept has been used for more than a century and many existing facilities rely on it. For example, large utility-scale recip power plants use compressed air for starting. Compressed air is stored in tanks on site and injected directly into the engine cylinders to initiate the start sequence. This allows starting sequences to occur with minimal power requirements when grid power is not available.

The same compressed air used to turn the crankshaft of a large recip can also be used to spin a turbine connected to a generator, though in a compressed air ES system much larger volumes of air are needed, and the generator(s) are often on the order of 100 MW or more. Compressed air storage is at present restricted to large underground salt caverns, abandoned mines/mineshafts, and other underground formations, which are generally considered "constant volume" CAES air storage, but can be extended to undersea facilities, which are considered "constant pressure" CAES air storage. Regarding compression and expansion of air, generally the compression process generates a large amount of heat, and the expansion phase cools the air being released. Dissipating the heat to the air with intercoolers reduces the energy required for compression, however expansion then requires additional heat input, which in some cases is provided by natural gas combustion. Efficiency increases if the heat is stored then released as needed for the expansion process, which is considered an adiabatic process.

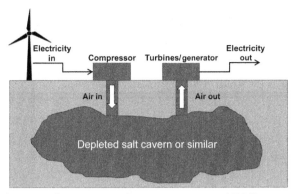

Figure 3.7 Schematic of a compressed air energy storage (CAES) system.

At present there are only three commercially operating CAES facilities. The 290 MW Huntorf plant in Germany (operational since 1978) uses a salt dome for compressed air storage. The McIntosh Alabama plant, United States (operational since 1991), 110 MW (26-hour storage) uses a salt cavern for air storage. These two plants have efficiencies in the 40%−50 + % range. A third plant in Gaines Texas, United States (operational since 2012) is much smaller at 2 MW but uses a more efficient isothermal process. The Texas plant is directly connected to wind turbines, using excess or low-cost renewable energy to power the compression system, then releasing energy when market prices are higher.

Constant volume CAES, like PH, requires specific geography. The sheer volume of compressed air needed for utility-scale applications limits application to a narrow range of sites in proximity to underground caverns and precludes application in most of the areas where ES is needed. Multiple new CAES plants are under development at the time of publication of this work, but it is difficult to present a clear picture of the amount of new CAES capacity the market can expect. The reader is encouraged to periodically review the literature to determine expansions in CAES capacity (Fig. 3.7).

Liquid air energy storage

Compressing air into a liquid dramatically reduces the storage volume requirement (700 L of ambient air = 1 L of liquified air) and a greater amount of energy is available for release during expansion, including the energy related to phase change from a liquid to a gas. Very similar to CAES, pressurized air is expanded through a turbine/generator that produces electricity. Liquid air energy storage (LAES) requires cryogenic storage of liquid air, which can be stored in commercially available tanks [similar in nature to the growing liquified natural gas (LNG) infrastructure]. The technology risk for LAES is low. The entire arrangement for an LAES system involves off-the-shelf, commercially mature components from the power generation and industrial gas sectors, simply arranged in a novel way for power generation. LAES systems have the potential to be scalable and can be placed anywhere. Component lifetimes are long (30 years or more) and the material used is mostly steel, which can be recycled. LAES applications are, at present, limited, but have the potential to serve as grid-scale ES. One benefit over CAES is that an LAES system is not reliant on underground caverns and can be sited anywhere [21].

One drawback to both CAES and LAES systems is that a generous amount of heat is produced during the compression/liquefaction process. Then, when MWh are needed, the working fluid expands causing dramatic temperature drops, necessitating additional heat. Modern LAES systems attempt to capture heat generated during compression/liquefaction and use that heat to assist in the expansion phase, increasing round-trip efficiency and precluding the need for combustion of fossil fuels. Even so, current LAES systems are being marketed for colocation with LNG terminals (with heat sinks to absorb compression heat) and/or thermal power plants, steel mills, and other industrial applications with surplus heat to assist in the expansion phase and improve LAES system cost and efficiency.

Trends in deployment of energy storage

At present there is no single clearinghouse for global installed capacity by ES type; however there are sources of data which may be incomplete but illustrate the major trends. For example, the US Department of Energy maintains a Global Energy Storage Database, with compiled information from over 60 countries [22].

The supermajority of existing ES projects are PH, either closed or open loop (Fig. 3.8). Thermal storage is also evident, but the majority of projects installed to date are ice or cold water storage and represent a form of load shifting and reduction as opposed to delivery of MWh to the grid. A wide array of storage types are represented in the data, but the technology with the greatest adoption rate in terms of MW (other than PH) appears to be battery storage (Fig. 3.9). The adoption rates of either PH or battery storage are region dependent. PH development in the United States stalled in the 1990s just as China's development was starting

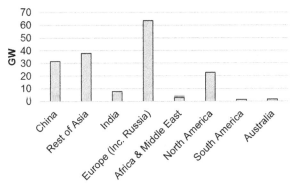

Figure 3.8 Geographic distribution of operating pumped hydro storage projects as of 2018 [22].

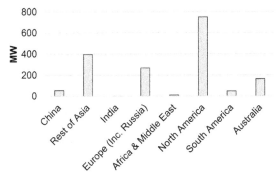

Figure 3.9 Geographic distribution of operating battery-storage projects as of 2018 [22].

to take off (Fig. 3.10). In the United States, battery-storage development accelerated after 2010, while development of the same seems to have plateaued in China, for now (Fig. 3.11).

Regardless of region or continent, the majority of battery installations to date are Li-ion. Both in the United States and China the supermajority of installations are based on Li-ion technology (Fig. 3.12), a trend that holds globally (Table 3.1)

Degradation issues

Anyone who owns a smart phone knows that as the phone ages, the battery inside the phone does not last as long between charges. The reason it does not last as long is degradation. Different ES technologies degrade at

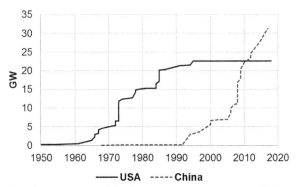

Figure 3.10 Cumulative pumped hydro storage capacity installed in the United States and China as of 2018 [22].

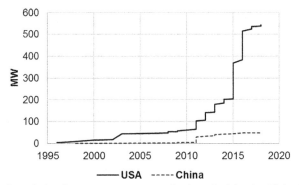

Figure 3.11 Cumulative battery-storage capacity installed in the United States and China as of 2018 (only accounting for deployed systems greater than 1 MW) [22].

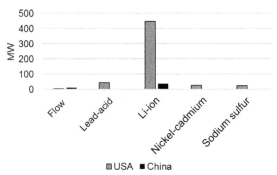

Figure 3.12 Major battery-storage technologies deployed in the USA and China (only accounting for storage systems greater than 1 MW) [22].

Table 3.1 Major battery energy storage technologies employed globally as of 2018 [22].

Battery type	MW	% of total
Lead-acid	59	3.7
Lithium-ion	1293	79.8
Nickel-based	30	1.9
Sodium-nickel	11	0.7
Sodium-sulfur	188	11.6
Flow battery	39	2.4
Total	**1620**	**100.0**

different rates and for different reasons. Most large-scale mechanical storage systems, such as PH, have long lifetimes, tens of thousands of cycles, with marginal degradation occurring through time. Flow batteries also have longevity and potential 20 + year lifetimes with little to no degradation [23]. Electrochemical battery-storage systems do degrade over time; however little detailed degradation information is available as their history, particularly for utility-scale applications is limited to a small number of applications. Li-ion systems have the largest pool of installed systems and their use is expected to increase, so there is a broader amount of information to draw from regarding degradation. Regardless of the type of ES being considered, utility planners should consult vendors for long-term degradation expectations as well as recovery of lost performance as maintenance procedures occur.

Li-ion batteries of multiple chemistry types have an experience base from both electric vehicle and utility-scale applications. Issues that influence degradation include the expected number of cycles per day, the depth of charge and discharge, and the temperature at which the system is maintained when operating. Most utility-scale systems are temperature controlled so degradation with temperature is less of an issue. Materials within the battery also degrade over time, leading to performance loss independent of use. The sheer number of varying types of Li-ion chemistries and their continual development make characterization difficult, but degradation is almost universally related to cycling duty. That is, a Li-ion system deployed for once-daily energy shifting will degrade less over a fixed time span than a system designed to cycle hundreds of times per day for regulation duty. In 2017 Xu et al. [24] showed that for a 20 MW, 12.5 MWh Li-ion system deployed in the ISO-NE market (north eastern

United States), battery life expectancy could range from two to ten years depending on the cycling duty.

Most battery systems are offered with metrics associated with shelf life and cycle life, and cycle life is often linked with cycle depth. For example, a battery manufacturer may specify a shelf life of 10 years and a cycle life of 3000 cycles at 80% cycle depth. Even so, there can be significant uncertainty in predicting actual battery life because operational dispatch of the system may cycle (charge/discharge) at different cycle depths, and degradation occurs at different rates depending on cycle depth. Some manufacturers are suggesting energy throughput as a more meaningful metric. Energy throughput refers to the total amount of MWh the battery can be expected to store and deliver through time, independent of number of cycles or depth of discharge.

Temperature, state of charge, number of cycles, depth of discharge, and aging of components all tend to degrade the capacity of a Li-ion battery system, which is referred to as "capacity fade." Capacity fade refers to the degradation in rated capacity through time and can vary dramatically from one application to another (and is dependent on the Li-ion chemistry as well). For planning purposes, understanding capacity fade is important as the full storage capacity cannot be assumed to be constant.

Whether performance is lost due to degradation from use or from capacity fade, utilities can implement strategies to maintain capacity. Overbuild and storage augmentation are options for maintaining the full capacity of a Li-ion storage system across a planning horizon. Let us assume a planner determines a need for 100 MWh (100 MW × 1 hour). The manufacturer guarantees at the end of 10 years the batteries will have a capacity of 80 MW (20 MW, or 20% assumed degradation). Assuming a linear degradation rate of 2% per year the utility may:

1. Overbuild storage capacity. Install 125 MW. By end of year 10 the system will degrade 80% on capacity, to 100 MW.
2. Sequential augmentation. Install 110 MW of capacity initially, knowing that it will degrade to approximately 100 MW by year 5, then install an additional 14 MW of storage.

Overbuild in this example will guarantee 100 MW of Li-ion capacity across the 10-year period but requires full purchase/investment upfront. Augmentation allows for a smaller upfront investment and a relatively minor investment 5 years into the project. If the capacity cost, $/MWh for battery capacity, is exactly the same every year, the net present value of the augmentation scheme will be lower than that for overbuild due to the time value of money. If the capacity is expected to be lower cost in future years, augmentation schemes can offer even better economics.

Reference metrics for common forms of energy storage

Typically for thermal resources there are a limited number of technology choices, but perhaps a number of potential suppliers with varying efficiencies, water consumption, capital, and maintenance costs. For integrated resource plans the various attributes are often collapsed to a handful of major capacity options (e.g., aero combustion turbines (CTs), combined cycle combustion turbines (CCCTs), and reciprocating engines (Recips). When it comes to ES, as we have seen there are far more technologies available. And each of these technologies may have a wide array of characteristics that are changing through time as new advances are made. To that end, it is difficult to characterize "energy storage" in one table; however, it can be done for informative purposes. Table 3.2 shows major attributes of the storage technologies discussed in this chapter. Please take care to use this information for comparative purposes only. The specific values for rating, duration, efficiency, etc., for different technologies may change with time and vary dramatically across manufacturers.

Resource planning considerations

Electric utility resource planners are increasingly interested in ES and at times being driven to include storage in their integrated resource plans (IRPs) by regulatory bodies [26]. Because ES is dramatically different from traditional resources, there are several factors that planners may have little to no experience with. For example, utilities that use load-duration curve approaches for long-term capacity expansion modeling are unable to quantify the value of storage. There is no mechanism in the process to inform arbitrage, costing, or dispatch of ES. More complicated chronological methods are required. If the case for storage is contingent upon real-time, subhourly calculations, more complex and computationally intense approaches are needed and may be outside the expertise of the resource planning staff. They may not have the software needed to do it. The true value of ES in a high renewable environment requires portfolio modeling to determine the influence of ES on everything else in the system, again requiring complicated capacity expansion and dispatch modeling. If the utility does not have access to the right tools, it is at a disadvantage and

Table 3.2 Major forms of energy storage commercially available in 2019 and their characteristics. Information is indicative [15,23,25].

Storage technology	Max rating (MW)	Upper end of discharge time at max rating (Duration)	Lifetime (years)	Max cycles	Round-trip efficiency (%)
Flywheel	20	minutes	—	20,000—100,000	70—85
Thermal	200	4 h	30	—	80—90
Lead-acid Battery	100	8 h	5—40	2000	80—90
Sodium-sulfur battery			10	4000	70—90
Nickel cadmium battery	100	8 h	20	2000	80—90
Li-ion battery	100	8 h	10	1000—10,000	90—95
Flow battery	100	12 h	15—20	12,000—140,000	70—85
Pumped hydro	3000	12 h	20—50	—	70—85
Compressed air	1000	12—24 h	20—40	—	40—70
Liquid air	100	2—12 h	10—30	—	40—70

will likely undervalue ES. Similar is true for regulatory bodies tasked with reviewing and approving IRPs. If they are not familiar with state-of-the-art computational approaches, they are not able to assess the IRPs presented to them by utilities. Finally, if ES is not included in the IRP as a capacity choice, it never gets modeled and has little to no chance of being chosen for new-build capacity.

Is storage even in the integrated resource plan?

Storage advocates and researchers have identified barriers to storage implementation as either lack of information on storage technologies, leading utilities to omit storage as an option [27] or, if storage is included in long range plans, parameters such as cost are incorrect [1]. ES, in particular Li-ion batteries, is undergoing extraordinary cost reductions due to emerging technologies and economies of scale. If the costs are too high today making storage infeasible, this may not be the case next year, or 5—10 years in the future. Resource planners need to include the forward cost curves in their planning models to ensure that ES technologies are selected appropriately. This underlies a fundamental reality for utilities that employ integrated resource planning. Long-term plans often specify the technology chosen to optimally fill the need, such that requests for proposals (RFPs) are written around that technology. If that technology is not storage, the chances of storage filling that need when the RFP is issued are severely compromised. The best chance for utilities to issue RFPs that are open to ES solutions is for utilities to correctly include ES as capacity choices in their long-term models.

Utility planners should employ best industry practices, consult with storage manufacturers and industry organizations, as well as with other utilities, to make sure they have the most accurate current and future cost and performance information. If their modeling approaches preclude quantification of the value of flexible capacity, they should move toward acquiring the assets and staffing required to accurately model their utility using chronological valuation approaches. The same is true for regulatory agencies tasked with modeling systems or verifying the suggestions made by utilities in their IRPs.

The case for real-time considerations

Many current ES projects in the United States were not the product of utility resource planning. As of 2016 more than half of the battery-storage capacity in the United States was owned by Independent Power Producers (IPPs), and three-quarters of the capacity was installed in two markets: PJM and CAISO [28]. One of the reasons for this trend is that IPPs do not install assets using a portfolio approach, where planners try to minimize the cost of the portfolio of all projects simultaneously. IPPs instead install capacity for profit maximization based entirely on location-specific economics unique to the project at hand. By focusing on a project, rather than a portfolio, IPPs can leverage every revenue stream and extract value from storage in ways traditional utilities cannot. For example, many of the first battery projects in the PJM market were installed to capitalize on revenue from ancillary service and real-time energy markets. Regulated utilities in the PJM market have historically NOT considered revenues from ancillary services or real-time energy in capacity expansion modeling or valuation of specific projects.

Within a regional market like PJM, utilities are responsible for maintaining capacity reserve margins and ensuring supply of MWh to meet customer load. But they are also connected to a grid that spans multiple states and utility jurisdictions. There are additional services needed to maintain reliability of the market/grid that fall outside of the jurisdiction of each of the utilities within the market. Energy supply and demand are met by hourly energy markets, then by real-time markets to correct for imbalances in hourly supply and demand. Real-time markets operate on 5 to 15-minute time scales. This continuous flow of MWh to and from the grid, from numerous utilities and across countless miles of transmission and distribution lines, can lead to instantaneous imbalance and voltage fluctuations that happen so fast and across such long distances that no single entity in the market can be responsible.

Regulation is a system-wide ancillary service to provide for voltage support on the grid and to correct for imbalances between electricity supply and demand on time scales of seconds or fractions of a second. Fast-response ES is well-suited for providing regulation. In markets such as PJM there are discrete regulation markets that pay providers for the ability to react quickly when needed and pay when resources are actually deployed. Developers have carefully studied the price of regulation relative to energy, found geographic pockets within the regional market allowing them to capitalize on the arbitrage; purchased low-cost MWh to sell into the regulation market at higher price. The gross revenue is used to pay down debt and operational costs and the remainder is profit. Profit levels from storage projects have been sufficient in markets like PJM to incentivize IPPs to invest in ES

Electric utilities that are not part of regional markets must also consider the need to supply ancillary services and real-time energy. Historically they have assumed there was sufficient capacity and capabilities to supply what was needed, and for almost a century that assumption was valid. However, as more VREs are added to the system, they now must account for volatility in their costs as well. While they do not respond to market pricing, their own economic dispatch systems provide for least-cost optimization. In general utilities attend to this challenge by performing traditional capacity expansion analyses [often load duration curve (LDC) based] then test the system with specialized subhourly software to find potential imbalances (met by regulation or real-time energy). If deficiencies are found, they then issue RFPs for ES or other flexible capacity specifically to meet these needs. While a workable solution, it is suboptimal as there are multiple and unrelated capacity optimization approaches happening in succession. The first step may install hundreds of MW of inflexible capacity necessitating additional flexible capacity to make up for the imbalance found in the secondary subhourly analysis. It is likely that a more comprehensive chronological capacity expansion approach would have installed a lower cost blend of flexible and inflexible capacity to begin with.

Regulation and real-time markets are difficult to characterize for utilities planning decades into the future. Historically, utilities did not consider real-time energy or ancillary services such as regulation at all when making capacity choices. Meanwhile IPPs, looking at real-time and ancillary service markets in great detail, are finding business cases for flexible ES. Furthermore, wind and solar capacity are known to increase volatility in pricing [29], leading to greater opportunities for ES. These opportunities may not make sense today but will become very relevant as VREs penetration increases. Knowing that ES is needed to meet decarbonization targets, many regulatory agencies are suggesting utilities must include subhourly valuation of ES projects, arguing that traditional approaches undervalue the true benefits of ES, and flexible capacity in general (e.g., [27,30]). Moving from legacy approaches to chronological subhourly valuation is a gigantic leap for resource planning teams, involving new analytical methods, different knowledge bases among staff, new software and far greater amounts of data, all of which require time and money to implement. Luckily there is an intermediate solution, bridging the legacy approaches and subhourly chronological valuation.

Chronological capacity expansion to value flexibility

Proper chronological capacity expansion modeling at hourly time resolution bridges legacy planning approaches and computationally intense real-time analyses. It can provide a first-tier approach toward proper integration of ES in IRPs. The notion that real-time, subhourly analyses are necessary to fully extract the value of ES is an artifact of the large portion of storage projects (to date) which were installed specifically to take advantage of subhourly markets. But it is not true that flexible capacity has little value outside of subhourly markets. Traditional resource planning approaches have long discounted the value of flexible capacity because they ignore even hourly chronology. Storage is not the only technology that has struggled to gain market share due to legacy planning approaches. Lessons learned from those other technology providers may be useful for advancing ES. The following discussion illustrates an approach used to advance the benefits of including flexible capacity at the front end of resource planning and describes how ES technologies can leverage the same.

Reciprocating engines are very flexible and capable of providing many of the same services as ES. Years before storage associations started influencing regulatory bodies suggesting trajectories for utility resource planning, reciprocating engine manufacturers had invested resources into a similar effort. Traditional LDC-based capacity expansion models (the root of many IRPs) generally favor two types of thermal capacity; the highest efficiency units for baseload and intermediate applications, typically CCCTs, or low-cost units for peaking, typically frame CTs. As we saw in the previous chapter, for utilities or markets experiencing even a modest increase in renewables, the residual net loads are more erratic than load, and are not at all properly represented by the load-duration curve. Utilities that install inflexible CCCTs and CTs to attend to volatile net loads in high renewable environments will find that despite their planning, the fleet is ill-suited to balance renewables. The consequences are as follows:

- higher costs than anticipated, which are passed on to ratepayers;
- insufficient capacity, necessitating emergency provision for capacity outside of the planning construct;
- reliability problems; and
- decreased portfolio efficiency, leading to higher CO_2 emissions than necessary.

Simply changing to a more advanced capacity expansion planning approach will net an increase in flexible capacity chosen in the IRP process and attend to the problems mentioned directly above, without a need for subhourly analyses. This can best be illustrated with an example.

One study explored the benefit of advanced chronological approaches using a representative utility in California [31]. The utility had 26 GW of installed capacity, anticipated load growth, 6 GW of forced retirements of boiler plants, and a need to comply with a 33% RPS. Two planning approaches were used across a 10-year horizon: traditional LDC-based capacity expansion simulations and state-of-the-art chronological capacity expansion simulations (both using the PLEXOS software package as described in [32]). The study was designed to compare the outcomes of LDC-based versus chrono approaches assuming a typical CT-based line-up of new-build capacity choices, then to compare the outcome of the more advanced chrono approach with more flexible assets (recips) added to the list of new-build choices.

For the first comparison (LDC vs chrono), both approaches installed 6−7 GW of new capacity over the 10-year planning horizon with slightly more than 3 GW of CCCTs in each. The chrono approach used hourly time resolution across the entire planning period and built almost 10% more capacity than the LDC, including 365 MW of aero CTs that were not built with the LDC approach. Aero CTs are considered more flexible than CCCTs or frame CTs. They have shorter start times, and minimal restrictions on minimum run or downtimes. Why the difference in buildout? Within any capacity expansion plan the simulations estimate the operational expense (Opex) of running the portfolio against load. LDC approaches are simplistic and have been found to be on the order of 10% lower than actual costs as calculated by more rigorous chronological dispatch simulations. When chronology is accounted for, elements of the chrono dispatch model are used to calculate annual Opex throughout the optimization. The more advanced chrono approach can then "see" the operational challenges of supporting high renewable penetrations and install the appropriate amount of flexible capacity to minimize the cost of the total buildout. In summary, the chrono capacity expansion model was able to more accurately quantify the value of flexible capacity relative to the LDC-based model and was more accurate in representing total cost.

The chrono capacity expansion model above was limited to CT-based new capacity choices. The model was run again with more flexible, higher efficiency recip capacity added to the list of new-build choices. As before, the model was not forced to install any particular technology but was simply allowed to choose from the list of available technologies. Results of this second comparison showed that simply adding recip technology resulted in a different buildout. The buildout still included close to 3 GW of CCCTs, but only 400 MW of frame CTs instead of 3 GW, no aero CTs, and 2.4 GW of recips. Overall, the chrono model with recips built 630 MW less capacity, the 10-year all-in net present value costs were close to 900 MUSD less than the CT-based build, and CO_2 emissions were reduced by close to 2%. Cost savings were attributable to [31]:

- reduction in start costs for CCCTs;
- fuel savings and CO_2 reductions. Flexible recips optimize operation of other assets, such as CCCTs; and
- less capacity needed. Flexible capacity has the ability to serve a wider array of challenges, so less is needed.

The last point, less capacity needed, is due primarily to the capabilities of flexible capacity. The most flexible capacity has wider operational ranges (from minimum to maximum output). If a utility needs 100 MW of flexible ramping to follow wind or solar, it can do that with 100 MW of infinitely flexible capacity that can move between 0% and 100% output. Or it can install 200 MW of less flexible capacity that can only ramp between 50% and 100% output. The more flexible the capacity, the less capacity that is needed.

The first two points, reduction in start costs and fuel savings, are elements of *portfolio optimization*. Adding flexible capacity tends to optimize the entire portfolio of assets. This particular study illustrated that (1) moving to state-of-the-art chronological planning approaches quantified the value of flexible capacity and that (2) simply including a flexible technology as a new-build resource will result in a suggested buildout that is both more flexible overall, and less expensive. Expressed another way, if a utility does not include certain technologies, the result could be a more expensive system and higher prices for ratepayers. *These are the same concerns proponents of ES would like to see addressed in the utility industry.*

The operational benefits proven for flexible thermal capacity are equally applicable to ES. This was demonstrated in a study by the United States National Renewable Energy Laboratory [33], which looked at a utility system spanning two balancing areas in the state of Colorado. The test system comprised 16 GW of capacity, including 4 GW of wind and solar. Using PLEXOS chronological dispatch simulations at hourly resolution, they calculated the annual Opex of the test portfolio as-is, then again assuming 300 MW of battery storage. The storage scenario netted an annual 11 MUSD decrease in fleet Opex relative to the same fleet with no storage at all. The cost savings were attributed to [33]:

- reduction in start costs for CCCTs and boiler plants;
- fuel Savings due to portfolio optimization.

Both aforementioned studies were done at hourly time scales. They clearly showed the value of flexible capacity because they used state-of-the-art chronological dispatch tools either directly (as in the Colorado study [33]) or as part of a chronological capacity expansion simulation (as in the California study [31]). Either form of these approaches (chronological dispatch or capacity expansion) is included in a growing number of software packages commercially available to utilities today.

In a practical sense, hourly chronological capacity expansion approaches fit within the paradigm of modeling that utilities are already familiar with and make use of readily available hourly data. One of the downfalls of chrono capacity expansion simulations is the computational time needed to converge on a solution, even using hourly data. Subhourly modeling requirements may be impractical until computational speed increases. Efforts to push utilities into adopting subhourly modeling could undermine capacity expansion optimization, moving planners to force storage into a system using one-off subhourly approaches for ES alone rather than the portfolio as a whole, thus missing the integrated optimum. This would also introduce bias by excluding other flexible capacity choices. The optimum build is better approximated by hourly chrono capacity expansion simulation, with all technologies in the mix of capacity the model can choose from. As algorithms increase in efficiency and computational resources increase in speed, subhourly discretization can be added.

The above discussion is specific to utilities that employ long-term IRP-type planning approaches. If a utility has limited new-build opportunities with known capacity needs and sites available, then it would be appropriate to employ chronological, subhourly dispatch simulations. Dispatch simulations only look at the operation of assets over a short time span, typically one year, and are far less computationally demanding as the user manually inputs all of the capacity in the model, including the new-build options (as opposed to a capacity expansion simulation, which has to also optimize new-build choices across 10−20-year horizons, a far more demanding problem to solve). By using subhourly analyses utilities can leverage potential savings or additional revenue from the assets attending to hourly and real-time energy as well as a host of ancillary services such as regulation. Ideally, each analysis will value the project based on the cost impacts to the portfolio of assets as a whole and not just the performance, dispatch, costs, and/or revenues of the standalone ES project.

Mandates and subsidies

It is not unheard of for governments to use taxpayer money to advance certain technologies considered useful for society, as has been demonstrated for solar and wind. Indeed, many governments have vibrant R&D programs searching for breakthrough technologies or they provide funding for academia and industry to do the same. Once technologies are established and promoted by society at large, their implementation rates may not be as great as considered necessary based purely on economics. In order to stimulate adoption, regulations (mandates) may order utilities to install specified amounts of storage, ensuring cost recovery or providing subsidized financing. Within the United States as of 2019, six states have legislated storage targets for future years [34]. The state of New Jersey has a storage mandate of 2000 MW by 2030, with an interim target of 600 MW by 2021. Depending on which storage technologies are employed and the extent of solar penetration, it has been estimated that incentives (subsidies) ranging from 140 to 650 MUSD will be needed to make the New Jersey investments whole [35]. The state of New York in 2019 directed New York's six investor-owned utilities to hold competitive procurements of at least 350 MW of utility-scale storage projects, and authorized 350 MUSD in bridge incentives to stimulate storage project development [36]. Many of these mandates and incentive programs in the United States are put in place, at present, in regions without significant renewable penetration (less than 30% of annual GWh met by VREs). Most of the incentives for ES in the United States are implemented at the state rather than the federal level, similar to Australia [37]. Nations such as China [38], India [39], and various European countries [40] are subsidizing ES projects directly or offering incentives for domestic manufacture of batteries (for use in vehicles, home, and utility-scale ES). In 2018 the World Bank committed 1 billion US$ to accelerate investments in battery ES for developing countries [41].

Most of the energy used to charge storage systems at present comes from traditional thermal fleets. And most of the benefits from ES projects come from dispatch against market signals for real-time energy and/or ancillary services. But this will change as utilities adopt greater levels of renewable penetration, yielding tremendous volumes of low to zero variable cost surplus, or "overgeneration," from VREs, thus driving the charging cost of ES down. In the meantime, mandates and subsidies will yield technology improvements and economies of scale, ensuring that ES is ready to provide flexibility and support to high renewable, low-carbon power systems. Most of these efforts emphasize and incentivize intermediate duration ES technologies with durations of 12 hours or less. Longerterm seasonal or multiday storage will more than likely be needed for most utility systems as they approach providing 80%−100% of their annual load with renewables. One option for long-term ES is renewable fuels.

References

[1] R. Cooke, A.L. Twitchell, A.B. O'Neill, Energy storage in integrated resource plans. PNNL-28627. <https://energystorage.pnnl.gov/pdf/PNNL-28627.pdf>, 2019.

[2] T. Jacobson, M.Z. Delucchi, M. Bazouin, G. Bauer, Z. Heavey, C. Fisher, et al., 100% clean and renewable wind, water, and sunlight (WWS) all-sector energy roadmaps for the 50 United States, Energy Environ. Sci. 1 (2015) 2093−2117.

[3] C. Barbosa, L.D.S.N.S. Bogdanov, D. Vainikka, P. Breyer, Hydro, wind and solar power as a base for a 100% renewable energy supply for South and Central America, PLoS One. 12 (2017) e0173820. Available from: https://journals.plos.org/plosone/article?id = 10.1371/journal.pone.0173820.

[4] K. Perez, R. Rabago, A radical idea to get a high-renewable electric grid: build way more solar and wind than needed, GreenBiz (2019). Available from: https://www.greenbiz.com/article/radical-idea-get-high-renewable-electric-grid-build-way-more-solar-and-wind-needed.

[5] S. Jenkins, J.D. Luke, M. Thernstrom, Getting to zero carbon emissions in the electric power sector, Joule 2 (2018) 2498−2510.

[6] J. Hampl, Concept of the mechanically powered gyrobus, Trans. Transp. Sci. 6 (2013) 27−38.

[7] K. Amiryar, M.E. Pullen, A review of flywheel energy storage system technology applications and their applications, Appl. Sci. 7 (2017) 286.

[8] Beacon Power, Stephentown, New York. <https://beaconpower.com/stephen-town-new-york/>, 2019 (accessed 15.03.19).

[9] Beacon Power, Hazle Township, Pennsylvania. <https://beaconpower.com/hazle-township-pennsylvania/>, 2019 (accessed March 15.03.19).

[10] H. Trabish, PG&E contracts for 75 MW of energy storage on its way to 580 MW of capacity, Utility Dive (2015). Available from: https://www.utilitydive.com/news/pge-contracts-for-75-mw-of-energy-storage-on-its-way-to-580-mw-of-capacity/410242/.

[11] M. Hutchins, Pilot project for flywheel storage underway in Hawaii, PV Magazine. <https://pv-magazine-usa.com/2018/03/14/pilot-project-for-flywheel-storage-underway-in-hawaii/>.

[12] F. Han, Y. Shen, B. Hu, H. Fan, Optimizing the performance of ice-storage systems in electricity load management through a credit mechanism: an analytical work for Jiangsu, China, Energy Procedia. 61 (2014) 2876−2879.

[13] Newcastle University connects first grid-scale pumped heat energy storage system, The Engineer. <https://www.theengineer.co.uk/grid-scale-pumped-heat-energy-storage/>, 2019.

[14] Lerwick Power Station, <https://www.reapsystems.co.uk/lerwick-power-station-battery-system>, (accessed 17.10.19).

[15] B. May, J.G. Davidson, A. Monahov, Lead batteries for utility energy storage: a review, J. Energy Storage 15 (2018) 1450157.

[16] H. Ogunniyi, E. Pienaar, Overview of battery energy storage system advancement for renewable (photovoltaic) energy applications, in: 2017 International Conference on the Domestic Use of Energy (DUE), Cape Town, South Africa, 2017. <https://ieeexplore.ieee.org/document/7931849>.

[17] A. Rathi, The world's largest "virtual battery plant" is now operating in the Arabian desert, Quartz. <https://qz.com/1536917/the-uae-has-the-worlds-largest-virtual-battery-plant/>, 2019.

[18] A. Hesse, C. Schimpe, M. Kucevic, D. Jossen, Lithium-ion battery storage for the grid: a review of stationary battery storage system design tailored for applications in modern power grids, Energies. 10 (2017) 2107.

[19] M. Rychcik, M. Skyllas-Kazacos, Characteristics of a new all-vanadium redox flow battery, J. Power Sources 22 (1988) 59−67.

[20] H. Mai, California ISO tests flow battery tech that could decrease bulk storage costs, Utility Dive (2019). Available from: https://www.utilitydive.com/news/california-iso-tests-flow-battery-tech-that-could-decrease-bulk-storage-cos/554682/.

[21] J. Fialka, To store renewable energy, try freezing air, Scientific American (2020). Available from: https://www.scientificamerican.com/article/to-store-renewable-energy-try-freezing-air/.

[22] U.S. Department of Energy Global Energy Storage Database <https://www.energystorageexchange.org/>, (accessed May 24, 2019).

[23] L. Aquino, T. Roling, M. Baker, C. Rowland, Battery energy storage technology assessment. <https://www.prpa.org/wp-content/uploads/2017/10/HDR-Battery-Energy-Storage-Assessment.pdf>.

[24] D. Xu, B. Zhao, J. Zheng, T. Litvinov, E. Kirschen, Factoring the cycle aging cost of batteries participating in electricity markets, IEEE Trans. Power Syst. 33 (2017) 2248−2259.

[25] J. Remillard, J.; Perkins, Facility scale energy storage: applications, technologies and barriers. <https://www.ers-inc.com/wp-content/uploads/2017/02/Facility-Scale-Energy-Storage.pdf>, 2017.

[26] J. Twitchell, A review of state-level policies on electrical energy storage, Curr. Sustain. Renew. Energy Rep. 6 (2019) 35−41.

[27] Advanced Energy Storage in Integrated Resource Planning (IRP). 2018 Update. <https://energystorage.org/wp/wp-content/uploads/2019/09/esa_irp_primer_2018_final.pdf>, 2018.

[28] U.S. battery storage market trends. <https://www.eia.gov/analysis/studies/electricity/batterystorage/pdf/battery_storage.pdf>, 2018.

[29] A. Deb, S. Asokkumar, A. Hassansadeh, M. Aarabali, Impacts of high variable renewable energy futures on wholesale electricity prices, and on electric-sector decision making. <https://eta-publications.lbl.gov/sites/default/files/report_pdf_0.pdf>, 2018.

[30] Resolution on modeling energy storage and other flexible resources, in: NARUC 2018 Annual Meeting Resolutions. <https://pubs.naruc.org/pub/2BC7B6ED-C11C-31C9−21FC-EAF8B38A6EBF>, 2018.

[31] J. Ferrari, Incorporating flexibility in utility resource planning. <https://cdn.wartsila.com/docs/default-source/power-plants-documents/downloads/white-papers/americas/wartsila-bwp---incorporating-flexibility-in-utility-resource-planning.pdf?sfvrsn = 63b6f145_8>, 2014.

[32] M. Nweke, C. Leanez, F. Drayton, G. Kolhe, Benefits of chronological optimization in capacity planning for electricity markets, in: 2012 IEEE International Conference on Power System Technology (POWERCON), Auckland, 2012, pp. 1−6.

[33] M. Denholm, P. Jorgenson, J. Hummon, M. Jenkin, T. Palchak, D. Kirby, et al., The value of energy storage for grid applications. NREL/TP-6A20-58465. <https://www.nrel.gov/docs/fy13osti/58465.pdf>, 2013.

[34] A. Zablocki, Fact sheet: energy storage. <https://www.eesi.org/papers/view/energy-storage-2019>, 2019.

[35] New Jersey Energy Storage Analysis (ESA) Final Report. <https://www.bpu.state.nj.us/bpu/pdf/commercial/NewJerseyESAFinalReport05-23-2019.pdf>, 2019.

[36] Energy Storage. New York State Energy Research and Development Authority. <https://www.nyserda.ny.gov/All-Programs/Programs/Energy-Storage>, 2019 (accessed 15.11.19).

[37] M. Maisch, Long read: state and territory subsidies for Australian storage, PV Magazine. <https://www.pv-magazine-australia.com/2018/12/08/long-read-state-and-territory-subsidies-for-australian-storage/>, 2018.

[38] China to boost energy storage capacity to fuel renewable power use, Reuters. <https://www.reuters.com/article/china-power-storage/china-to-boost-energy-storage-capacity-to-fuel-renewable-power-use-idUSL4N1MN1NA>, 2017.

[39] Y. Sharma, Subsides soon to make batteries in India, The Economic Times. <https://economictimes.indiatimes.com/news/economy/policy/subsides-soon-to-make-batteries-in-india/articleshow/70526760.cms>, 2019.

[40] Germany launches battery subsidy package, Energy Reporters <https://www.energy-reporters.com/storage/germany-launches-battery-subsidy-package/>, 2019.

[41] World Bank Group commits $1 billion for battery storage to ramp up renewable energy globally. <https://www.worldbank.org/en/news/press-release/2018/09/26/world-bank-group-commits-1-billion-for-battery-storage-to-ramp-up-renewable-energy-globally>, 2018.

CHAPTER 4

Renewable fuels for long-term energy storage

Introduction

Fossil fuels powered the world for more than a century. Clean, renewable, carbon-free, and carbon-neutral generation will power the coming centuries. The transition we are experiencing brings multiple challenges related to power security, reliability, environmental impact, and cost. One of these challenges is a belief that the only way forward is through sole reliance on renewables, understood by the general public as wind and solar, perhaps supported by energy storage (ES). As discussed in the previous chapter traditional ES technologies are designed for durations ranging from minutes to hours, a time scale that is not commensurate with longer duration storage needs of power systems with deep, 80%–100% decarbonization.

Electric utilities are responsible for reliability, ensuring secure power supply under all conditions, including multiday winter storms that cover solar panels with snow, crippling lulls in wind power, and droughts compromising hydropower. They need firm reliable electricity sources whether wind, solar, or hydro is there or not. Building enough battery or other traditional ES to deal with multiday absence and seasonal variations in renewable energy is theoretically feasible but could be prohibitively expensive. For example Jenkins et al. [1] reviewed 40 studies of various pathways towards deep decarbonization, published between 2014 and 2018, and found "Even at $100 per kWh of installed energy capacity (less than a third of today's costs), enough Li-ion batteries to store 1 week of United States electricity use would cost more than $7 trillion, or nearly 19 years of the total United States electricity expenditures." To attain a high if not 100% renewable energy state longer-term storage paradigms are needed at much lower cost than battery, pumped hydro, or similar traditional storage technologies. There is a growing school of thought that considers renewable synthetic fuels the key to this puzzle.

Electric Utility Resource Planning
DOI: https://doi.org/10.1016/B978-0-12-819873-5.00004-6

Synthetic fuels are chemically similar to fossil fuels, only they are not extracted from the ground and are not fossil-based. They are manufactured using renewable feedstocks and, ideally, renewable energy to power the process. Fuels such as synthetic methanol, diesel or methane, are carbon-neutral when the carbon in the fuel comes from biological sources or from direct air capture (DAC). Carbon-neutral fuels are analogous to their fossil-fuel counterparts in terms of chemical composition. Except for hydrogen, they use storage and delivery systems already in place and can be used in existing combustion turbine (CT) and reciprocating engine (Recip) technologies, which utilities are very familiar with. Hydrogen is carbon-free and can be used to generate MWh from fuel cells and newly emerging Recip and CT technologies, but will require a purpose-built hydrogen infrastructure for storage and delivery of the fuel.

Synthetic fuels are considered renewable when their formation is powered by renewable energy. Any system designed to rely 100% on renewables will have excess generation beyond immediate loads. Some of this energy will be used to charge ES for day-to-day time-shifting and for system balancing. Another portion could be used to power electrolysis to generate hydrogen from water, DAC of carbon, and other fuel production processes. Methanizers combine hydrogen and carbon to form hydrocarbons of choice, from methane (CH_4) to aviation and transportation fuels. These fuels are carbon-neutral from a climate change perspective if the necessary carbon is harvested from the air. The carbon is simply recycled, with no net increase in atmospheric CO_2 concentration. The carbon-neutral aspect is important and is aligned with the International Panel on Climate Change (IPCC) recommendation that to avoid irreversible climate change impacts society must reach a carbon-neutral state by 2050 [2].

Renewable fuels as long-term energy storage

Most ES technologies are sub-24-hour duration and are typically committed for daily power shifting, shifting excess solar during peak production at mid-day toward night time, or for shorter duration voltage regulation and grid support. Potential revenues and costs are understood across short time scales such as minutes or hours, for which plenty of data is available. This data is used to manage existing resources or to construct the business case for specific ES projects.

While storage complements and enables renewables, most ES technologies are not equipped for durations spanning days. The typical battery system is considered ideal for short-term time-shifting but less than ideal for seasonal shifting [3]. Compressed air energy system or pumped hydro can be designed for longer durations but are limited to regions with suitable geography. Installing enough of any of these could be cost-prohibitive and impractical.

Periods of low variable renewable energy (VRE) production and seasonal trends must be accounted for. To illustrate seasonality some examples are provided using data from the United States. The US Energy Information Agency records and makes public the total monthly capacity factor of all renewable installations larger than 1 MW in size (Fig. 4.1, showing 2014–18). Solar output is maximized in summer months and minimized in the winter. Wind patterns are more variable but generally peak in the winter and are minimized in the hottest summer months. Hydro output follows seasonal trends in precipitation and ice melt and tends to "dry out" during the hot summer months. Hydro is also subject to broader scale perturbations related to drought. For example, California experienced drought conditions of varying intensities from December 2011 lasting through March 2019, with extreme drought occurring during 2014–16 [4]. The capacity factor for California's 14,000 MW of hydro capacity fell dramatically during those same years (Fig. 4.2).

Researchers in industry and academia have studied the impacts of seasonality and drought on renewables to understand the best way to attend to these fluctuations, particularly for power systems moving toward 100% renewables. Some advocate there is no need for storage; the solution is to simply build so much wind and solar that enough energy is always available (e.g., refs. [7–9]). The amount of land required and the total system

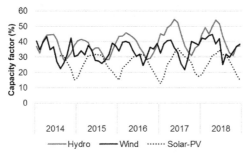

Figure 4.1 Seasonal variation of monthly capacity factors for all United States installations of hydro, wind, and solar-PV (> 1 MW) from 2014 to 2018, based in US EIA data [5].

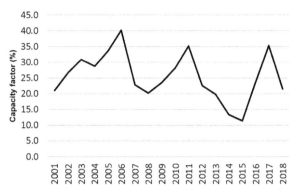

Figure 4.2 Annual capacity factor for 14 GW of hydro resources for the state of California, 2001−18 [6], with lowest capacity factors 2014−15 time frame a result of drought conditions.

cost would be prohibitive for most utilities to consider this approach, in which case ES is needed.

The allure of renewable fuels is that they use excess renewable energy to synthesize a carbon-free or carbon-neutral fuel, which can be stored indefinitely. Renewable fuels can be stockpiled and drawn upon as needed, using power plant technology utilities already own or are at least familiar with. Renewable fuels are generally referred to as the product of "power to X" (PtX), where the fuel type is referenced as X: X = G if the fuel is gas, hydrogen or methane, or L for any liquid fuel such as diesel, aviation fuel, or methanol. For electric utility systems, their major benefit is for use as long-term ES, to attend to seasonal fluctuations (e.g., refs. [10−12]). Global analyses of PtG roles in 100% carbon-neutral power systems indicate PtG has greatest potential in colder climates and those dominated by wind, whereas equatorial countries with high diversity of resources and ample hydro resources will have the least potential [13]. The focus here will be on gaseous fuels, as the majority of utility systems are currently more reliant on natural gas and less reliant on liquid fuels for power generation. Renewable liquid fuels, however, do have promise for the transportation sector.

What about biofuels?

Renewable fuels as described earlier are a relatively new and viable pathway, but one form of renewable fuels has been produced for some time now, biofuels. Biofuels fall into three classifications: direct combustion, recycled, and synthetic. The distinction is important as biofuel type dictates their utility to the resource planner and their place in policy discussions.

Direct combustion

Direct combustion refers to using biomass as a fuel in lieu of fossil fuels. This can occur in a boiler plant where wood waste is burned to produce steam, which spins a steam turbine generator. Black liquor is a by-product of paper/pulp processing, has a high heat content, and can be used as well. In 2018 biomass and waste, including landfill gas, provided 2% of the electricity in the United States, of which 60% was generated using wood waste/black liquor as a fuel [14]. In 2016 in the European Union wood supply from forestry accounted for more than 60% of all biomass sources for energy production [15]. Wood products can be burned directly or, more often, pelletized for standardized shipping. While direct combustion of biomass is carbon-neutral from a climate change perspective, the carbon accounting for using wood/biomass directly requires assessment of the entire chain. If fossil fuels are used to harvest the biomass and transport it to a power plant, the net carbon emissions will be positive. For example, wood pellets have been considered a renewable fuel for power generation in Europe for some time, yet large parts of the supply are shipped across the Atlantic Ocean from the United States. Carbon emissions from forestry activities and shipping, as well as increased logging to meet demand, lead many to question the viability of wood as a carbon-neutral source of renewable energy [16].

Another potential source of fuel for direct combustion is bagasse, the residue left from sugarcane processing. Cuba has a long history of sugar plantations feeding bagasse to power plants for electricity production. As of 2015 Brazil had installed over 10,000 MW of power plant capacity fueled by sugarcane by-products [17]. India also has over 2000 MW of bagasse-fuelled plants. Many sugar mills produce all the power and heat needed using residues from the milling process, with excess to spare. There are few if any policy-drivers pushing generators to use bagasse. It is simply readily available in abundant supply, and the economics are favorable relative to energy purchase from the grid or via generation using fossil fuels. From a resource planning perspective, sugar mills would be considered industrial loads supplying most of their MWh needs through self-generation. Otherwise, a boiler plant fuelled by bagasse could be a new build option to consider assuming the economics of bagasse supply were understood.

Recycled biofuels

Recycled biofuels are taken from sources that generate methane and have traditionally vented it to the atmosphere, such as landfills, wastewater treatment plants, and livestock operations. From a climate change perspective, methane is a far more potent greenhouse gas than CO_2. Recovering or recycling methane from these sources both mitigates climate change and allows utilities to leverage carbon-neutral fuels in their portfolios. Some jurisdictions explicitly recognize recycled biofuels as a form of renewable energy, equivalent to wind and solar.

Raw biogas quality can vary significantly among sites, and even within a site from day to day, necessitating gas upgrading to ensure the cleaned gas meets standards for injection into natural gas pipelines. Recycled biofuel processes have been in use for some time, not just at the industrial scale but at the scale of individual houses and farms. Local production of recycled biogas for heating and cooking offsets the need for wood, electricity, or other fuels. In India in 2014 there were close to 5 million farm-sized biogas plants [18].

Synthetic biofuels

Synthetic biofuels use crop-based biomass or algae as feedstock to generate hydrocarbon fuels. Processes may synthesize feedstocks into liquid fuels catalytically or via biological methanation. First the bio-feedstock is gasified into a stream of carbon and hydrogen-rich gas called syngas. In catalytic synthesis, syngas is fed into a catalytic reactor where it is converted via the Fischer-Tropsch process to liquid hydrocarbons such as biodiesel, but the process can be modified to generate methane. Alternately the syngas can be fed to a biological process that produces hydrocarbons, often referred to as "bio-methanation." Food crops such as corn can be fermented to produce ethanol, which is blended with gasoline to reduce fossil-fuel use. The synthetic biofuel market has been primarily dedicated to production of liquid fuels for transportation purposes. Feedstocks for biodiesel can range from palm oil to soybeans and sunflowers, cotton seeds, rapeseeds, and coconuts. The price of biodiesel on the open market has at times actually been lower than traditional fossil-based diesel [19].

The utility of biodiesel for an electric utility is dependent upon whether they can substitute this fuel for fossil-based diesel based on economics.

Resource planning considerations

Biofuels can be used for power generation, but their utility and efficacy are dependent on the source and type. Direct combustion is an economic decision, but carbon-neutrality must be determined on a case-by-case basis. Recycled biofuels are often methane-based, considered renewable, and can be directly substituted for natural gas. This allows planners to retain thermal plants and burn biogas directly in a renewable fashion, or to credit their carbon accounting by subtracting the carbon emissions equivalent of the biogas from their total fuel burn. Biodiesel can be used in dual fuel power plants, either as a substitute for natural gas or if the economics are favorable over biogas. Synthetic biofuels have great promise but have been primarily dedicated to liquid transportation fuels. Still, synthetic biogas may be available in sufficient quantities to compete with recycled biogas and if so, the comparative economics should be explored.

Direct combustion and synthetic biofuel production may face limits in future years. In terms of using wood for direct combustion the Natural Resources Defense Council (NRDC) contends that "Burning wood for electricity accelerates climate change, destroys forests and increases emissions of dangerous air pollutants" [20]. Synthetic biofuels rely on both food and nonfood crops as a feedstock, raising concerns over land use changes and food prices. As more land is cleared and cultivated for feedstock crops, less land is available for natural forests and wetlands, housing, and agriculture for food crops. This can lead to increases in land and food prices. These and other concerns generally lead global analyses of energy transition to place upper bounds on the potential of biogas and other biofuels [13]. In addition, their use for balancing seasonal variations in solar, wind, and hydro may be limited by local conditions. Therefore there is a perceived need for synthetic, renewable fuels that are not location-dependent and can be made just about anywhere. The easiest such fuel to produce is hydrogen.

Hydrogen

Hydrogen is the lightest element in the periodic table and the most abundant substance in the universe. French chemist Antoine Lavoisier named the element in 1783 from the Greek words "hydro" (water) and "genes" (forming) because the product of hydrogen combustion is water. Seventeen years later, English scientist William Nicholson used electrolysis to break water into its main constituents, hydrogen and oxygen. Later that same year German physicist Johann Wilhelm Ritter performed a similar electrolysis experiment but altered the arrangement of the electrodes, allowing for collection of the two gases as independent streams of hydrogen and oxygen. The power of hydrogen became widely recognized in later years, notably so in the classic novel "The Mysterious Island" by Jules Verne in 1874 [21] where in a dialog between characters we have the following:

Yes, but water decomposed into its primitive elements.... and decomposed doubtless, by electricity, which will then have become a powerful and manageable force, for all great discoveries, by some inexplicable laws, appear to agree and become complete at the same time. Yes, my friends, I believe that water will one day be employed as fuel, that hydrogen and oxygen which constitute it, used singly or together, will furnish an inexhaustible source of heat and light, of an intensity of which coal is not capable

One hundred and twenty-one years later, in 1995, the US Secretary of Energy's Hydrogen Technical Advisory Panel (HTAP) reported [22]:

Hydrogen and electricity, ultimately derived from renewable technologies, will serve as the clean, inexhaustible energy carriers in the rapidly approaching next century

And by 2018 the International Renewable Energy Agency (IRENA) recognized that renewable fuels, specifically hydrogen, can provide the "missing link" for deep decarbonization [23]. Renewable fuels provide far more than seasonal or long-term time-shifting of renewable energy. They can be used directly to decarbonize transportation, home heating and cooking, and other sectors of society that may prove difficult to decarbonize through electrification. Hydrogen is considered a primary renewable synthetic fuel. It also serves as a building block for all other synthetic hydrocarbon fuels.

Power to hydrogen

At present the global hydrogen production is in the range of 500 billion cubic meters per year [24], and more than 90% of that is produced by steam reformation. Steam reformation is a multistep process in which steam at high temperature and pressure reacts with hydrocarbons (natural gas or other fossil fuels) in the presence of a catalyst to produce hydrogen.

Fossil sources supply the necessary heat and power and the primary reaction waste product is CO_2. While steam reformation has proved cost-effective due to low-price fossil fuels, in a decarbonized future hydrogen will need to come from a process with carbon-free reaction feedstocks, powered by renewable energy.

Advances on this front are already being made. The first project using wind energy to produce hydrogen was installed in 2013 by the German utility Uniper [25]. Currently, the most promising method for broad-scale hydrogen production that does not rely on fossil-based feedstock is electrolysis of water into its constituent gases, oxygen and hydrogen. Electrolytic hydrogen production is a mature industry. More than 400 industrial electrolyzers were in commercial operation by the early 1900s [24], mainly for the chemical industry. Electrolysis of water requires significant energy so commercial systems use various electrolyte solutions and catalysts to improve reaction kinetics and thermodynamics. Alkaline electrolyzers were developed in the 1920s and proton exchange membrane (PEM) technology emerged in the 1970s. There is a third approach based on solid oxide electrolysis cells (SOECs) that is emerging that promises higher efficiency, but is still in the development phase [26]. Various review articles are regularly occurring in the literature and point to the promise of SOEC for large-scale hydrogen production (e.g., ref. [27]). For this work the two commercially available technologies will be reviewed, alkaline and PEM.

Alkaline electrolyzers

Pure water electrolysis at room temperature and pressure splits water into hydrogen and oxygen but is inefficient and can suffer from inexact separation leading to gas mixing and reduced gas purity. Significant energy input is required because pure water is a poor conductor of electricity. Alkaline water electrolysis uses aqueous KOH or NaOH electrolytes to conduct electricity more readily and improve electrolyzer efficiency. Alkaline electrolyzers separate anodes and cathodes, which can be from a variety of materials, by a thin diaphragm that is nonconductive to electrons, while allowing hydroxyl ions (OH^-) to pass through the pores of the diaphragm. Diaphragms are made of state-of-the art materials that minimize gas mixing, so that hydrogen output streams are relatively pure.

Alkaline electrolyzers are well developed and relatively low cost, using porous membranes, nonprecious catalysts, and design principles and advances tested across almost a century. Standard designs require equal pressure over the anode and cathode to prevent gas crossover across the membrane. The constant-pressure requirement limits their ramping ability, making it difficult to control production in an adaptive way, such as responding to direct solar power on a cloudy day when solar generation fluctuates. They are also reportedly difficult to shut down and start up on a regular basis. Improvements to design methodology include use of two-step electrolysis, with one step dedicated to oxygen production and the other step dedicated to hydrogen production. Two-step alkaline electrolysis holds promise for dynamic low-cost hydrogen production (e.g., ref. [28]), but is still early in the development phase.

Proton exchange membrane electrolyzers

PEM electrolyzers use solid polymer electrolytes and are more compact and simpler to construct than alkaline systems. During operation water decomposes into oxygen and protons (hydronium ions, H^+) at the anode, and protons migrate across the membrane to the cathode where they are reduced to hydrogen gas. During this process, molecules of solvation water accompany the protons, a process described as the electro-osmotic flow. Electro-osmotic flow is a sign of inefficiency in the system; hence advancements over the prior few decades have been made to minimize this effect (e.g., ref. [29]).

One promising feature of PEM systems is that they can idle in standby mode and swing hydrogen production up and down as needed either to meet a variable demand, or to capitalize on intermittent renewable energy. Their flexibility has led some to consider them a form of highly flexible demand response. This reactive ability could allow them to provide ancillary services to assist in integrating renewables [30]. The higher pressure of hydrogen gas output from PEM systems (Table 4.1) is considered advantageous as most downstream uses will require compression.

Comparison of alkaline and proton exchange membrane electrolyzers

Alkaline electrolyzers are a more mature technology and at present are considered less expensive than PEM systems. PEM systems require less space to construct and are more dynamic. Table 4.1 compares performance characteristics. A review of 128 power-to-gas projects in Europe [31] indicates a trend toward larger electrolyzer systems (greater than 1 MW) and the majority of larger systems are PEM.

Table 4.1 Performance characteristics of alkaline and PEM electrolyzers.

Technology		Alkaline	PEM
Metric	Unit		
Efficiency	kWh per kg hydrogen	49−51	52−58
Efficiency	%, LHV	65−68	57−64
Lifetime	Operating hours	80k−90k	40k−50k
Lifetime	Years	20	20
Output pressure	Bar	Atm. to 15	30−60
Load range	%	15−100	0−160
Start time (hot/cold)	Minutes	1−10	1 s/5
Shutdown time	Minutes	1−10	Seconds
Ramp up/down	%	0.2−20	100

Source: Data adapted from Hydrogen from renewable power, Abu Dhabi. https://www.irena.org/-/media/Files/IRENA/Agency/Publication/2018/Sep/IRENA_Hydrogen_from_renewable_power_2018.pdf, 2018. Study on early business cases for H_2 in energy storage and more broadly power to H_2 applications. https://www.fch.europa.eu/sites/default/files/P2H_Full_Study_FCHJU.pdf, 2017.

Hydrogen to power

Any discussion of hydrogen as a form of ES requires understanding how hydrogen can be converted to useable power for utility purposes. The first technology to discuss in this context is the fuel cell.

Fuel cells

Fuel cells in essence run the electrolysis reaction in reverse. The history of fuel-cell development starts in 1839, when Welsh inventor Sir William Robert Grove mixed hydrogen and oxygen in the presence of an electrolyte to produce water and electricity. More than a century later, Francis Thomas Bacon, a British engineer, developed the first practical hydrogen-oxygen fuel cell, which was further refined and developed for use on the Apollo moon missions, where hydrogen and oxygen were already available for propulsion and the by-product water could be used for drinking and to humidify the capsule.

Fuel cells come in different forms and chemistries, but the basics are the same. Hydrogen is split into protons (H^+) and electrons at the anode, an electrolyte carries protons through a membrane to the cathode, and electrons cannot penetrate the membrane and are forced through a circuit to the cathode. Finally, protons combine with the previously stripped electrons and oxygen from ambient air at the cathode to produce water.

The flow of electrons through the circuit provides the electric current required to produce MW. Fuel-cell types include:

- Alkali, which generally uses a solution of potassium hydroxide in water as the electrolyte.
- Molten carbonate use high-temperature sodium and magnesium carbonate as the electrolyte.
- Phosphoric acid fuel cells use phosphoric acid as the electrolyte.
- Solid oxide fuel cells use a hard metal or ceramic compound as the electrolyte.
- PEM fuel cells use thin permeable polymer sheets as the electrolyte.

Efficiencies range from 50% to 70% depending on fuel-cell chemistry. To date fuel cells have been used in small industrial power applications but plans for larger facilities are on the horizon. From 2014 to 2016 between 150 and 200 MW of fuel-cell power generation equipment was delivered worldwide for stationary generation purposes [33]. The cumulative installed global base of operating stationary fuel cells was approaching 1000 MW in 2015 [34], and more than 200,000 residential home heating fuel-cell systems were installed as of 2018 [35]. In 2016 there were 56 1 MW or larger fuel-cell installations in the United States [36], with the majority of them stripping hydrogen from low-cost natural gas streams to fuel the device.

Combustion turbines and reciprocating engines

Utilities already own these technologies for power generation using natural gas. Existing CTs can utilize hydrogen blends ranging from 20% to as high as 90%, depending on the turbine technology, control systems, and other factors. As of 2019 several large CT manufacturers (e.g., General Electric, Mitsubishi Hitachi Power Systems, Siemens, Ansaldo Energia) have successful track records of running CTs on varying hydrogen blends with natural gas, with plans to offer CTs running on 100% hydrogen within the next decade [37]. EUTurbines, an association of Japanese and European CT manufacturers, claims the industry "is committed to provide CTs that can handle a share of 20% hydrogen by 2020 and gas turbines operating with 100% hydrogen by 2030" [38]. Several projects have been announced for construction of CTs with contractual agreements for firm 100% hydrogen burn dates. Recip manufacturers have tested blends as high as 35%–50% and are also engaging in R&D to develop engines that can run on 100% hydrogen.

Resource planning considerations for hydrogen

While hydrogen holds great promise for zero-carbon, renewable power generation, the policy and market forces driving hydrogen development go far beyond the power generation space and include vehicle fuels and home heating and cooking [35]. These additional demands are expected to accelerate adoption of hydrogen electrolyzers, storage and transport technologies beyond what could be driven solely by utility demand for power generation.

Heating value and energy density

Hydrogen has one of the highest energy contents of any fuel on a weight basis, making it a fuel of choice for space exploration, where weight equals cost. For earth-bound power generation hydrogen energy density on a weight basis is compromised by the low density of hydrogen on a volume, or kg/m^3 basis, such that a volume of hydrogen gas contains less energy than the equivalent volume of alternate fuel such as methane. Practically speaking this means units designed to burn hydrogen will consume much larger volumes of hydrogen relative to natural gas. Every fuel releases a specific amount of energy during combustion, which is determined experimentally. The energy released is measured as higher heating value (HHV) or lower heating value (LHV). The difference between HHV and LHV represents the heat of vaporization, of converting liquids in the fuel, including water, to gas. Natural gas is bought and sold in the market on an HHV basis, while liquid fuels are often transacted on an LHV basis. Utility planners should take care in noting the basis for heating value, energy density, and pricing (HHV or LHV), for hydrogen or any other fuels. The efficiencies (%) and heat rates (kJ/kWh) original equipment manufacturers provide for power generating equipment may also be provided on an HHV or LHV basis. Figs. 4.3—4.5 show representative HHV and LHV heating content, energy density (gas fuels only), and energy density in liquid state of hydrogen and other common fuels, respectively [39].

Hydrogen has an excellent heat content (kWh/kg) but lags behind other fuels in energy density. Methane, methanol, and diesel may also be formed from renewable sources. Heat content and energy density are important considerations when planning for broad-scale hydrogen power generation as these features dictate how the fuel is transported and delivered to site.

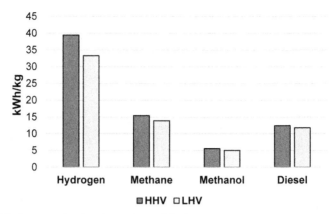

Figure 4.3 Comparative heating values of fuels.

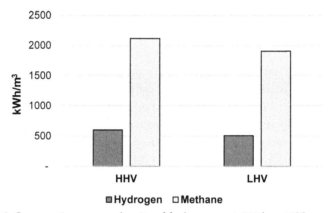

Figure 4.4 Comparative energy density of fuels as gas at 200 bar, 15°C.

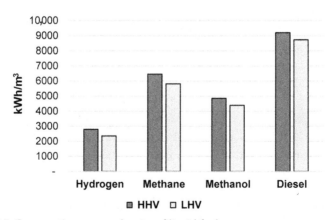

Figure 4.5 Comparative energy density of liquid fuels.

Storage and transport

Most regions have well-established fossil-fuel storage, transport, and delivery systems that can accommodate renewable fuels with similar characteristics without modification. Synthetic methane and methanol and synthetic or biodiesel can be stored, transported, and used in systems designed for their fossil counterparts. Hydrogen is completely different. For vehicles/transportation the fuel must be compressed or liquified at high pressure. For power plants, converting pipelines from natural gas to hydrogen service requires complete redesign and replacement. Accelerated corrosion of pipeline steel in the presence of high hydrogen concentrations and leakage of hydrogen from seals intended for methane are major issues. Leakage is more prevalent in distribution lines, posing a hazard in confined spaces [40]. Utility planners considering hydrogen as a means for decarbonization need to make sure the infrastructure is in place to support the effort. While fuel storage/delivery infrastructure is often outside the control of electric utilities, it is not outside of the purview of regulators and policy makers. That is, utility planners looking to capitalize on hydrogen energy production may need assistance from government programs and legislation to socialize the costs.

Water consumption for hydrogen production from electrolysis

Water consumption is another factor that warrants attention. Assuming ideal collection of hydrogen from water splitting via electrolysis, 9.1 kg (2.4 gallons) of water are consumed as feedstock to produce 1 kg of hydrogen gas [41]. Approximately 378 kg (100 gallons) of water are needed to produce hydrogen from electrolysis to generate 1 MWh of electricity from a 60% efficient fuel cell. This assumes the electrolyzer feedstock water conforms to water chemistry requirements with no water treatment needed, which would increase the water consumption to account for blowdown from water conditioning/treatment. Comparatively speaking, in the United States hydroelectric plants evaporate 68,000 kg (18,000 gallons) per MWh of electricity used by consumers [42], while the power generation industry as a whole withdrew on average 49,200 kg (13,000 gallons) per MWh in 2017 and accounted for 40% of all water withdrawals in the country [43]. Water withdrawal for evaporative cooling of thermoelectric power plants has been declining in the United States as older coal plants retire and new thermal units are built using closed-loop radiator or air-cooled condenser technology. While water consumption for hydrogen production appears rather small relative to hydropower or traditional thermal generation, the success of hydrogen production will rely on siting at or near water sources, as well as societal acceptance (regulatory and otherwise) allowing for enough water withdrawal. Local and regional conditions will dictate the manner in which water withdrawal is permitted relative to other needs such as preservation of ecological and hydrologic regimes, water needed for public water systems and agriculture.

Electrical conversion efficiency

A 100% efficient electrolyzer will use 39 kWh of electricity to produce 1 kg of hydrogen [44]. Assuming a 50% efficient alkaline or PEM electrolyzer, the electricity needed to make 1 kg of hydrogen is double the ideal amount, or 78 kWh per kg of hydrogen. The 78 kWh input would produce the equivalent of 39 kWh of fuel energy. If consumed in a 60% efficient fuel cell, each kg of hydrogen would produce 23.4 kWh of electricity to the grid. Therefore in an ideal system with 50% electrolyzer efficiency and using a 60% efficient fuel cell, the amount of electrical energy that can be delivered to the grid is 30% of the energy used to fuel the process. While round trip efficiency is on the order of 30%, far less than battery or other forms of storage, the advantage of hydrogen is that it can be stored in massive quantities indefinitely. Another advantage is that the renewable energy ideally used for electrolysis would otherwise have been curtailed and never used in the first place, so round trip efficiency for hydrogen or other renewable fuels is not so easy to characterize and is not always directly comparable to other forms of storage.

Global hydrogen production facilities and electrolyzer costs

A large number of hydrogen production facilities exist to serve the chemical and agricultural industries, but facilities dedicated entirely to power generation have only recently started to gain traction. A comprehensive survey of all power-to-gas projects globally was published in 2019 [45] and found 153 facilities, 86 of which were dedicated to hydrogen production, the remainder dedicated to synthetic methane production. Estimated capital costs on a Euro/kW basis were provided for current and future pricing trends (Table 4.2). Other sources provide alternate future cost expectations (e.g., ref. [23]) with lower costs than those shown in Table 4.2, reflecting a difference in cost calculation methodology and perhaps the data sources drawn from.

Table 4.2 Estimated capital costs by electrolyzer type and by year out to 2050 [45], in Euro/kW, where kW refers to the power draw of the electrolyzer.

Electrolyzer type	Year		
	2020	2030	2050
Alkaline	500−1000	500−800	300−400
PEM	500−1300	300−1300	300−700

For comparison, tables documenting the cost of well-established thermal power plant technologies such as CTs will also have a wide variance depending on the data and assumptions used. What can be taken from future cost curves is that economies of scale are expected to drive electrolyzer prices below 500 Euro/kW for alkaline processes, while PEM technologies appear to have slightly higher cost, but also have the potential to fall below 500 Euro/kW. As with any generation technology, larger project sizes are expected to enjoy economies of scale with lower project costs, driving the cost of hydrogen on a Euro/kg basis lower over time. In 2019 Glenk and Reichelstein [46] analyzed market trends in Germany and Texas, United States. They found that current hydrogen production costs on the order of 3.23 Euro/kg are expected to fall to 2.5 Euro/kg within a decade. Others suggest hydrogen costs could fall as low as 1.3 and 0.73 Euro/kg by 2030 and 2050, respectively [47]. While there appears to be disparities in hydrogen production costs going forward 20−30 years, all sources indicate with higher adoption rates through time production costs will fall. These trends are useful for utilities to understand, but utilities considering hydrogen production in their long-range plans should consult vendors and get localized costing and performance.

Blending hydrogen with natural gas

Excess renewable energy can be used to generate hydrogen for injection into the natural gas pipeline system, creating a blended fuel. The intent is not to fill the pipes with hydrogen rather than methane, rather the intent is to have the pipeline gas have a certain percentage of hydrogen, which ultimately reduces the carbon footprint of the blended gas relative to natural gas alone. It is generally believed that hydrogen blends in the 5%−15% range (by volume) would pose minimal safety or reliability concerns and could be burned in most existing devices, from home heating and cooking to industrial uses and power generation, with little to no difference in performance relative to pure natural gas [40]. Hydrogen blended with methane at low concentrations produces the desired heat or power with reduced CO_2 emissions relative to that from pure natural gas combustion.

Some utility systems are already, or soon will be, blending hydrogen into natural gas pipelines. The Australian Renewable Energy Agency announced a project in 2018 to generate renewable hydrogen for injection into the gas grid near Sydney in concentrations up to 10% [48]. The European gas transport group Snam planned in 2019 to increase hydrogen concentrations in its natural gas network from 5% to 10% near Salerno in southern Italy [49]. In 2019 the town of Schopsdorf in Saxony-Anhalt, Germany, announced it would be blending up to 20% green hydrogen from PtG processes into their natural gas distribution network [50]. And in 2020 a pilot project became operational in the United Kingdom blending 20% hydrogen into a local gas network in and around Keele University, with the press release noting "If a 20% hydrogen blend was rolled out across the country it could save around 6 million tonnes of carbon dioxide emissions every year, the equivalent of taking 2.5 million cars off the road." [51].

Utility resource planners in other jurisdictions may also be able to leverage hydrogen blends into existing gas infrastructure. As renewable portfolio standards or other mandates force decarbonization, more solar and wind will be installed to offset thermal generation. Existing natural gas assets may be needed for some time for reliability purposes, yet subject to strict CO_2 emissions limits or carbon taxes. Using hydrogen blended into natural gas streams provides electric utilities with a near-term means for reducing CO_2 while retaining needed generation capacity. CT and Recip manufacturers can supply the necessary information on hydrogen limits their equipment can manage without performance or maintenance problems.

Direct air carbon capture

Synthetic fuels include hydrogen on its own, or more complex fuels such as methane and methanol. Hydrogen is a building block for all of them, but they need a carbon source. For synthetic methane or methanol to be considered "carbon-neutral" they require the carbon be taken from the atmosphere, such that subsequent combustion yields no net increase in atmospheric CO_2 concentrations. Beyond hydrogen, two additional steps are needed: DAC of carbon and a process to combine hydrogen and carbon to form hydrocarbons, a process called methanation. Here we discuss DAC.

Calls for DAC began in 1999, with Hashimoto et al. [52] advocating for synthetic fuel production using DAC of CO_2 specifically to halt or prevent anthropogenic climate change. That same year, Lackner et al. [53] explored large-scale capture of atmospheric CO_2 to manage climate risks. Later, in 2005, Nobel Laureate George Olah advocated for synthetic methanol production as an alternative to a hydrogen economy, specifically for replacement of liquid fossil fuels [54]. More recently, research and development of synthetic methane production using DAC CO_2 have gained momentum.

In Switzerland in 2017 Climeworks began operating what is claimed to be the world's first commercially operating DAC plant, with energy provided to the process by waste heat from an incinerator and production costs on the order of 400 US\$/metric ton [55]. In 2018 Climeworks opened a DAC facility in Troia, Apulia (Italy) designed to collect 150 tons of CO_2 per year, which is combined with hydrogen to make methane. In 2019 Carbon Recycling International signed an agreement to build a methanol plant in China designed to capture 150,000 tons of CO_2 and generate 180,000 tons of liquefied methane and methanol, with commissioning expected in 2021 [56]. This list of projects and companies associated with DAC and renewable methane or methanol is by no means exhaustive, but highlights that DAC is moving beyond the pilot stage into large-scale industrial applications.

DAC systems consist of a contact area across which air flows, some form of solvent or sorbent, and a regeneration module [57]. There are presently two commercially scalable technologies, high-temperature aqueous solution (HTAS) and low-temperature solid sorbent (LTSS).

High-temperature aqueous solution direct air capture

HTAS DAC consists of two simultaneous processes, adsorption and regeneration. In the adsorption process, ambient air is mixed with a spray of sodium hydroxide (NaOH), which reacts with CO_2 to form a solution of sodium carbonate (H_2O and Na_2CO_3). CO_2-depleted air leaves the system. The Na_2CO_3 solution is sent for regeneration where it is mixed with calcium hydroxide ($Ca(OH)_2$) to form solid calcium carbonate ($CaCO_3$) and NaOH. NaOH is recycled back to the adsorption process, while the $CaCO_3$ is heated to release CO_2 and CaO. The CO_2 is collected and the CaO is mixed with water to regenerate $Ca(OH)_2$. Some processes use potassium hydroxide (KOH) instead of NaOH. Calcium carbonate must be heated to 800°C−900°C to release CO_2 and is the most energy-intensive part of the HTAS DAC process.

The energy needs of HTAS DAC include electricity for the fans and pumps and other equipment and thermal energy for heat. At present, commercial and pilot facilities use the lowest-cost form of thermal energy, natural gas, which in turn releases CO_2, albeit not as much as harvested by the process. Use of fossil fuels for heat is counter to the sensibilities of decarbonization, and the system could be fully electrified. One study estimates the total energy need for a KOH system would be on the order of 1500 kWh_{el} per ton of CO_2 [58], while another estimates the total energy need in the range of 1300−1500 kWh_{el} per ton of CO_2 [57]

Low-temperature solid sorbent direct air capture

LTSS DAC requires a two-step batch process. In the first step, air is passed over a sorbent mesh or filter that binds CO_2, and in some cases may also bind water from air moisture. Multiple sorbent types are available or under development. This binding step is halted when the sorbent is saturated with CO_2. The sorbent is then heated to 100°C, releasing a stream of CO_2 as well as any water that may have been adsorbed. The process repeats itself once the sorbent mesh has cooled to ambient temperature. Typical cycle times are 4−6 hours, although newer approaches using sub-atmospheric saturated steam as a heat transfer fluid can achieve cycle times of 30 minutes or less [57]. Similar to HTAS DAC, the LTSS process requires electrical energy and heat. Amine-based sorbent systems have energy needs on the order of 200−300 kW_{el} and 1500−2000 kW_{th} per ton of CO_2 [57]. As systems decarbonize, the kW_{th} can be replaced by kW_{el} supplied from renewable overgeneration.

Resource planning considerations for direct air capture

The economics and costs of DAC systems are evolving so rapidly from pilot to the industrial stage that installed costs are difficult to characterize. Expected cost ranges vary, but all reports indicate that greater adoption rates will lead to economies of scale, continually driving costs down. Fasihi et al. [57] report HT and LT DAC system installed costs in the range of 700−800 Euro per ton of CO_2 harvested per year, falling to 200 Euro per ton-year by 2050.

Delivered costs of CO_2 vary depending on the type of DAC, project scale, and local factors. Keith et al. [58] provided detailed engineering and cost estimates of a 1 million-ton-of-CO_2-per-year DAC plant, based on mature commercially available technologies, estimating levelized cost of 90−200 US\$/ton. In 2019 Breyer et al. [10] performed a study for the Maghreb region of northern Africa, Algeria and Morocco, exploring pathways to 100% renewables by the year 2050. They expect DAC costs to fall to the range of 55−100 Euro per ton of CO_2 captured, based on existing commercially deployed DAC technologies and expected cost reductions as technology deployment accelerates. Cost predictions vary, but large-scale facilities, harvesting hundreds of thousands to millions of tons of CO_2 per year, are generally expected to incur costs in the range of 20−200 US\$/ton [59].

Methanation: combining hydrogen and carbon

Methanation is the core process combining hydrogen and CO_2 to make hydrocarbons such as methane via the power-to-gas process (PtG) and methanol via the power-to-liquid (PtL) process. The first methanation attempt was proposed by Paul Sabatier and Jean-Baptiste Senderens in 1902, and since then numerous projects have used methanation to remove CO and CO_2 from the ammonia synthesis process. Similarly, refineries and even hydrogen plants use methanation to remove CO that can be harmful to catalysts. The use of methanation to create fuels is also well established, although historically the carbon source was not from DAC, but rather from fossil fuels such as coal. For example, the Great Plains Synfuels Plant in North Dakota, which came online in 1984, processes 16,000 tons per day of lignite coal and converts it to synthetic methane for injection into gas pipelines [60]. Integrated gasification combined cycles (IGCCs) use coal feedstock to produce high-quality gas for use in traditional combined cycle combustion turbines and have been in use globally for decades. Using coal as a feedstock for methanation processes is generally falling out of favor due to environmental concerns, the falling price of natural gas in many locations, and the movement of electric utilities toward higher renewable penetration and decarbonization. Still, technology advances made over the decades can be leveraged for production of renewable fuels using carbon from DAC or biological sources. The process of methanation generally follows one of two pathways: catalytic/thermochemical or biological.

Catalytic/thermochemical methanation

Catalytic/thermochemical methanation uses metal catalysts, typically nickel, to promote the reactions necessary to produce the desired fuel. The reactions are optimized at temperatures of 200°C—550°C and pressures of as high as 100 bar. Since they use elements of the process first suggested by Paul Sabatier, catalytic/thermochemical methanation is broadly referred to as the Sabatier process. The Sabatier process is sensitive to feedstock purity, as impurities can poison the catalysts. The reader is encouraged to review the literature on various Sabatier approaches that have been researched and developed over decades.

Biological methanation

Biological methanation replaces metallic catalysts with biocatalysts, methanogenic microorganisms. Bio-methanation generally works in the temperature range of 35°C—70°C and pressures of 1—15 bar. Methanogenic organisms are less sensitive to feedstock purity but require more space to achieve the same production as a comparably rated Sabatier process. Bio-methanation can occur in continuously stirred tank reactors where the methanation occurs in the biological stew, but the mixing requirements generally require a larger MW_{el} need relative to Sabatier processes [61]. Newer bio-methanation processes are emerging that reduce or eliminate the power needed for mixing, increasing efficiency. Note that the term bio-methanation in the literature often refers to direct synthesis of biofuels using biomass as the carbon source, while biological methanation as discussed in this section uses CO_2 as a feedstock and biocatalysts to perform the methanation step.

Resource planning considerations for methanation

From an electric utility resource planning perspective, methanation is a component of the PtG and PtL pathways for renewable fuel production, where the intermittent nature of available renewable energy must be considered. Fossil-based synthetic gas production processes were developed to run on a continuous, or steady-state basis. In high renewable energy systems the synthesis of renewable fuels may be more sporadic and subject to availability of excess carbon-free MWh. Sabatier processes experience temperature swings during dynamic operation, starting, stopping, and restarting, that can lead to catalyst failure, so research into more accommodating reactor designs is underway [61] and should be considered for the design basis of any PtX projects for high renewable systems. In 2017 Southern California Gas Company and the National Renewable Energy Laboratory (NREL) launched the first power-to-gas facility in the United States that included a bio-methanation process for CH_4 production to be injected into the gas grid. One of the goals of the project is to "... answer questions like whether the bioreactor can be operated efficiently and economically to follow solar- and wind-generated electricity profiles" [62]. The efficiency of this project is reported as 50%−60%; for every 100 MWh_{el} used for electrolysis, 50−60 MW_{th} of methane is generated [63]. Internationally, a study done in 2019 [45] identified 67 methanation projects for PtG, the majority of which are in Germany, Denmark, and the Netherlands. Of the methanation projects reviewed [45] the carbon source varied, with at least 15 using bio and sewage gases, while some were referred to as using DAC.

Final thoughts on renewable fuels

Biofuels are renewable and can provide a piece of the decarbonization puzzle. They should be used to their full advantage, but have practical limitations as outlined earlier in this chapter. Additional power-to-fuel approaches are needed to help fully decarbonize power systems and other parts of the economy, providing the "missing link." The critical steps for power to hydrogen (PtH) and power to methane (PtM) have been addressed: electrolysis for hydrogen, DAC for carbon, and methanation to combine hydrogen and carbon into methane. The fuels become completely decarbonized when process energy comes from renewables and feedstocks are not fossil-based. Fig. 4.6 shows an idealized PtM process powered entirely by excess renewable energy. Steep learning curves and economies of scale will drive down installed and production costs of PtH and PtM in coming years, similar to the rapid declines in wind, solar, and battery storage costs [64].

While the cost of producing renewable fuels today may seem expensive relative to the low cost of fossil fuels (many ask why would we make synthetic fuels if oil and gas are low cost now?), policy shifts toward decarbonization will soon make comparison between the fuels irrelevant. Rather, PtM or PtH will be evaluated in a 100% renewable context with their contribution or efficacy assessed relative to solar, wind, hydro, pumped hydro storage, battery storage, etc. ES will time-shift excess renewable energy for time scales ranging from seconds to minutes to

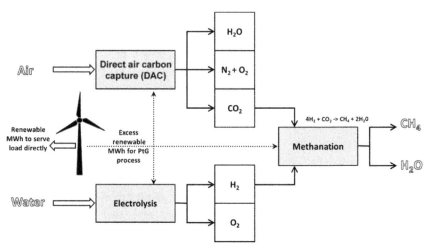

Figure 4.6 Idealized representation of carbon-neutral methane production via the power-to-methane process. If hydrogen were required instead, only the electrolysis part is needed. Final products (CH_4, H_2, or a combination of the two) injected into fuel storage and distribution networks or delivered directly to an asset that can use the fuel.

attend to supply volatility, and for hours to handle day-to-day net load fluctuations. PtM pathways appear to be most economical for longer-term storage necessary to cover seasonal variations, drought years for hydro, and unforeseen but not atypical extreme weather events that compromise VREs for days or weeks. For these scenarios, the combination of PtM with thermal resources can provide lower ratepayer costs and higher reliability than traditional ES. The optimal amount of PtM will vary regionally and by utility and must be assessed with rigorous and complex optimization approaches, such as found in state-of-the-art long-term capacity expansion simulations, which should form the basis of electric utility long-term or integrated resource plans.

Initial studies indicate that PtM is most applicable for power systems exceeding 80% of their energy directly from renewables and where PtM attends to long-term and seasonal shifting [10,64−67]. Power-to-gas facilities act as new loads specifically designed to absorb excess wind and solar MWh [68−73]. In a 100% renewable system load is first served directly by wind, solar, and hydro. The amounts of wind and solar required will necessarily be in excess of demand for most hours of the year. Kotter et al. [70] analyzed a section of the German electrical system under 100% renewable scenarios and found PtM to be the preferred long-term storage technology relative to Li-ion batteries. Belderbos et al. [66] evaluated the

Belgian power system and found that PtM is optimal as long-term storage in high renewable systems relative to other storage pathways. Child and Bryer [74] evaluated the Finnish power system under 100% decarbonization and found similar, that PtG serves as a crucial piece in a cost-optimized portfolio. Laslett et al. [67] studied the southwestern interconnected system of Australia and also determined for high renewable penetrations ($>80\%$) PtM played a crucial role for long-term seasonal shifting, in particular for wind. Ferrari [75] showed that PtM provided for optimal ratepayer costs (lowest \$/kWh) in a 100% carbon-neutral system relative to an all-renewable and Li-ion approach to decarbonization. The above references are by no means exhaustive and represent a snapshot of the research available in the literature indicating a growing interest in PtM for decarbonization. Similar results have been obtained for power to hydrogen in terms of advantages for long-term storage over batteries or traditional ES, see Eveloy and Gebreegziabher [76] for a review. One challenge for PtH is that, at present, no broad-scale storage and delivery systems exist for hydrogen and the technologies that can burn it at scale are still emerging. Methane storage and delivery systems exist now, at least in power systems presently reliant on gas.

The studies noted above all look at some future state with high or complete renewable penetration. First, we must get from here to there while simultaneously maintaining reliability and controlling costs for ratepayers. A big challenge facing utility planners during this transition will be integrating the mass of existing utility assets into that 100% renewable future in such a way as to avoid stranded assets, or investment in technologies needed today that become unable to contribute to capacity or energy needs as 100% target dates approach, but that ratepayers have already paid for (and will continue to pay for after they are no longer allowed to be used if they burn fossil fuel). PtM provides a means for utilities to leverage existing natural gas generators as carbon-neutral assets when the transition is made. In addition, if PtM is considered a renewable fuel source according to Renewable Portfolio Standard (RPS) or other renewable mandates, utilities can consider installing standard CT or Recip technology to meet today's power needs without fear of them becoming stranded assets once RPS target dates approach.

Once 100% RPS target dates are met, a system utilizing power to fuels "sees" the thermal fleet acting as a sort of giant "battery." With battery systems the amount of MW that can be delivered to the grid is controlled by the size of the inverter, and the duration is a function of how many battery cells are present in the system. With renewable fuels in a 100% carbon-neutral system, the thermal assets are no longer reliant on fossil fuels. Instead they act as the inverters, converting the energy potential of renewable fuels to electricity, and their duration is a function of available fuel storage. One study [75] showed that a small electric utility in the state of New Mexico could reach carbon-neutrality by converting 955 MW of existing thermal capacity into a giant distributed "battery" with a duration of 554 hours (23 days!) at full output, based on the amount of fuel that could economically be produced using the PtM process shown in Fig. 4.6. In this sense, utility resource planners will be valuing renewable fuels not as an alternative to fossil fuels based on costs, but rather they will be weighing the cost of renewable fuel production combined with existing thermal fleets against the cost and performance of other forms of ES. Determining the optimal mix of any technology types against regulatory regimes is far more complex than many imagine and requires sophisticated resource planning approaches.

References

[1] S. Jenkins, J.D. Luke, M. Thernstrom, Getting to zero carbon emissions in the electric power sector, Joule 2 (2018) 2498–2510.
[2] Summary for policymakers of IPCC Special Report on Global Warming of 1.5°C approved by governments. Intergovernmental Panel on Climate Change. <https://www.ipcc.ch/2018/10/08/summary-for-policymakers-of-ipcc-special-report-on-global-warming-of-1-5c-approved-by-governments/>, 2018.
[3] F. Clerjon, A. Perdu, Matching intermittency and electricity storage characteristics through time scale analysis: an energy return on investment comparison, Energy Environ. Sci. 12 (2019) 693–705.
[4] Drought in California. <https://www.drought.gov/drought/states/california>, (accessed 04.03.19).
[5] Electric Power Monthly. U.S. Energy Information Agency. <https://www.eia.gov/electricity/monthly/epm_table_grapher.php?t = epmt_6_07_b>
[6] California Hydroelectric Statistics and Data. <https://ww2.energy.ca.gov/almanac/renewables_data/hydro/index_cms.php>, (accessed 22.05.19).
[7] T. Jacobson, M.Z. Delucchi, M. Bazouin, G. Bauer, Z. Heavey, C. Fisher, et al., 100% clean and renewable wind, water, and sunlight (WWS) all-sector energy roadmaps for the 50 United States, Energy Environ. Sci. 8 (2015) 2093–2117.
[8] C. Barbosa, L.D.S.N.S. Bogdanov, D. Vainikka, P. Breyer, Hydro, wind and solar power as a base for a 100% renewable energy supply for South and Central America, PLoS One. 12 (2017). Available from: https://journals.plos.org/plosone/article?id = 10.1371/journal.pone.0173820.
[9] K. Perez, R. Rabago, A radical idea to get a high-renewable electric grid: build way more solar and wind than needed, GreenBiz (2019). Available from: https://www.greenbiz.com/article/radical-idea-get-high-renewable-electric-grid-build-way-more-solar-and-wind-needed.

[10] A. Breyer, C. Fasihi, M. Aghahosseini, Carbon dioxide direct air capture for effective climate change mitigation based on renewable electricity: a new type of energy system sector coupling, Mitig. Adapt. Strateg. Glob. Change 25 (2020) 43−65. Available from: https://link.springer.com/article/10.1007/s11027-019-9847-y.

[11] J. Gielen, D. Bazilian, M.D. Medlock, K.B. Logan, Power-to-X in the German experience: another in the list of growing energy transition strategies, Forbes (2019). Available from: https://www.forbes.com/sites/thebakersinstitute/2019/05/08/power-to-x-in-the-german-experience-another-in-the-list-of-growing-energy-transition-strategies/#53852c175514.

[12] Powerfuels: missing link to a successful global energy transition current state of technologies, markets, and politics − and start of a global dialogue. <https://www.powerfuels.org/fileadmin/gap/Publikationen/Green_Paper/Global_Alliance_Powerfuels_Powerfuels-A_missing_link_to_a_successful_global_energy_transition.PDF>, 2019.

[13] C. Bogdanov, D. Farfan, J. Sadovskaia, K. Aghahosseini, A. Child, M. Gulagi, et al., Radical transformation pathway towards sustainable electricity via evolutionary steps, Nat. Commun. 10 (2019). Available from: https://www.nature.com/articles/s41467-019-08855-1.

[14] F. Mayes, Increases in electricity generation from biomass stop after a decade of growth, Today in Energy (2019). <https://www.eia.gov/todayinenergy/detail.php?id=39052> (accessed 16.12.19).

[15] Brief on biomass for energy in the European Union. <https://publications.jrc.ec.europa.eu/repository/bitstream/JRC109354/biomass_4_energy_brief_online_1.pdf>, 2019 (accessed 16.12.19).

[16] R. Drouin, Wood pellets: green energy or new source of CO_2 emissions? Yale Environ. 360 (2015). Available from: https://e360.yale.edu/features/wood_pellets_green_energy_or_new_source_of_co2_emissions.

[17] T. Bayar, Biomass is booming in Brazil, Power Engineering International. <https://www.powerengineeringint.com/2015/05/29/biomass-is-booming-in-brazil/>, 2015.

[18] F. Scarlat, N. Dallemand, J.-F. Fahl, Biogas: developments and perspectives in Europe, Renew. Energy. 129 (2018) 457−472.

[19] M. Zahan, K.A. Kano, Biodiesel production from palm oil, its by-products, and mill effluent: a review, Energies. 11 (2018). Available from: https://www.mdpi.com/1996-1073/11/8/2132.

[20] Investigation shows forests destroyed to supply biomass. <https://www.nrdc.org/media/2019/190618>, (accessed 16.12.19).

[21] J. Verne, The Mysterious Island, Charles Scribner's Sons, New York, NY, 1920.

[22] The Green Hydrogen Report. <https://www.hydrogen.energy.gov/pdfs/greenhyd.pdf>, 1995.

[23] Hydrogen from renewable power, Abu Dhabi. <https://www.irena.org/-/media/Files/IRENA/Agency/Publication/2018/Sep/IRENA_Hydrogen_from_renewable_power_2018.pdf>, 2018.

[24] M. Rashid, M. AlMesfer, M. Naseem, H. Danish, Hydrogen production by water electrolysis: a review of alkaline water electrolysis, PEM water electrolysis and high temperature water electrolysis, Int. J. Eng. Adv. Technol. 4 (2015) 80−93.

[25] F. Simon, Four energy storage projects that could transform Europe, Euractiv. (2019). Available from: https://www.euractiv.com/section/energy/news/four-energy-storage-projects-that-could-transform-europe/.

[26] S. Schmidt, O. Gambhr, A. Staffell, I. Hawkes, A. Nelson, J. Few, Future cost and performance of water electrolysis: an expert elicitation study, Int. J. Hydrog. Energy 42 (2017) 30470−30492. Available from: https://www.sciencedirect.com/science/article/pii/S0360319917339435.

[27] S. Pandiyan, A. Uthayakumar, A. Subrayan, R. Cha, S.K. Krishna Moorthy, Review of solid oxide electrolysis cells: a clean energy strategy for hydrogen generation, Nanomater. Energy 8 (2019) 2−22.

[28] Y. Chen, L. Dong, X. Wang, Y. Xia, Separating hydrogen and oxygen evolution in alkaline water electrolysis using nickel hydroxide, Nat. Commun. 7 (2016). Available from: https://www.nature.com/articles/ncomms11741.

[29] A. Naimi, Y. Antar, Hydrogen generation by water electrolysis, in: M. Eyvaz (Ed.), Advances in Hydrogen Generation Technologies, 2018.

[30] M. Eichman, J. Townsend, A. Malaina, Economic assessment of hydrogen technologies participating in california electricity markets. <https://www.nrel.gov/docs/fy16osti/65856.pdf>, 2016.

[31] P. Wulf, C. Linben, J. Zapp, Review of power-to-gas projects in Europe, Energy Procedia. 155 (2018) 367−378.

[32] Study on early business cases for H₂ in energy storage and more broadly power to H₂ applications. <https://www.fch.europa.eu/sites/default/files/P2H_Full_Study_FCHJU.pdf>, 2017.

[33] J. Curtin, S. Gangi, Fuel cell technologies market report 2016. <https://www.energy.gov/sites/prod/files/2017/10/f37/fcto_2016_market_report.pdf>, 2016.

[34] I. Bobmann, T. Staffell, The shape of future electricity demand: exploring load curves in 2050s Germany and Britain, Energy. 90 (2015) 1317−1333.

[35] K. Staffell, I. Scamman, D. Abad, A. Balcombe, P. Dodds, P.E. Ekins, et al., The role of hydrogen and fuel cells in the global energy system, Energy Environ. Sci. 12 (2019) 463−491. Available from: https://pubs.rsc.org/en/content/articlelanding/2019/ee/c8ee01157e#!divAbstract.

[36] Fuel cell power plants are used in diverse ways across the United States. <https://www.eia.gov/todayinenergy/detail.php?id = 35872#>, 2018.

[37] S. Patel, High-Volume Hydrogen Gas Turbines Take Shape, Power. <https://www.powermag.com/high-volume-hydrogen-gas-turbines-take-shape/>, 2019.

[38] Spotlight on: turbines and renewable gases!. <https://www.euturbines.eu/publications/spotlight-on/spotlight-on-turbines-and-renewable-gases.html>, 2019 (accessed 13.11.19).

[39] Hydrogen properties. <https://www1.eere.energy.gov/hydrogenandfuelcells/tech_-validation/pdfs/fcm01r0.pdf>, 2001.

[40] M. Melaina, M. Antonia, O. Penev, Blending hydrogen into natural gas pipeline networks: a review of key issues. NREL Technical Report NREL/TP-5600-51995. <https://www.nrel.gov/docs/fy13osti/51995.pdf>, 2013.

[41] M. Webber, The water intensity of the transitional hydrogen economy, Environ. Res. Lett. 2 (2007).

[42] R. Torcellini, P. Long, N. Judkoff, Consumptive water use for U.S. power production, NREL/TP-550-33905. <https://www.nrel.gov/docs/fy04osti/33905.pdf>, 2003.

[43] Water withdrawals by U.S. power plants have been declining, in: Today in Energy. <https://www.eia.gov/todayinenergy/detail.php?id = 37453>, 2018 (accessed 23.09.19).

[44] D. Gardner, Hydrogen production from renewables, RenewableEnergyFocus.com. <http://www.renewableenergyfocus.com/view/3157/hydrogen-production-from-renewables/>, 2009.

[45] M. Thema, M. Bauer, F. Sterner, Power-to-gas: electrolysis and methanation status review, Renew. Sustain. Energy Rev. 112 (2019) 775−787.

[46] S. Glenk, G. Reichelstein, Economics of converting renewable power to hydrogen, Nat. Energy 4 (2019) 216−222.

[47] J. Mathis, W. Thornhill, Hydrogen's plunging price boosts role as climate solution, Bloomberg News. <https://www.bloomberg.com/news/articles/2019-08-21/cost-of-hydrogen-from-renewables-to-plummet-next-decade-bnef>, 2019.

[48] Hydrogen to be trialled in NSW gas networks. <https://arena.gov.au/news/hydrogen-to-be-trialled-in-nsw-gas-networks/>, 2018 (accessed 03.01.20).

[49] Italy's Snam looking to raise hydrogen mix in its pipelines, Reuters.com. <https://www.reuters.com/article/us-snam-hydrogen/italys-snam-looking-to-raise-hydrogen-mix-in-its-pipelines-idUSKBN1WP2KZ>, 2019.

[50] Hydrogen levels in German gas distribution system to be raised to 20 percent for the first time. <https://www.eon.com/en/about-us/media/press-release/2019/hydrogen-levels-in-german-gas-distribution-system-to-be-raised-to-20-percent-for-the-first-time.html>, (accessed 06.12.19).

[51] HyDeploy: UK gas grid injection of hydrogen in full operation.<https://www.itm-power.com/news/hydeploy-uk-gas-grid-injection-of-hydrogen-in-full-operation>, 2020 (accessed 03.01.20).

[52] K. Hashimoto, K. Yamasaki, M. Fujimura, K. Matsui, T. Izumiya, K. Komori, et al., Global CO_2 recycling—novel materials and prospect for prevention of global warming and abundant energy supply, Mater. Sci. Eng. A 267 (1999) 200−206. Available from: https://www.sciencedirect.com/science/article/abs/pii/S0921509399000921.

[53] P. Lackner, K. Ziock, H.-J. Grimes, Carbon dioxide extraction from air: is it an option? Report # LA-UR-99-583. <https://www.osti.gov/servlets/purl/770509>, 1999.

[54] G. Olah, Beyond oil and gas: the methanol economy, Angew. Chem. Int. Ed. 44 (2005) 2636−2639.

[55] B. Magill, World's first commercial CO_2 capture plant goes live, Climate Central. <https://www.climatecentral.org/news/first-commercial-co2-capture-plant-live-21494>, 2017.

[56] Agreement signed for CRI's first CO_2-to-methanol plant in China. <https://www.carbonrecycling.is/news-media/co2-to-methanol-plant-china>, 2019 (accessed 04.12.19).

[57] C. Fasihi, M. Efimova, O. Breyer, Techno-economic assessment of CO_2 direct air capture plants, J. Clean. Prod. 224 (2019) 957−980.

[58] K. Keith, D.W. Holmes, G. St-Angelo, D. Heidel, a process for capturing CO_2 from the atmosphere, Joule 2 (2018) 1573−1594. Available from: https://www.sciencedirect.com/science/article/pii/S2542435118302253.

[59] A. Ishimoto, Y. Sugiyama, M. Kato, E. Moriyama, R. Tsuzuki, K. Kurosawa, Putting costs of direct air capture in context. <https://www.american.edu/sis/centers/carbon-removal/upload/fcea_wps002_ishimoto.pdf>, 2017.

[60] Great Plains Synfuels Plant. <https://www.netl.doe.gov/research/Coal/energy-systems/gasification/gasifipedia/great-plains>, (accessed 02.12.19).

[61] T. Gotz, M. Lefebvre, J. Mors, F. Kock, A.M. Graf, F. Bajohr, et al., Renewable power-to-gas: a technological and economic review, Renew. Energy. 85 (2016) 1371−1390.

[62] SoCalGas power-to-gas project selected by U.S. Department of Energy's National Renewable Energy Laboratory to Receive Funding. <https://www.sempra.com/newsroom/press-releases/socalgas-power-gas-project-selected-us-department-energys-national>, 2017.

[63] SoCalGas and Electrochaea announce commissioning of new biomethanation reactor system pilot project, PR Newswires. <https://www.prnewswire.com/news-releases/socalgas-and-electrochaea-announce-commissioning-of-new-biomethanation-reactor-system-pilot-project-300901080.html>, 2019.

[64] C. Gorre, J. Ortloff, F. van Leeuwen, Production costs for synthetic methane in 2030 and 2050 of an optimized power-to-gas plant with intermediate hydrogen storage, Appl. Energy. 253 (2019).

[65] A. Walker, S.B. Mukherjee, U. Fowler, M. Elkamel, Benchmarking and selection of power-to-gas utilizing electrolytic hydrogen as an energy storage alternative, Int. J. Hydrog. Energy 41 (2016) 7717–7731.

[66] E. Belderbos, A. Virag, W. D'haeseleer, E. Delarue, Considerations on the need for electricity storage requirements: power versus energy, Energy Convers. Manag. 143 (2017) 137–149.

[67] D. Laslett, Carter, C. Creagh, P. Jennings, A large-scale renewable electricity supply system by 2030: solar, wind, energy efficiency, storage and inertia for the South West Interconnected System (SWIS) in Western Australia, Renew. Energy. 113 (2017) 713–731.

[68] N. Qadrdan, M. Abeysekera, M. Chaudry, M. Wu, J. Jenkins, Role of power-to-gas in an integrated gas and electricity system in Great Britain, Int. J. Hydrog. Energy 40 (2015) 5763–5775.

[69] Y. Liu, W. Wen, F. Xue, Power-to-gas technology in energy systems: current status and prospects of potential operation strategies, J. Mod. Power Syst. Clean Energy 5 (2017) 439–450. Available from: https://link.springer.com/article/10.1007/s40565-017-0285-0.

[70] R. Kotter, E. Schneider, L. Sehnke, F. Ohnmeiss, K. Schroer, Sensitivities of power-to-gas within an optimised energy system, Energy Procedia 73 (2015) 190–199. Available from: https://www.sciencedirect.com/science/article/pii/S1876610215014381.

[71] M. Varone, A. Ferrari, Power to liquid and power to gas: an option for the German Energiewende, Renew. Sustain. Energy Rev. 45 (2015) 207–218.

[72] L.M. Gutierrez-Martin, F. Rodrigues-Anton, Power-to-SNG technology for energy storage at large scales, Int. J. Hydrog. Energy 41 (2016) 19290–19303.

[73] J. Lund, P.D. Lindgren, J. Mikkola, J. Salpakari, Review of energy system flexibility measures to enable high levels of variable renewable electricity, Renew. Sustain. Energy Rev. 45 (2015) 785–807.

[74] C. Child, M. Breyer, Vision and initial feasibility analysis of a recarbonised Finnish energy system for 2050, Renew. Sustain. Energy Rev. 66 (2016) 517–536.

[75] J. Ferrari, Pathways towards 100% carbon reduction for electric utility power systems. <https://www.wartsila.com/energy/towards-100-renewable-energy/optimising-power-systems>, 2019.

[76] T. Eveloy, V. Gebreegziabher, A review of projected power-to-gas deployment scenarios, Energies 11 (2018).

CHAPTER 5

Long-term capacity expansion planning

Introduction

Electric utilities are tasked with providing reliable and affordable electricity to their customers. Reliable means customers are not plagued with blackouts, which can compromise public safety and cause economic harm. Utilities deliver reliability by providing redundancy in the system, which can be quantified by metrics such as reserve margin. Affordable means people are not forced into "energy poverty" by paying a disproportionate amount of their income for electricity. Affordability is somewhat subjective, but utilities strive to provide least-cost. The task for electric utility resource planners is to demonstrate and quantify that their long-term expansion plans are indeed the lowest cost solutions (Fig. 5.1).

The capacity expansion planning process can be as simple as a spreadsheet or involve state-of-the-art dispatch simulation and optimization algorithms that converge on least-cost solutions. Any model is only as accurate as the information that goes into it. And capacity expansion models require a good amount of input data, information, and assumptions related to costs.

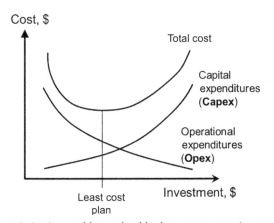

Figure 5.1 The optimization problem solved by long-term capacity expansion efforts.

Electric Utility Resource Planning
DOI: https://doi.org/10.1016/B978-0-12-819873-5.00005-8

Costs in capacity expansion

A utility's costs for power generation fall into three major categories:
* operating expenditures (Opex);
* fixed operations and maintenance (FOM); and
* capital expenditures (Capex).

Operating expenditures

Opex is the annual expenditure related to fuel and other consumables, including electricity purchase. Major Opex costs are as follows:
* Fuel: often the most expensive operating cost (for thermal plants).
* Energy: purchase of MWh from the market, or via contractual arrangement with a generator owned by another utility or independent power producer (IPP).
* Emission control consumables: reagents consumed for control of air pollutants such as nitrogen oxides.
* Variable operations and maintenance (VOM): day to day operations costs and minor maintenance activities.
* Water: many power plants require large volumes of water. Water can be needed for evaporative cooling systems, emission control systems, power augmentation, and makeup water for boilers.

Opex is often determined at the plant level and calculated for the entire portfolio as a cost per MWh.

Fixed operations and maintenance

FOM costs are annual fixed costs a utility must pay independent of asset use. Typical FOM costs include:
* Staffing: power plants of any type, from thermal to hydro to renewable typically have some level of permanent staffing. Positions such as plant manager or maintenance technician or control room operator are salaried positions with benefits, a fixed cost independent of how the plant runs.
* Annual maintenance costs: whether it is a solar farm that needs regular panel cleaning or annual maintenance activities on a thermal plant, these costs occur annually and may vary in intensity from year to year.
* Phone, internet, sewer connections: needed for plant operations, often set as fixed annual or monthly fees.
* Property taxes: must be paid annually independent of generation.

Capital expenditures

Utilities must continually update, replace, and/or expand their fleet of assets. Every power plant has capital costs which can be broken down as follows:

- Equipment cost: the cost of manufacture, assembly, and delivery to site of all equipment needed to build a functioning plant;
- EPC cost: engineering, procurement, and construction of the facility;
  - civil works, foundations, buildings, parking lots, fencing, etc.,
  - provision of bulk materials such as concrete, piping, cabling, and any other material or machinery not included in the equipment cost, and
  - plus all labor and engineering.
- Owners cost:
  - land,
  - electrical interconnection studies and permits,
  - environmental permitting,
  - payment for any owners engineering services by third parties,
  - Interest during construction; the payment of interest charges during the construction phase when interest is accruing while no revenues are being generated,
  - Interconnection costs to the transmission or distribution system, fuel pipelines if applicable, water/sewer connections.
- Major overhauls: Major overhauls are not part of the cost of building a power plant but can be considered a Capex depending on the utility business model and local regulatory structure. Regulated investor-owned utilities may consider major overhauls an infrequent capital expenditure for rate recovery. Other utilities may levelize the costs over multiple years and either include it in FOM or calculate it as a $/MWh adder to the VOM part of Opex.

The utility must pay for all elements listed above to successfully build and operate a power plant, either purchasing it outright or borrowing some or all the money needed and securing loans to cover the balance. The Capex portion of a utility's accounting is often a 10- or 20-year fixed annual fee, the sum of which, when fully repaid, covers the entire cost of the plant plus whatever interest is due. The annual Capex is often referred to in modeling contexts as an *annualized build cost*, calculated for each plant and reported individually and as a cumulative total for each year.

For nonenergy professionals Capex and FOM costs can be understood by looking at an electricity bill from a utility. Electricity bills often have several components. These can include a variable charge ($/kWh) and a fixed "capacity" charge. The variable charge is dependent on how much energy you use. If you use zero kWh that month, your variable charge is zero. But even if you use no energy at all, you still have a capacity charge. The capacity charge represents how utilities recover FOM and Capex costs.

Cost information is included in IRPs typically in tabular format and used as input data into any associated capacity expansion analysis. Often the capital cost in the table is the EPC cost, although it is more accurate to apply an adder reflecting owners cost as well. The magnitude of the adder can be based on detailed cost estimates or, more often, an assumed percent of the EPC cost, where the percentages are guided by experience. For newer technologies such as Li-ion battery storage, forward curves on expected prices in future years may be used as well.

The supply stack and marginal cost

The FOM and Capex portions of a long-term resource plan are easily grasped. Most readers understand that whether or not you use energy, somebody is spending money for you to have the ability to turn your light on with a flip of the switch, and you pay them for this service.

Opex is also conceptually simple and it would be easy to calculate if this was 1930 and your utility only had one 100 MW coal power plant. You could calculate how many tons of coal at a certain price ($/ton) are required to generate 100 MWh of electricity and show the result in the units of $/MWh. This would represent the majority of the Opex and give a clear idea of the operational cost of electricity. But how do you determine the cost of electricity when the utility has dozens of generators of widely differing technology types using different fuels, or no fuel at all? How do you capture energy storage which is reliant on the MWh generated by some other source? And how to calculate this when different generation assets only run certain hours of the day? The answer to this tricky question depends on how "day-ahead forecasting" ties together with the "supply stack."

Day-ahead forecasting is the way utilities and grid operators estimate hourly load for the next day and schedule the dispatch of power plants to meet load. Why hourly and not every minute? Mainly because hourly forecasts are easily understandable and only require 24 data points per day, and most generators (historically) have start times and other restrictions measured in hours. Load forecasting is an art and a science fueled by utility experience. They know daily and weekly load patterns. They know how the load patterns shift with the seasons. They also know the typical electric use trends for homes and for commercial and industrial facilities. Based on this in-depth understanding of their system they are pretty good at estimating the hourly load for tomorrow. They must also forecast the combined output of variable renewable energy (VREs) such as wind and solar (Fig. 5.2A).

Once hourly loads are estimated, the utility must determine which power plants will run and at what times, and to do this they rely on the supply stack. The supply stack is simply the rank ordering of all assets in a utility portfolio by their size (MW) and Opex ($/MWh). The sum of MW from the supply stack that just meets load, and their corresponding Opex cost, defines the cost of serving load for that hour. The last unit added to meet load for that hour sets the clearing price (Fig. 5.2B). Historically a utility dominated by thermal assets would have a fixed supply stack. However, when VREs are added to the system, the supply stack changes by the hour depending on the availability of low Opex VREs (Fig. 5.3).

The time-dependent nature of VREs introduces an added level of complexity to the supply stack concept. No longer can utilities and grid operators make firm plans from day to day based on existing assets. They must now account for how VREs will supply MWh throughout the day, which is both weather dependent and fluctuates seasonally. With

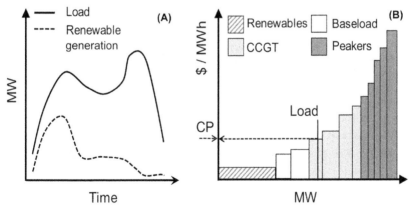

Figure 5.2 Utility load and renewable generation for a hypothetical 24-h day (A) and supply stack (B) showing the load for a given hour and corresponding clearing price (CP) for that hour.

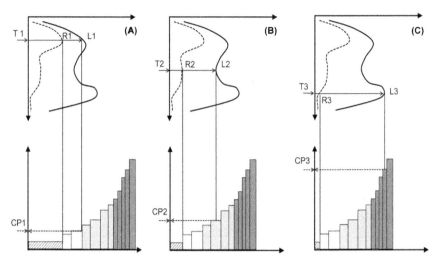

Figure 5.3 Utility load and renewable generation at times T1, T2, and T3 (A, B, and C, respectively). Loads (L1, L2, L3) and renewable output (R1, R2, R3) are used together with the supply stack to determine the corresponding clearing prices (CP1, CP2, CP3). Note that the width of the renewable portion of the supply stack (bottom panels) varies with time throughout the day.

increased weather forecasting accuracy utilities can reduce uncertainty, but we all know that weather forecasts are not 100% accurate.

One additional term is worth mentioning, marginal cost. Marginal cost is the clearing price for each hour, set by the last and most expensive generator in the supply stack to come online to serve load. For a given hour, every unit at or below the marginal cost will be dispatched to serve load. By combining the day-ahead load and VRE forecasts with the supply stack, utilities can make an hourly schedule for the power plants for the next day. Each plant is assigned specific run hours according to least-cost dispatch principles.

Utility marginal cost data by hour may not be made public. In regional energy markets multiple utilities contribute to a pool of resources to meet system, or market-wide load. Every generator gets paid the marginal cost which may vary from location to location within the system, in which case it is referred to as the locational marginal price (LMP). For a given generator dispatched at a given hour, the difference between actual generation cost and marginal cost (or LMP) is the gross revenue the utility receives for that generator for that hour. Gross revenues are used to pay down annualized build costs and FOM, the remainder is referred to as net revenue, or profit. Generators that set the marginal cost are referred to as the marginal unit, or the unit on the margin. In a competitive market the marginal unit only gets paid for its operational cost and is making zero gross revenue. No power plant owner wants to operate and cause wear and tear on a facility with no revenue. It is for this reason some generators will inflate their VOM, and ultimately their Opex, in bids to the grid operator. Providing a higher Opex will reduce the number of hours they run in the market but assures they enjoy larger than zero gross revenue for the hours they do run as the marginal unit. The ensemble of units that only run sporadically are on or close to the margin and are considered peaking units. It can be the case that peaking units do not earn enough revenues from market operations to pay off annualized build costs and/or FOM, in which case the "missing money" is supplied by other mechanisms to keep them in the market. They are kept in the market to maintain reliability.

Net load and the supply stack

The impact of VRE generation on load and the resultant net load has been shown in prior chapters. Here, net load is presented in the context of the supply stack. Wind and solar generally have two features: (1) they are not strictly dispatchable, their output varies hour to hour, day to day; and (2) their variable cost, the Opex part, is close to zero, assuring MW from these sources are utilized first to meet load before any other assets are dispatched. Because of these features, it is common to simply adjust the load by subtracting the renewable output, with net load as the result. Net load is the load which dispatchable resources "see" and are dispatched to serve. If net load is used, then the variable width of the renewable generation in the supply stack (Figs. 5.2 and 5.3) goes away and the clearing price is simply that at which the net load at a specific hour intersects the supply stack. If net load is zero, it implies all load is served by renewables and the clearing price is close to zero.

If the net load (Fig. 5.4B) is used instead of load and the supply stack is shown without renewable capacity on the X-axis, clearing prices (Fig. 5.5) are equivalent to those shown in Fig. 5.3.

Real-time dispatch

Typically, utilities first estimate load and renewable output one day ahead of time, then provide instruction to power plants to run specific hours of

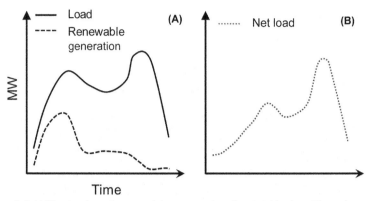

Figure 5.4 Utility load and renewable generation for a 24-h day (A) and resultant net load (B), where net load equals (from A) load minus renewable generation.

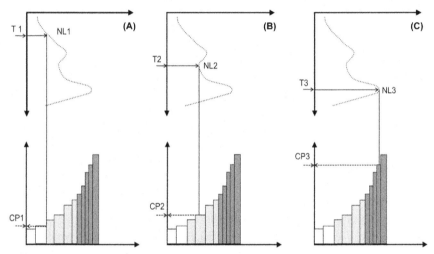

Figure 5.5 Utility net load for a hypothetical 24-h day. At times T1, T2, and T3 (A, B, and C, respectively) the net loads (NL1, NL2, NL3) are used together with the supply stack to determine the corresponding clearing prices (CP1, CP2, CP3).

the next day based on the marginal cost concepts outlined above. Every plant that generates at or below the marginal cost is dispatched for that hour. Of course, when the next day rolls around customers do not behave exactly as expected and wind and solar experience deviations from the day-ahead forecasts. Even if load and VRE are exactly as forecasted in terms of hourly values, they can vary quite a bit within an hour, such that generators set to meet hourly loads will either be overgenerating or not supplying enough energy to meet instantaneous demand. Real-time markets are used to attend to the deviations between hourly expectations and the actual loads in real time.

For real-time dispatch, generators are committed to serve load as per the supply stack concepts noted above, only now their operational status is included. If a certain plant is at full load, it cannot supply more MWh and additional generators will need to come on-line in real-time. These decisions are usually made on timescales of 5—15 minutes. Generators not committed to day-ahead hourly dispatch can be called upon to provide energy for as little as 5 minutes. Other generators committed to the hour by day-ahead dispatch may receive new dispatch orders coming in multiple times within the hour.

While many utilities are not in an organized market, dispatch decisions are still made based on the supply stack and least-cost dispatch concepts. Generally, their hourly and real-time prices are not publicly available. For utilities in an organized market, it is possible to see day ahead hourly and real-time energy prices, if not for a utility, then for the market as a whole. Most organized markets have websites showing pricing in real time for a given day and provide access to historical hourly and real-time price data.

While real-time markets are essential for keeping the lights on, they are rarely considered in long-range or integrated resource plans. Capacity expansion models are rarely run at less than hourly resolution. What is becoming more popular today is for utilities to do their traditional capacity selection with long-range planning models, then take the resultant portfolios and run them through sophisticated real-time dispatch models, accounting for energy and ancillary services (spin reserve, regulation). The purpose is to assess whether the portfolio is flexible enough to handle what it will be subjected to. If any deficiencies are found, for example not enough ramp capacity to attend to intrahour variations, then additional capacity is needed. Most often this additional capacity is selected based on the experience of the resource planners and operational staff at the utility, it is not necessarily the product of long-term cost optimization.

Capacity factors

The capacity factor is the ratio of actual MWh produced to the maximum possible MWh that could be produced, typically on an annual basis. For planning purposes, utility planners often assume capacity factors for different technology types based on experience. That experience is drawn from the interplay between loads, net loads, and supply stacks over time periods of multiple years.

Generally units that run all the time are considered "baseload," units that run at intermediate levels (in terms of hours per year) are considered "intermediate," and finally, units that only run a few hours per year (generally less than 1000) are considered "peakers." The most expensive peaking unit would only be needed a few hours per year to meet the highest peak loads. This information on expected run hours and technology bins (baseload, intermediate, peaking) can be coupled together with levelized or annual cost curves (ACCs) for different technology types to create screening curves.

Screening curves

Utilities can use historical data or simulations of expected future net loads to create screening curves which are used for long-term planning purposes. Screening curves come in multiple formats, two of which include levelized cost of energy (LCOE) and ACCs. Both can be displayed as a function of hours across a year, ranging from 0 to 8760. LCOE is calculated as follows:

$$\text{LCOE (\$/MWh)} = \frac{\text{Total Cost}}{\text{Total Output}}$$

$$\text{Total Cost} = \sum_{t=1}^{n} \frac{I_t + M_t + F_t}{(1+r)^t}$$

$$\text{Total Output} = \sum_{t=1}^{n} \frac{E_t}{(1+r)^t}$$

where
I_t = investment and other fixed costs for year t
M_t = operations and maintenance costs for year t
F_t = fuel costs for year t
E_t = electrical output (MWh) for year t
n = expected lifetime of the facility, years
r = discount rate
The annual cost (AC) is simpler to calculate and based on the following:

AC(\$/year) = Annual Fixed Cost + Total Variable Cost
Annual Fixed Cost = Capital repayment + All fixed costs (such as FOM)
Total Variable Cost = Sum of all Fuel and other variable costs for the year

Levelized cost is a function of run hours, and generally the more hours a plant runs per year, the lower the LCOE. This is so because fuel and other variable costs are relatively constant and calculated as a cost per MWh which does not change. Fixed cost is the same every year (in $) and when expressed as $/MWh goes down with higher run hours. AC, in contrast, is anchored at the annual fixed cost at zero hours, indicating the minimum cost required to have the plant available, and increases for every run hour as the sum of all fuel and other variable costs. More efficient plants will have a shallower slope with increasing run hours. Both metrics can be plotted for several technologies as a function of expected annual run hours or capacity factor. Table 5.1 lists several technologies and their indicative costs. Figs. 5.6 and 5.7 show the corresponding ACCs and 20-year LCOE as a function of run hours respectively.

The ACC (Fig. 5.6) for zero hours represents the annual fixed costs, and the lower the capital cost the lower the intercept with the Y-axis. The slope of the cost curves is dependent on sensitivity to fuel costs, which are a function of both efficiency and cost of fuel. For a fixed fuel price, higher efficiency units have smaller slopes. Renewable generators have given fixed costs but very flat representations as there is little added cost associated with higher capacity factors. The LCOE (Fig. 5.7) conveys similar information but incorporating a 20-year net present value calculation. Note that for all technologies the LCOE decreases with increasing run hours. Here 20-years was used as a common basis as is the case in many evaluations, but it is acceptable to set the term of the LCOE calculation equal to either the technical or financial life of the asset. Large hydroelectric dams may have 50-year lifetimes while some battery-storage facilities may have lifetimes as short as 10 years.

What both the ACC and LCOE shown in Figs. 5.6 and 5.7 is that for high run hours baseload coal is the lowest cost resource (in this example).

Table 5.1 Indicative performance and cost metrics for several technologies for use in calculating annual cost and/or levelized cost of energy.

Technology	Coal	CCGT	Recip	CT	Renewable
Owners cost ($/kW)	2070	1125	920	690	2070
Efficiency (%)	35	55	47	38	NA
FOM (MUSD/year)	2	2	2	2	0.4
VOM ($/MWh)	3	3	3	3	0.25
Fuel cost ($/MBtu)	2	5	5	5	NA

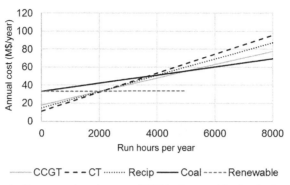

Figure 5.6 Illustrative annual cost curves (ACCs) of several technologies as a function of annual run hours. Renewables are cut off beyond 5000 h/year (approximately 60% capacity factor), which is an upper limit for wind and solar.

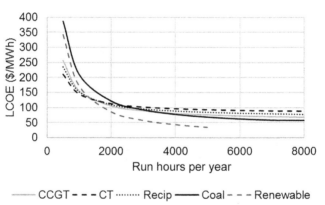

Figure 5.7 Illustrative levelized cost of energy (LCOE) of several technologies as a function of annual run hours. Renewables are cut off beyond 5000 h/year (approximately 60% capacity factor), which is an upper limit for wind and solar. Weighted average cost of capital 5%.

For peaking needs with low run hours low Capex thermal capacity is lowest cost, such as simple cycle combustion turbines (CTs). While simple cycle CTs are not very efficient, if they are rarely called upon to run the Opex is less important. In the 1000–4000 hours, high-efficiency medium speed reciprocating engines (Recips) can offer lower costs than CTs and even combined cycle combustion turbines (CCCTs). Of course, the exact composition of the ACC and LCOE plots are highly dependent on the underlying assumptions and need to be developed on a utility-by-utility basis. However, independent of parameterization, the ACC and LCOE plots show that even if VREs have near-zero variable cost when represented in the supply stack, fixed, and quasifixed costs are not zero, and hence renewable energy is not "free."

The ACC and LCOE are representations of the estimated costs to build, maintain, and run generation assets. Some utilities may choose to offset purchase of generation assets and instead arrange contractually, through power purchase agreements (PPAs), for MWh to be delivered from facilities built and owned by IPPs. The cost for the utility is often set close to the LCOE, plus a profit margin for the IPP.

Some utilities do not utilize the entire LCOE or ACC curve but opt to bin certain technologies into baseload, intermediate, and peaking and assign a capacity factor to them. For example, it is not uncommon for utilities to lump CTs and Recips together as "peaking technology" and assess their ACC or LCOE based on an assumption of 10% (or similar) capacity factor. While this simplifies the tabulation of technologies in a screening process, it loses certain information. For example, Recips are more efficient than CTs and have lower Opex, which means they generally run more hours in a utility system than CTs. Comparing the two technologies at a fixed capacity factor is not an accurate reflection of their ACC or LCOE. The disparity is greater with increasing fuel prices where efficiency has a greater impact on ACC or LCOE.

In IRPs along with cost and performance data for new-build assets, estimates of ACC or LCOE may be included as well. The ranking of costs can inform initial prescreening of technologies. For example, a wide variety of potential capacity choices can be entertained, while only those with the lowest ACC or LCOE are retained for subsequent and more detailed evaluation. In some cases, the ACC or LCOE can be the sole determinant of new-build technology selection.

Load duration curve

The load duration curve (LDC) is simply the hourly load over the course of a year sorted from maximum to minimum. A utility planner can look either at the duration curve of the load itself, or the duration curve of the net load. If the duration curve of load is used, the LDC shows the total GWh the utility needs to serve for the year. If the duration curve is of net load, the LDC shows the total GWh the utility needs to serve with dispatchable resources after a portion of the load is already met by VREs.

Using the load duration curve for long-term planning

A utility combines estimates of future load patterns, including future peak load expectations, to create LDCs of future states (going out 10, 20, or more years). They then must answer two questions:

1. Do they have enough capacity to meet load?
2. If not, what types of new capacity do they have to build and when?

To answer these questions, they plot a future year expected LDC, then divide it into baseload, intermediate, and peaking (Fig. 5.8). This provides an estimate of the amounts of each type of capacity needed (Bar plot to the right in Fig. 5.8) to compare to the existing portfolio. If the portfolio needs 1000 MW of peaking and the utility currently owns 500 MW, then they will need to install an additional 500 MW of peaking assets, similar for intermediate and baseload.

The ACC or LCOE curves are often used to determine the hour cut-offs for each type of capacity, shown as less than 1000 hours for peaking, greater than 7000 hours for baseload, and intermediate between 1000 and 7000 in Fig. 5.8. There is no common definition of these terms so the definition of hour ranges is indicative, different definitions can be found in any number of IRPs and academic texts. The technologies represented and the cost curves (ACC or LCOE) vary from region to region

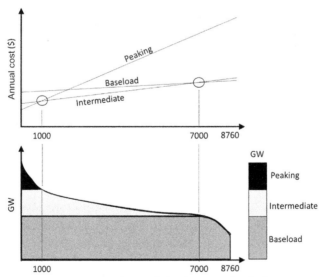

Figure 5.8 Screening curve together with load (or net load) duration curve to estimate the amounts of peaking, intermediate, and baseload capacity needed to serve load.

depending on local costs, meaning that each utility should derive the screening curves for their location and purposes.

Generic five-step capacity expansion framework, traditional approach

There are no established frameworks for long-term capacity expansion planning, but the approach can be characterized with a generic five-step process (Fig. 5.9). This basic process applies to the traditional approach as well as more complicated approaches. Within the traditional approach, the LDC plus the screening curves are used for steps 1–3, the

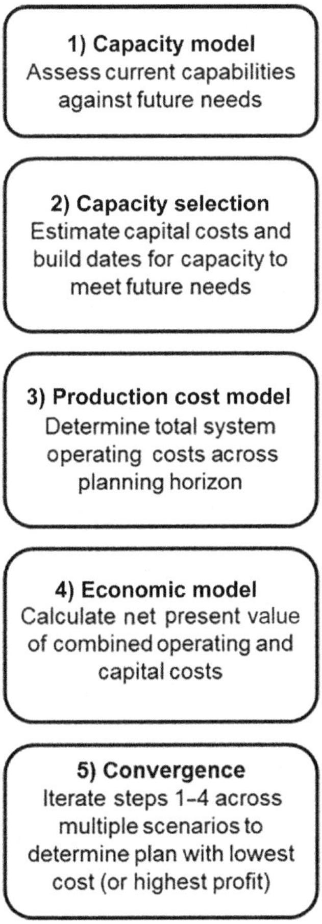

1) Capacity model
Assess current capabilities
against future needs

2) Capacity selection
Estimate capital costs and
build dates for capacity to
meet future needs

3) Production cost model
Determine total system
operating costs across
planning horizon

4) Economic model
Calculate net present value
of combined operating and
capital costs

5) Convergence
Iterate steps 1–4 across
multiple scenarios to
determine plan with lowest
cost (or highest profit)

Figure 5.9 Basic process of electric utility long-term capacity expansion planning.

determination of what types of capacity to install and when. The third step involves production cost models, used to calculate Opex for the portfolio of assets across the planning horizon. Opex can be determined using basic LCOE or ACC curves and estimates of run hours (derived from the LDC) or through use of more sophisticated simulation tools called dispatch simulators or, more broadly, production cost models. The fourth step, the economic model, can be as simple as a table or spreadsheet of basic net present value (NPV) calculations on annual Capex and Opex costs reported by steps two and three respectively.

Software packages exist that automate steps 1−4 testing various convolutions of capacity types, searching for the lowest cost to serve load over the planning horizon, and ultimately doing the work of step 5 (Fig. 5.9). The choices the model can select from are provided by new-build resource tables listing technology type, unit or plant sizes, and associated costs, performance, construction times, and other parameters. If the utility is small with only a few assets, the approach in the preceding paragraph may be sufficient. If the utility is large, with dozens to hundreds of assets, finding the correct mix of new capacity to minimize costs is not an easy problem to solve. It requires complex mathematical optimization routines which form the heart of commercially available planning software.

Commercial optimization packages iteratively solve for solutions, and the solution is found when the simulation converges. Convergence is determined by criteria specified by the user. One criterion almost universally used is gap size. Gap size is a measure of how much better the current solution is for a given iteration relative to the last. At some point additional computations will not provide any better of an answer. Setting a threshold gap size is a way to define the cutoff. The smaller the gap size, the longer it takes to converge to a solution. But if gap size is set too high, to speed up calculations, nonunique solutions can occur. That means if you run the model 10 times you can get 10 different portfolios. They may not be dramatically different from each other, but they will be different. Generally, gap size is set through experience to yield unique, optimal solutions without excessive run times.

Gap size is a setting in optimization platforms. Each solution being evaluated is the answer to an equation called the objective function. The objective function is a representation of costs and any number of constraints that must be satisfied for a solution to be feasible. Defining an objective function is beyond the scope of this work, detailed descriptions can be found in documentation accompanying capacity expansion simulation tools. But it is generally the case that the fewer the constraints, the easier it is (computationally) to calculate the value of the objective function for any given iteration. Because the LDC approach to a large extent ignores the chronology of load, net load, and does not consider unit start times, minimum run times, etc., which are all constraints, it is capable of converging on a solution very quickly and without the need for advanced computational capabilities.

It is also the case that utilities may not solve for one optimal capacity expansion. They may explore numerous outcomes across projections of varying fuel price, load growth, extreme weather patterns, etc., and create tables of alternate portfolios under varying assumptions. The choice of the preferred solution (to guide investment) may be based on the experience and intuition of utility planning staff and management. For example, a utility may calculate portfolios based on low, mid and high fuel price trajectories, and decide (based on the individual judgment of staff and management) that the mid fuel price scenario is the most likely based on their current understanding of fuel markets. Other more complicated approaches exist where solutions are plotted relative to an efficient frontier, where optimal portfolios are decided based on the interplay between costs and risk (e.g., see [1]).

Convergence contingent on reserve provision and reliability

Preferred portfolios must also satisfy reliability expectations. The mathematical problem utilities are solving for is not simply the amount and type of capacity needed to meet load. The solution can also account for things such as operational reserve provisions, capacity reserve margins and loss of load probabilities (LOLP). These factors can be added to the problem formulation as constraints.

Operational reserves refer to the need to maintain capacity in reserve to cover voltage fluctuations and power swings that accompany the mismatch between expected and actual load, expected and actual VRE generation, etc. A special form of operational reserve is called a contingency reserve. Contingency reserves are generally set at the size of the largest generator or transmission line which, upon failure, must be accounted for by other units capable of supplying power within a short time frame, typically 10 minutes or less.

Operational reserve provision has historically been ignored in the long-term planning phase as the amounts needed were rarely more than a few percent of load and relatively fixed in magnitude. With the emergence of higher VRE penetrations, regulation and other forms of load following reserves have more impact than previously experienced by utilities. In planning models, if operational reserves are accounted for, they can be set as a percentage of load or as a percentage of VRE output. The time dependence of operational reserves, however, makes traditional LDC-based approaches ill-suited for their inclusion in the analysis. More advanced approaches (discussed later in this chapter) are better suited for rolling operational reserves into the objective function. In the traditional approach, operational reserves and their costs can be included in postcapacity-expansion-simulation production cost models (also discussed later in this chapter).

The capacity reserve margin is more of a reliability metric, it attends to the risk of peak load occurring while one or more plants are down for maintenance or on forced outage. The utility must maintain more capacity than the highest peak load to act as a safety margin. Capacity reserve margins are typically in the range of 15% and are most often set as a constraint in the modeling process. Capacity reserve margins are rather easy for capacity expansion models to handle as the constraint is simply whatever capacity (MW) is needed for peak load, the solution must have 15% (or whatever the desired value) more MW.

Other metrics exist to quantify reliability such as LOLP. LOLP is a statistical analysis of numerous "what if" scenarios involving one or multiple power plants going off-line simultaneously for any number of reasons. Utilities must maintain a diversity of resources with differing risk profiles to ensure that portfolio LOLP does not violate expectations, typically one event every 10 years. Not all capacity expansion models are capable of LOLP or other reliability calculations, requiring resource planners to post-process preferred portfolios for reliability assessments.

One of the first software packages designed for electric utility long-term capacity expansion planning using LDC architecture was created by the Electric Power Research Institute [2]. Called the electric generation expansion analysis system (EGEAS), it has been on the market for decades. The mathematical optimization approaches first used by EGEAS have formed the backbone of many subsequent software packages and combine all five basic elements shown in Fig. 5.9. EGEAS is an example of a planning tool that calculates reliability metrics such as LOLP and capacity reserve margin and requires preferred portfolios to meet expected reliability norms.

Production cost models

Estimating Opex is typically reserved for the domain of production cost models. If utility planners set expected capacity factors by technology type based on the LDC, the Opex can be determined using the same information required to calculate the LCOE: variable costs associated with fuel, purchased MWh, consumables, etc. Production costing can be as straightforward as calculating the annual Opex using simple assumptions. This approach is most applicable for small utilities with few assets and limited renewable penetration.

For larger utilities with complex portfolios and VRE penetrations beyond 10%−30% of annual GWh, more sophisticated production cost models are required. Production cost models are often referred to as dispatch models as they determine which plants are running at each time interval, basically automatically calculating the supply stack, determining the marginal unit, and committing that and all lower cost units for that time interval before moving on to the next. Advanced simulators are designed to compare expected load against the supply stack for varying

Table 5.2 Assumptions of historical production costing in LT capacity expansion planning.

Assumption	Rationale for assumption
Use representative days or weeks, instead of annual simulations of all days of the year	Good representation of peak and off-peak conditions, which were considered as "bookends" to the Opex problem, no perceived need to simulate more.
Use 4- to 12-hour time steps	No perceived need to go to finer time scales, results considered adequate. Also, going to finer time scales was difficult given computational limitations.
Ignore dynamic features of the technologies considered (start, stop, and run constraints)	Associated constraints and costs of dynamic features considered too small/ unimportant to sway capacity decisions. Early production cost models did not allow for their inclusion.
Ignore operational reserves	Historically, operational reserves were understood as simply a small percentage of load, and their provision was considered insufficient to sway capacity decisions. Early production cost models did not allow for their inclusion.

time intervals (e.g., subhourly, 1-, 4-, or 12-hour blocks) and time horizons (weeks, months or years), to determine which units will dispatch (and how often) as well as their individual operating costs and the clearing price for each period. They then summarize total generation costs over weekly, monthly, or annual time periods. The effort requires an entire library of information on every existing and proposed generator, and a means to evaluate them all simultaneously. Load can have values that do not fit cleanly within the full-load outputs of generators, so the approach must be able to determine, for any given time, if one or more units will need to run at part load. Further complexity arises when taking dynamic features into account, such as limitations on unit start times, minimum up and down times, etc. Determination of production cost is a mathematical optimization problem, which becomes even more computationally challenging if operating reserve provision is accounted for.

Historically, production cost problems have been difficult to solve, mainly due to limitations in computational power and use of optimization algorithms that were still in early stages of refinement. Traditional methods of long-term planning, if they use a dispatch or production cost model at all, have historically made simplifying assumptions. Common assumptions and reasoning are given in Table 5.2.

Concerns related to traditional approaches, particularly for systems with variable renewable energy

The LDC, screening curve, and the traditional approach in general represent the bulk of conventional long-term planning approaches used to justify utility investment decisions for more than half a century. In the past, the industry was set on the central facility mindset, with preference given toward larger facilities which enjoyed lower $/kW pricing and higher efficiencies than smaller plants. The types of technologies considered could be drawn from a small pool of well-defined options. The mathematical problem could literally be done by hand using pen and paper, as it was before computers became commonplace. While the traditional approach does not provide all information regarding system needs, it does provide a good approximation [3], *particularly for systems without appreciable amounts of wind and solar.*

Global sustainability concerns and changing economies of scale have, however, produced a rapid acceleration of utility-scale wind and solar VRE deployments. VREs add an element of time-dependency to the supply stack that never existed before, which leads to increased volatility in clearing prices, dramatic changes to operational profiles of existing (non-VRE) assets, growing relevance of dynamic features of technology options and operational reserve modifications necessary to attend to VRE volatility. Ignoring these realities can lead to a number of concerns and problems (Table 5.3).

Table 5.3 references several studies that identify basic shortfalls of the traditional approach and the typical assumptions therein (Table 5.2). Numerous other works substantiate these concerns. For example Nweke et al. [11] showed in an analysis of the South Australian electrical system that using more detailed chronological long-term planning models, which inherently take dynamic features and short time-step resolution into the investment decision, build future capacity mixes that are different from that proposed by traditional LDC approaches. The LDC approaches over-value renewables and do not provide adequate balancing capacity. Ferrari et al. [12] evaluated the CAISO system (California), comparing operational costs of a system determined using traditional approaches to a system where inflexible technologies were replaced with flexible assets, and found significant reliability improvements, cost-savings to ratepayers, and reduced CO_2 emissions. The difference in results implies the traditional approach delivered a system that was not a least-cost solution. Ferrari et al. [9] compared traditional planning approaches against newer chronological long-term capacity planning methods for the Southern California Edison utility area (California) and found that for a fixed amount of

Table 5.3 Concerns and problems using traditional approach to long-term planning exercises for systems with growing levels of renewable penetration.

Assumption	Concerns/problems
Use representative days or weeks, instead of annual simulations of all days of the year	No consistent criteria for day/week selection, selected days/weeks may not be representative of annual needs [4,5]
Use 4- to 12-hour time steps	Suboptimal investment in flexibility needed to support renewables [6]
Ignore dynamic features of the technologies considered (start, stop, and run constraints)	Overinvestment in inflexible resources leading to increased costs and CO_2 emissions that would be avoided if flexible resources selected instead [7—9]
Ignore operational reserves	Resultant portfolios inadequate for net load ramping or renewable balancing [10], leading to increased costs and CO_2 relative to the optimal capacity buildout

VREs added to the system, the portfolio suggested by the traditional LDC approach was significantly less flexible and more expensive than that suggested by more advanced approaches. Poncelet et al. [13] performed a literature review and determined that traditional approaches, in general, tend to overestimate renewable performance, place greater emphasis on baseload or inflexible resources, and tend to neglect the value of flexible capacity, a trend that is reversed when dynamic features and finer detail time resolution is employed. More recent work, although not directly related to long-term planning, highlights the growing need for flexible operating reserves as VRE penetrations increase (e.g., Mohandes et al. [14]). It is precisely the flexibility features that high VRE systems need which are ignored by traditional approaches. These features are almost universally related to fast-response characteristics of non-VRE assets, which require simulations at short time scales, preferably hourly [15].

Importance of dynamic features

"Dynamic features" is a term used to describe an ensemble of technical aspects of generating technologies that are traditionally ignored in the planning process. These features represent additional constraints that more advanced simulation tools can incorporate. Here they are described in more detail and their relevance made clear. Dynamic features of any generating technology can be categorized as follows (Table 5.4)

In alignment with the "central plant" mindset, many utility portfolios have relied on large coal, nuclear, and CCGT facilities for bulk power delivery. The owner of such a plant would prefer to let the units run as many hours as possible and minimize the number of starts and stops. In traditional power systems, prior to the late 1990s, this was not an issue as the load patterns were stable year to year and plants were built accordingly without serious strain related to the dynamic features discussed here.

In the early 2000s renewables such as wind and solar began to gather momentum in the market, gaining regional adoption where incentivized by legislated mandates and/or government subsidies. In general, if a utility gets less than 10% of its annual MWh from wind and solar, the net load is scarcely different from load, and the balance of fleet does not really experience any difference in operational profiles. When utilities start to push 10%−30% of their annual MWh from variable renewables, the dynamic features can no longer be ignored. Practically every analytical study assessing expanding VRE penetration documented several factors common to

Table 5.4 Dynamic features.

Start cost	Certain technologies designed for baseload or intermediate use [boiler plants, some combined cycle combustion turbines (CCCTs)] are not designed for frequent starts (one or multiple times per day). If they are forced into a pattern of frequent starts they incur additional maintenance costs, which are often characterized as a "start cost," or a maintenance penalty associated with a start. These "start costs" are independent of other start costs such as start fuel, the fuel required to get the unit to full load. Certain peaking technologies (industrial CTs) also incur additional start costs if required to start multiple times per day.
Start time	Many plants, from coal or gas boilers to nuclear facilities to combined cycles, may require significant time to get to full load; in some cases, as long as 12−24 h. A gradual start sequence is required to avoid thermal and mechanical stresses incurred by faster loading.
Minimum run time (MRT)	Some facilities, typically larger in size, once started, must run for several hours to ensure thermo-mechanical equilibrium. If the plant is shut down before MRT is reached, damage, and maintenance penalties can occur.
Minimum down time (MDT)	Similar to MRT, once units come off-line, they must cool down to a specified state before the next start sequence is initiated or incur potential damage and increased maintenance costs.

non-VRE generation (almost all fossil-based thermal), all related to the fact that the dispatchable fleet had to attend to net loads which were more volatile than the basic load profile, including:

- decreased run hours;
- increased cycling (starts and stops); and
- increased volume of hours at part loads, to have capacity available for net load ramps.

The first factor, decreased run hours, occurs because renewables are providing more MWh, which tends to push the VRE part of the supply stack further to the right (as per Fig. 5.3), or, conversely, net loads are smaller than loads and so the amount of load to be met with thermal resources is reduced. Furthermore, the dispatch algorithms used for least-cost dispatch must account for real-life physical and financial issues related to dynamic features (Table 5.4). If net load is such that dispatchable resources must come on line, but are only needed for 1 hour (or less), baseload assets with low operational costs cannot start/stop or satisfy other constraints within that dispatch and must be passed over for assets that can start/stop without start costs or run time limitations. These are typically fast-start Recips, combustion turbines, or energy storage. It may also be necessary to run large baseload plants at minimum load for hours at a time as it is less costly than starting and stopping them. If planning models do not account for dynamic features, utilities risk installing inflexible capacity that cannot meet the challenges of real-life dispatch.

Attempted fixes to the traditional approach

Dynamic features may have been ignored in the past with little consequence, but as systems adopt more VREs, dynamic features become more important and influential. Many utilities have invested in software for long-term capacity planning, with entire teams of staff trained and well versed in their use and hesitant to incur the cost of implementing new tools. But they are cognizant of the shortfalls of simplistic dispatch models and know they do not provide an accurate estimate of the Opex portion of NPV calculations. Some opt to update Opex using more advanced least-cost dispatch simulation tools (Fig. 5.10).

While the use of updated Opex estimates derived from more accurate production cost modeling can appear attractive, the drawback is that the capacity mix used to update production cost (Step A, Fig. 5.10) is based on the traditional model. This approach provides greater accuracy in Opex costs related to inflexible assets that were already chosen by the modeling process, as opposed to a true least-cost capacity expansion optimization.

An alternative approach is to perform the traditional analysis and then assess reliability of the resultant least-cost portfolio. If the portfolio is short on ramping capabilities, provision of operational reserves, or flexibility in general, then screening curves are used to add specific assets as needed throughout the planning horizon. Because these additional capacity choices occur outside of the optimization process, the outcome is by definition "suboptimal" and costs more than necessary. Fortunately, a new wave of planning tools is emerging, designed to account for volatility caused by renewables and the consequent flexibility needs. These are generally referred to as chronological capacity expansion models.

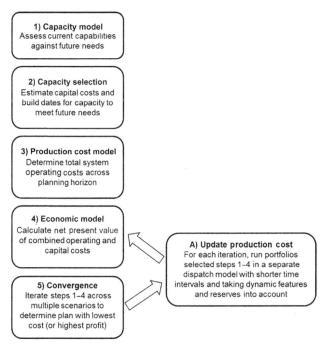

Figure 5.10 Basic five-step process of electric utility long-term capacity expansion planning, with additional step A to more accurately assess operational expenditures (Opex).

Advanced approaches—chronological long-term planning models

Traditional LDC approaches sort raw load or net load data, which can be quite erratic, from maximum to minimum, removing the time dimension from the problem. The LDC illustrates basic realities of the load, the area under the LDC curve represents the GWh, or energy requirements, the utility must satisfy. It also allows for intuitive understanding of concepts such as peaking and "baseload" and can be coupled quite neatly with screening curves. However, all-time information that would allow observance of rate and magnitude of change is lost during sorting. Chronological approaches skip the LDC decomposition and rely on the load or net load data directly, including their time dependence (hence the name "chronological," or Chrono for short). *LDC approaches are designed to assess capacity needs, while Chrono approaches are designed to assess capacity and capability needs simultaneously.*

The size and complexity of Chrono long-term capacity expansion problems is far greater than traditional LDC approaches, and large computational problems need significant computational resources. Hence the development and implementation of Chrono approaches was a function of the computational capabilities available to researchers and, later, to utility planners wishing to employ such approaches using commercially available simulation tools. In 2012, Nweke et al. [11] described how advances in the computational world allowed the use of Chrono long-term expansion planning in ways that would not have been possible only a few years prior outside of academia or institutions with affordable access to super-computing facilities.

The basic framework of a Chrono capacity expansion exercise is similar to the traditional approach (Fig. 5.9) with major differences occurring in steps 2 (capacity selection) and 3 (production cost model), as per Fig. 5.11.

Chronological long-term capacity expansion models are more difficult to grasp than basic LDC approaches because they attempt to solve multiple problems at different time scales simultaneously, a process only tractable in recent years with increases in computing power. Furthermore,

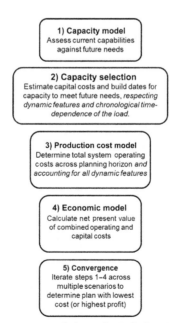

Figure 5.11 Basic five-step process of chronological electric utility long-term capacity expansion planning.

most of these models are proprietary and not open source. One of the earliest such simulation engines provided to the market was Energy Exemplar's PLEXOS software package. PLEXOS contains individual blocks or phases that can be run independently or together (Table 5.5).

Any one of the phases can be run independently. For example, a user may use only the ST functionality for detailed Opex simulations. A full "chronological" long-term capacity expansion plan using PLEXOS is enabled when the LT plan phase is fully integrated with the PASA, MT, and ST phases, such that the resultant capacity expansion plan takes account of the full temporal chronology across the entire planning horizon. This multistage functionality allows for accurate accounting of VREs, and the complete cost accounting for resources required to manage volatility, from flexible thermal to energy storage, as well as any other resources considered in the evaluation.

Other chronological capacity expansion models have come to the market with similar underlying optimization approaches, including Aurora [17] and PowerSimm [18]. Additional tools are constantly under development. Different tools include different features, including provision of

Table 5.5 Major elements of long-term capacity expansion planning using PLEXOS [16].

LT plan	Long-term plan least-cost expansion planning.
PASA	Projected assessment of system adequacy. Scheduled maintenance events to maintain optimality of available capacity and assesses risks related to random forced outage events. Information from this phase can be used to inform the LT plan.
MT schedule	Medium-term schedule. The MT phase is based on load duration curves at user-defined daily, weekly, or monthly resolutions. Assesses constraints that related to long- and medium-term energy storage and energy limits (e.g., reservoir hydro annual or monthly energy budgets), emissions limitations, and fuel contracts. Information from MT is bridged to ST to allow allocations from MT to be passed into detailed dispatch determinations in the ST simulations.
ST schedule	Short term schedule (chronological dispatch engine). The ST phase is the chronological dispatch simulator, estimating the supply stack and cost optimal dispatch or resources for each time interval (user-defined down to 1-minute granularity). Accounts for all dynamic features (start times, start costs, minimum up/down times) and any other energy or other constraints passed into ST from the MT phase.

regional databases that include basic network representations for transmission as well as libraries of all existing generators within the region. For example, a utility in a regional electricity market must constantly assess cost of self-generation versus market purchase of MWh, which is highly dependent on the asset mix and operations of every utility and IPP in the market. It is no longer sufficient for a utility in this context to model its own resources, it must model the entire regional market to understand how its own resources are impacted by the market as a whole, which influences new capacity decisions. For example, if the market is flooded with low price energy and a utility needs new capacity for capacity reserve margins, the capacity expansion calculations may choose the lowest cost capacity for reliability, knowing it will rarely need to run. A market database of assets is a convenient feature for utilities, consultants, regulatory commissions, or academics first delving into chronological long-term planning. The database alone can save users countless hours of research and manual data entry. However, databases included with commercial software are often compilations of publicly available data which may or may not be correct or complete. Wise users will review and vet data appropriately.

Some software packages include the basic elements of other chronological capacity expansion models but emphasize stochastic (hypothetical) simulations, exploring numerous "what if" scenarios. While a Chrono long-term plan is more properly able to minimize cost and CO_2 emissions with high VRE penetrations, they are often reliant on fixed annual wind and solar data sets, either some representation of average VRE performance, or a specific hourly profile for a year. Some consider the solutions of such models to be deterministic. They are deterministic because they use static profiles for VRE output. Static data sets do not account for dissimilar weather years which have nonzero probabilities of occurring. Stochastic modeling can perform the capacity expansion simulation using a typical weather year, then test the resultant portfolio(s) against any number of alternate data sets representing other weather years. The intent is to determine shortfalls in load-serving abilities or cost overruns utilities could expect due to fluctuations in VRE output relative to the static data set initially used.

A recent work [19] evaluated the power systems of Turkey and Guinea-Bissau in West Africa, applying a capacity expansion model to each using a typical meteorological year for hourly wind and solar data. They then ran the resultant portfolios against two dozen alternate data years for each. ACs and emissions for the West African system exceeded that suggested by the planning model for all 24 years. For the Turkish system, the annual expenses exceeded that expected for half of the 24 years and led to time periods of unmet demand. In both cases, cost and emissions overruns and unserved loads were related to VRE generation different across a variety of weather years than the static data set used to design the portfolios. In a broader context, if a utility in a northern clime used representative solar data, and that data only showed one 3-day period of low solar activity, how would that utility fare if a severe blizzard covered solar panels with snow for a 10-day period? That severe blizzard may not be typical, but utilities need to account for atypical weather conditions influencing wind and solar output. One way to do so is to perform stochastic analyses on resultant portfolios. Note that the need for stochastic evaluations is driven primarily by the growing reliance on energy from VREs. In the Guinea-Bissau example solar contributed 28% of the annual MWh and in the Turkish system VREs contributed 21%. As systems move toward 100% renewables the impact of atypical years or events will only become more pronounced.

The chronological capacity expansion modeling tools mentioned above are representative and do not include a full listing of all available options available to utility planners. As demand for Chrono tools increases additional products are expected to come to market. One of these is the open-source SWITCH 2.0 platform [20]. In addition, the makers of traditional planning tools may update their capabilities to incorporate additional features. The major takeaway is that Chrono long-term planning tools are a recent addition to the resource planning toolbox and are necessary for least-cost planning in high VRE environments.

Capacity expansion models for regional and policy initiatives

Long-term capacity expansion models are an integral part of the resource planning process, not just for electric utilities, but also for policymakers. Various tools and models are used to address different questions at different geographic and temporal scales. Table 5.6 provides a sampling of models used to assess long-term policy questions related to increased renewable penetration, the role of battery and other forms of storage, and the impact of hydrogen and other renewable fuels. These analyses are not intended to dive deep into operational details but instead seek to find

Table 5.6 Sampling of regional capacity expansion planning tools and their use of representative time periods for Opex calculations during the optimization.

Model	Representative times used for dispatch simulations/OPEX
European Long-Term Investment Model for the Electricity System (LIMES-EU)	6 representative days [21]
National Energy Modeling System (NEMS)	LDC used directly, no chronological dispatch [22]
Regional Energy Deployment System (ReEDS)	17 days (4 days from each of 4 seasons, plus a peak time slice) [23]
Resource Planning Model (RPM)	17 days (4 days from each of 4 seasons, plus a peak time slice) [24]

equilibrium long-term outcomes. Due to the sheer size of the systems, operational details may not be practical to include in their entirety. This sampling of broad-scale expansion models shows that most use a handful of representative days or rely on LDCs directly.

The above characterization of model types for regional/policy assessments is not meant to be exhaustive. Rinkjob et al. [25] provided a listing and comparison of 75 capacity expansion models, including the regional models listed. Selected comparisons of models in [25] show that LDC-based and models using small samples of data instead of full chronology have a high risk of overestimating contribution from VREs and underestimating the need for balancing resources to attend to net load ramps and operational reserves. Differences are most pronounced for systems with higher VRE penetration. While large regional analyses may address policy questions, if they rely on simplifying assumptions and legacy approaches there is a risk that the end-states they envision based on model output may be out of phase with the investment drivers for the utilities responsible for complying with policy.

Final considerations for resource planners and analysts

There is a growing consensus that LDC-based approaches, use of representative days with coarse time resolution and omission of dynamic features in Opex valuations yield the following:

- an exaggerated view of the contribution of VREs;
- underestimation of flexible capacity needs to balance VREs;

- emphasis on binary choices for thermal assets—choosing either the most efficient for energy production or the lowest capital cost for peaking resources; and
- underestimation of total system cost.

Nonetheless, LDC-based capacity expansion tools have enjoyed widespread use in evaluation of energy policy, particularly regarding the impact of expanding penetrations of wind and solar. Typically, a myriad of simplifying assumptions are made, including:

- lumping all generators (existing and proposed) into broad classes each with similar operational and capital cost attributes;
- use of linear-relaxation, which means the model does not select from discrete unit sizes that are commercially available, but rather solves for the optimal number of MW of each technology type; and
- ignoring the detailed operational and dynamic features of various technology types such as start times, start costs, MRT, MDT.

These simplifying assumptions allow for greater computational speed and review of numerous scenarios, allowing policymakers to explore questions at the scale of an entire state or country, multistate electricity markets, or at the continental scale related to market design changes, the broad cost impacts of varying renewable portfolio standards (RPS) standards, and the like. These models and applications, however, are not strictly concerned with the least-cost investment decisions that must be made at the electric utility level, nor do they respect real-life constraints. For example, the wind integration study for New England (United States) from 2011 [26] was a regional study assessing the feasibility of higher wind penetrations. The conclusion was that yes, operationally the electric power system across the states within New England could support higher wind penetrations, but it was unclear if market revenues would be enough to maintain the thermal generation needed to support wind. The report answered the question being asked, can we add wind so that it produces so much energy per year relative to load, without serious reliability problems? Resource planners are often given a constraint, for example that by a certain year 50% of energy must be served by VREs (via an RPS). The question they must answer is as follows—what is the best resource capacity mix, both VREs and otherwise, that minimizes cost or meets certain revenue targets, complies with all constraints and maintains reliability? The utility is answering a different question with capacity expansion analyses than the policy analyst.

Utility long-range plans (LRPs) or integrated resource plans (IRPs) must consider a greater level of detail in serving loads and maintaining reliability and must demonstrate that investment decisions yield the lowest cost for consumers. Therefore, utility planners cannot lump technologies together and must instead account for the contributions and capabilities of each existing or potentially new resource. They must account for dynamic details of all technologies at the unit level and they must assess their plans with as much detail to the chronology of intermittent VRE resources as possible. Some of the legacy approaches and tools are unable to support the granularity required. Newer Chrono capacity expansion planning approaches are available to bridge these gaps.

Utilities may appear slow to make the transition to newer modeling paradigms, even in the face of mounting evidence that newer approaches are necessary. However, the transition from legacy approaches to state-of-the-art is a complicated and lengthy process. Utility staff needs funding for new software and computational resources, training, and time to become proficient and confident in the use of new approaches. Regulatory staff tasked with reviewing and approving IRPs must also become proficient in the concerns associated with increasing VRE penetration and the newer capacity expansion planning paradigms. Not just to ensure higher levels of decarbonization directly with VREs, but to ensure policies and incentives are in place to support the energy storage, renewable fuels, and flexible capacity needed to achieve success.

References

[1] Energy Exemplar, Risk constrained integrated resource planning with LT plan. <https://energyexemplar.com/wp-content/uploads/Risk-Constraited-IRP-with-LT-Plan.pdf>, 2020.
[2] Electric Power Research Institute. <https://www.epri.com/#/?lang = en-US>, (accessed 22.02.20).
[3] P. Sullivan, K. Eurek, R. Margolis, Advanced methods for incorporating solar energy technologies into electric sector capacity-expansion models: literature review and analysis. NREL/TP-6A20-61185. <https://www.nrel.gov/docs/fy14osti/61185.pdf>, 2014.
[4] F.J. De Sisternes, M.D. Webster, Optimal selection of sample weeks for approximating the net load in generation planning problems. <https://dspace.mit.edu/handle/1721.1/102959>, 2013.
[5] K. Poncelet, H. Hoschle, E. Delarue, A. Virag, W.D. D'haeseleer, Selecting representative days for capturing the implications of integrating intermittent renewables in generation expansion planning problems, IEEE Trans. Power Syst. 32 (2016) 1936–1948.
[6] N. Helisto, H. Kiviluoma, H. Holttinen, L.D. Lara, B. Hodge, Including operational aspects in the planning of power systems with large amounts of variable generation: a review of modeling approaches, WIREs Energy Environ. 8 (2019) e341.

[7] B. Palmintier, M. Webster, Impact of unit commitment constraints on generation expansion planning with renewables, in: 2011 IEEE Power and Energy Society General Meeting, IEEE, Detroit, MI, 2011.

[8] M. Welsch, P. Deane, M. Howells, B. O'Gallachoir, F. Rogan, M. Bazilian, et al., Incorporating flexibility requirements into long-term energy system models − a case study on high levels of renewable electricity penetration in Ireland, Appl. Energy. 135 (2014) 600−615.

[9] J. Ferrari, Incorporating flexibility in utility resource planning. <https://cdn.wartsila.com/docs/default-source/power-plants-documents/downloads/white-papers/americas/wartsila-bwp---incorporating-flexibility-in-utility-resource-planning.pdf?sfvrsn = 63b6f145_8>, 2014.

[10] M. Villavicencio, A capacity expansion model dealing with balancing requirements, short-term operations and long-run dynamics. CEER Working Paper #25. <http://www.ceem-dauphine.org/working/fr/A-CAPACITY-EXPANSION-MODEL-DEALING-WITH-BALANCING-REQUIREMENTS-SHORT-TERM-OPERATIONS-AND-LONG-RUN-DYNAMICS>, 2017.

[11] C. Nweke, F. Leanez, G. Drayton, M. Kolhe, Benefits of chronological optimization in capacity planning for electricity markets, in: 2012 IEEE International Conference on Power System Technology (POWERCON), Auckland, 2012, pp. 1−6.

[12] J. Ferrari, M. Backman, J. Leino, R. Paldanius, W. Huang, N. Zhang, et al., Power system optimization by increased flexibility. <https://cdn.wartsila.com/docs/default-source/power-plants-documents/downloads/white-papers/americas/wartsila-bwp---power-system-optimization-by-increased-flexibility.pdf?sfvrsn = 5eb6f145_8 >, 2014

[13] K. Poncelet, E. Delarue, D. Six, J.D. Duerinck, Impact of the level of temporal and operational detail in energy-system planning models, Appl. Energy. 162 (2016) 631−643.

[14] B. Mohandes, M.S. El Moursi, N. Hatziargyriou, S. El Khatib, A review of power system flexibility with high penetration of renewables, IEEE Trans. Power Syst. 34 (2019) 3140−3155.

[15] N. Ludig, S. Haller, M. Schmid, E. Bauer, Fluctuating renewables in a long-term climate change mitigation strategy, Energy 36 (2011) 6674−6685.

[16] PLEXOS Market Simulation Software. <https://energyexemplar.com/solutions/plexos/>, (accessed 14.11.19).

[17] AURORA electric modeling forecasting and analysis software. <https://energyexemplar.com/products/aurora-electric-modeling-forecasting-software/>, (accessed 01.03.20).

[18] PowerSIMM™ Planner. <https://www.ascendanalytics.com/products/planner>, (accessed 22.02.20).

[19] A.P. van Loon, D. Chattopadhyay, M. Bazilian, Atypical variability in TMY-based power systems, Energy Sustain. Dev. 54 (2020) 139−147.

[20] J. Johnston, R. Henriquez-Auba, B. Maluenda, M. Fripp, Switch 2.0: a modern platform for planning high-renewable power systems, SoftwareX 10 (2019) 100251.

[21] B. Knopf, P. Nahmmacher, E. Schmid, The European renewable energy target for 2030 − an impact assessment of the electricity sector, Energy Policy. 85 (2015) 50−69.

[22] The electricity market module of the national energy modeling system: model documentation 2018. <https://www.eia.gov/outlooks/aeo/nems/documentation/electricity/pdf/m068(2018).pdf>, 2018.

[23] W. Short, P. Sullivan, T. Mai, M. Mowers, C. Uriarte, N. Blair, et al. Regional energy deployment system (ReEDS). NREL/TP-6A20-46534. <https://www.nrel.gov/docs/fy12osti/46534.pdf>, 2011.

[24] T. Mai, E. Drury, K. Eurek, N. Bodington, A. Lopez, A. Perry, Resource planning model: an integrated resource planning and dispatch tool for regional electric systems. NREL/TP-6A20-56723. <https://www.nrel.gov/docs/fy13osti/56723.pdf>, 2013.

[25] H.-K. Rinkjob, P.M. Haugan, I.M. Solbrekke, A review of modelling tools for energy and electricity systems with large shares of variable renewables, Renew. Sustain. Energy Rev. 96 (2018) 440–459.

[26] New England Wind Integration Study. ISO-New England.<https://www.iso-ne.com/static-assets/documents/committees/comm_wkgrps/prtcpnts_comm/pac/reports/2010/newis_report.pdf>, 2011

CHAPTER 6

Illustrating concepts with examples

Resource planning is becoming more complicated, with a variety of renewable and other technology options available today that were not feasible in years past, the emergence of volatility driving electricity markets, distributed energy replacing the central-station mindset, and so on. It can be difficult to envision all of these aspects simultaneously to make sense of the whole. It may be worthwhile to explore individual factors in more detail, then take a closer look at what they all mean together. First an example is provided showing how and why flexibility is necessary for utilities to absorb variable renewable energy (VRE) generation efficiently, and how this can improve the business case and costs associated with high renewable penetrations. The impact of renewables on market pricing and volatility is then demonstrated using data from several regional markets in the United States, showing trends across time as VRE penetration is increasing. How utilities can make sense of this shifting market is described through several examples of methods utilities are using to recognize and quantify the value of flexible capacity. The sum of these factors is then presented in the context of a new resource planning approach that seeks to integrate capacity and transmission and distribution (T&D) planning simultaneously.

How flexibility reduces curtailment and maximizes the value of variable renewable energy sources

Many utilities looking to expand renewable penetration start from a position of thermal dominance in their portfolios and aim to replace with clean generation. The process is not instantaneous, it can take years, as older thermal units retire and are replaced with VREs, flexible thermal and energy storage. During this transition utilities often have inflexible capacity that can limit how much renewable energy they can absorb. It might be a must-run nuclear or geothermal facility that is unable to start, stop, or cycle effectively. Or it could be legacy thermal plants that cannot contribute to some aspects of grid reliability without also generating electricity [1], meaning

Electric Utility Resource Planning
DOI: https://doi.org/10.1016/B978-0-12-819873-5.00006-X

they must run at part load to be able to ramp when needed to support renewables This is especially true for inflexible capacity with long start, minimum run, and down times, making it impractical to shut them off completely if they are needed a few hours later. In some jurisdictions, legacy rules written around older inflexible technologies require units to be running to provide ramp support, but disallow newer, faster thermal generation to provide the same services from a nonspin state. Batteries or other forms of storage could step in to fill the void as their response rates are almost instantaneous;, however, their duration adds a new dimension. A 30-minute storage system may not be adequate for a 3-hour net load ramp. Regardless, any thermal units that must run at part load to support renewables force carbon-positive MWh into the system at the expense of clean VRE MWh. They effectively place a lower net load bound on the system. The following example illustrates this point.

Imagine a utility with a 100 MW peak load on a given day and hundreds of MWs of VRE capacity. VRE generation is nonzero throughout the 24-hour day, but peaks in mid-day due to the contribution from solar. If every MWh from VREs was used to serve load, 52% of the daily load would be met with carbon-free renewable energy. Now let us imagine that utility has 40 MW of "must run" thermal capacity. Net load for this day can then never be below 40 MW (Fig. 6.1A). Reducing the must

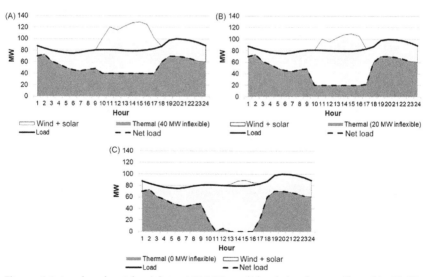

Figure 6.1 Load and net load for a 100 MW peak load day for a utility with 40 (A), 20 (B), and 0 (C) MW of inflexible must-run capacity.

run requirements to 20 MW (Fig. 6.1B) and to 0 MW (Fig. 6.1C) leaves more room for the utility to maximize VRE utilization.

In this example, the utility with zero MW of inflexible capacity could reach 51% of load served directly by VREs (Table 6.1) versus the maximum of 52%. In a broader context, this example shows how retention of baseload or other inflexible resources that cannot start/stop at least once daily compromises the utilities' ability to take full advantage of VRE output. Conversely, *systems with adequate flexible capacity maximize the utilization rate of VREs.*

In the early phase of transition, with still-modest VRE penetration, energy storage or renewable fuel production could absorb overgeneration, but the business case/economics are not ideal as the amount of overgeneration, which is in essence low-cost energy, may not be enough to support the investment. A better investment may be to lay the groundwork for future VRE expansion by replacing inflexible fossil assets, at least in part, with flexible thermal assets. Providing this flexibility also ensures the optimal economic case for VREs.

Many in the public, and in the industry as well, believe VREs have a fixed value or cost-independent of context, but is this true? At present, a common metric for showing the cost of VRE generation is the levelized cost of energy (LCOE). Overgeneration and curtailment of VREs causes the LCOE to increase, although this is rarely discussed or considered in planning or policy discussions. To demonstrate how curtailment changes the business case for VREs (based on LCOE), let us assume the utility in question had the same load and renewable profiles every day of the year. This is not realistic, but it simplifies the calculations and demonstrates the

Table 6.1 Energy balance for representative day assuming utility has 40, 20, and 0 MW of inflexible capacity.

Inflexible capacity (MW)	40	20	0
Reference figure	1A	1B	1C
Load (MWh)	2025	2025	2025
Full energy from VREs (MWh)	1052	1052	1052
VRE energy serving load (MWh)	753	912	1026
Curtailment (MWh)	299	140	26
Thermal energy serving load (MWh)	1272	1114	999
% Load served by VREs	37%	45%	51%
% of VRE MWh curtailed	28%	13%	2%

principle. Then let us assume that the VRE capacity is a blend of solar and wind with the following characteristics;

VRE capacity installed	120 MW
VRE installed cost	1200 $/kW
Weighted average cost of capital	7%
Interest rate	7%
VRE capacity factor	36.5%

The VRE capacity factor typically used by utilities and developers is based on the full potential annual MWh the resource could produce under ideal conditions and assuming no curtailment. In this case the unconstrained capacity factor is 36.5%. However, when solar and wind are forced to curtail, they are denied the ability to generate MWh. For LCOE the numerator is cost, in this example, United States dollars (USD), and the denominator is MWh. For the same cost, curtailment reduces the MWh and in effect increases the LCOE. In this example, the ideal case of full energy utilization yields an LCOE of 35.4 USD/MWh, while the presence of a 40 MW fixed, inflexible floor on net load (Table 6.1) reduces the capacity factor and increases the LCOE to 49.4 USD/MWh (Table 6.2). That is, a project valued at 35.4 USD/MWh for capital recovery assumes every MWh generated is used. Curtailment increases the USD/MWh the facility needs to get paid just to break even. Contractually, some independent power producers (IPPs)

Table 6.2 Levelized cost of energy for VRE capacity as a function of curtailment caused by inflexible capacity relative to the ideal of no curtailment.

Inflexible capacity (MW)	40	20	0	Ideal
Reference figure	1A	1B	1C	–
VRE energy serving load (daily MWh)	753	912	1026	1052
Annual VRE MWh	274,891	332,736	374,408	383,880
Annual capacity cost (MUSD for each of 20 years)	13.6	13.6	13.6	13.6
Present value capex (MUSD over 20 years)	154.1	154.1	154.1	154.1
Present value of MWh generated over 20 years	3,116,053	3,771,759	4,244,141	4,351,506
Levelized cost of energy ($/MWh)	49.4	40.9	36.3	35.4

Only capital costs are considered in this example as variable operations and maintenance is relatively small for VREs and other fixed costs are equivalent across scenarios.

who sell wind or solar energy to utilities are covered by various forms of make-whole payments. The intent is to make sure the IPP recovers its investment and returns and provides reliable clean energy to the utility. A utility that owns the asset is paying the same for capital and maintenance whether all or part of the energy is used. Ratepayers are paying, in the end, for the full cost either way, including the cost of more expensive thermal generation that is running, while VRE MWh are being curtailed.

The need for curtailment is utility- and system-dependent. Studies show the penetration levels at which curtailment occurs can be as low as 15% and as high as 75% [2]. Generally, the fewer baseload assets a utility has the more renewables they can install without running into curtailment issues. This is, of course, dependent on the inherent flexibility of other assets in the portfolio. The less flexible the balance of fleet, the greater the probability of overgeneration and curtailment.

Utility planners should strive to make sure the balance of fleet is flexible enough to minimize overgeneration. This can be accomplished using chronological capacity expansion models. These models inherently minimize curtailment as part of the cost optimization problem, doing so by leveraging the near-zero Opex cost of VREs. If utilities are required to meet renewable portfolio standard (RPS) targets, the targets and dates can be added to the simulation as constraints. A chronological model will then choose the appropriate blend of flexibility and efficiency to minimize costs.

The impact of increasing variable renewable energy penetration on day ahead and real-time pricing

Theoretically, as more VREs are added to the system, clearing prices should go down as well. But we also know that for any hour and within the hour VRE output is dependent on atmospheric conditions, which can be quite variable. So, while pricing is going down with higher VRE penetrations, we should also expect the pricing to become more volatile. Simulation exercises predicted falling prices with increasing VRE penetration years before systems began mass deployment of VREs. However, the variability issue had not been adequately addressed due to several factors: simulations only using static or fixed profiles for VREs, clearing prices calculated using crude approximations with fixed VRE behavior, and clearing prices calculated as monthly or annual averages assuming fixed conditions within each time period. As electric utility systems install greater amounts of VREs they are generally finding that the expectation of falling prices is well founded. However, they are also experiencing much greater volatility in pricing that was not predicted or expected, which adds a new dimension to the resource planning problem.

To demonstrate these principles, data are provided here for three large, independent markets in the United States (Table 6.1, Fig. 6.1). Each of these is referred to as an ISO, as they are managed by independent system operators (ISOs). Each of the ISOs is a nonprofit independent agency tasked with dispatch of all generators within their footprint, which may include the territory of any number of investor-owned utilities, government or municipal utilities, electric cooperatives, and/or IPPs. The three ISOs were chosen as they are experiencing rapid VRE deployment (Fig. 6.2; Table 6.3).

System operators manage two energy markets: day ahead (DA) and real time (RT). The 24-hour DA energy market solves for locational marginal prices (LMPs) at hundreds to thousands of pricing nodes across the ISO footprint. The location of the nodes is a function of transmission system topology and the location of substations, such that the calculation of LMPs also accounts for network complexities related to transmission. Dispatch is based on least-cost principles with constraints accounted for to maintain reliability. The supply stack for each hour of the following day is

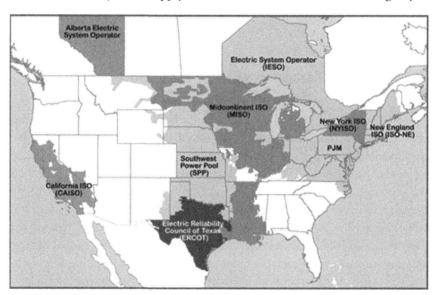

Figure 6.2 Geographic location of independent system operators in the United States and Canada [3].

Table 6.3 Characteristics of ERCOT, SPP, and CAISO markets, three (of seven) independent system operators operating in the United States.

	ERCOT	SPP	CAISO
Location in the United States	Southwest	Mid–west	West
Geographic area (km²)	522,449	1,414,140	339,808
VRE dominant type	Wind	Wind	Solar
Total capacity (GW)	78	90	73
Wind capacity (GW)	21	21	6
Solar capacity (GW)	1.5	0.2	9

informed by the pricing bids of every generator in the system as well as forecasts of load and VRE generation for the next day. Generator bids also include important constraints such as start time to full load, minimum run time, minimum down time, energy budgets for hydro that may restrict run hours, states of charge, and charge/discharge rates for energy storage systems, all of which must be respected in dispatch scheduling. The DA market is an hourly market.

The RT energy market is designed to make up for differences between DA expectations and what happens in RT. If load is different from expected, generators must alter output to accommodate. If the DA forecast predicted 10 GW of solar in hour 12 and only 8 GW was available, additional generation must be secured to fill the gap. Since fluctuations do not happen in hourly increments, this continuous re-dispatch of the system to correct for imbalances must happen in "real time." Instead of re-dispatching the entire system every second, ISO markets generally define RT in increments of 5−15 minutes.

In practice, this means that 24 hours ahead of time generators in the system are given schedules for the following day on an hourly basis. On the next day the generators dispatch to the schedule. However, when discrepancies occur between expectations and reality, generators scheduled for DA operations may, in RT, have their output ramped up or down relative to the scheduled output. Additional units may also be turned on or off (in 5- or 15-minute increments) to address imbalances in RT. These additional units are generally those that were not selected for dispatch in DA for the hour in which RT energy is needed. Of course, imbalances happen at even shorter timescales (millisecond to second) and these are attended to by ancillary services (AS) such as regulation.

Every utility outside of an ISO market operates assets to meet load using the DA and RT energy market constructs in one form or another, dispatching based on least-cost principles. The ISO market acts as the dispatch center for the numerous utilities within its footprint. One advantage of looking at the impact of renewable energy on pricing at the ISO scale is that it inherently accounts for geographic diversity of VRE resources given the broad areas that ISOs encompass. ISOs generally provide full transparency by maintaining publicly accessible information on historical DA and RT LMP pricing, load, and generation by fuel type (e.g., hydro, nuclear, coal, gas, geothermal, wind, solar, etc.). The same information for a stand-alone utility is generally not available to the public. The following figures for the Electric Reliability Council of Texas (ERCOT), Southwest Power Pool (SPP), and California Independent System Operator (CAISO) systems were constructed using data collected from refs. [4−6], respectively, with assistance from ref. [7]. The plots (Fig. 6.3) show monthly VRE penetration, the proportion of each month's load served by VREs.

As can be seen in Fig. 6.3, DA and RT pricing (monthly averages) converge as expected. Months with higher percentages of load met by VREs tend to have lower LMPs, and vice versa. These trends become clearer when we plot monthly average DA and RT prices as a function of VRE penetration (Fig. 6.4). In all three systems average pricing trends downwards as VRE penetration increases. Pricing still shows quite a bit of

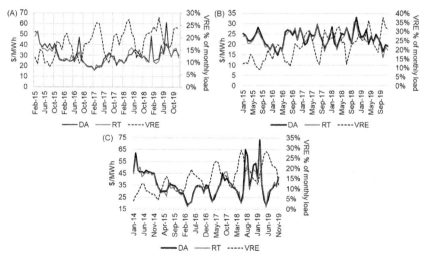

Figure 6.3 Day ahead (DA) and real-time (RT) system-wide average monthly locational marginal prices and VRE penetration across time for ERCOT (A), SPP (B), and CAISO (C) systems in the United States.

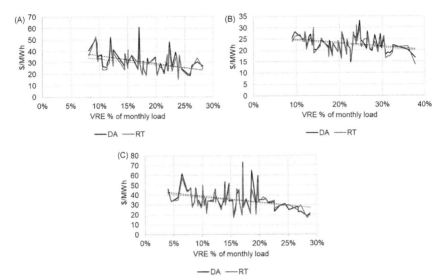

Figure 6.4 Day ahead (DA) and real-time (RT) pricing and linear trend lines (dashed) as a function of VRE penetration within ERCOT (A), SPP (B), and CAISO (C) systems in the United States.

variability for any VRE level as pricing is influenced by numerous additional factors such as load, weather, fuel pricing, maintenance outages, and transmission congestion. But in general, the trends show falling prices with higher VRE penetration.

Another way to look at the influence of VREs on pricing is to plot monthly DA and RT price volatility along with VRE penetration (Fig. 6.5). Here volatility is defined as the standard deviation in pricing for each month, divided by the average price for the month. Standard deviation is a statistical measure of how far the values within a month vary from the mean. If pricing is constant, standard deviation and hence volatility are zero.

In general volatility for both DA and RT LMPs increases with increasing VRE penetration, although the effect is far more pronounced for RT pricing (Fig. 6.5). This trend can be seen more clearly by plotting price volatility directly against VRE penetration, where the trend lines indicate that RT pricing is more sensitive to VRE penetration (Fig. 6.6). Again, for any level of VREs the volatility can vary quite a bit as fuel pricing, congestion, load, weather, and numerous other factors influence pricing as well. The main point is that increasing amounts of VREs tend to reduce average pricing and make pricing more volatile, a rule of thumb that is

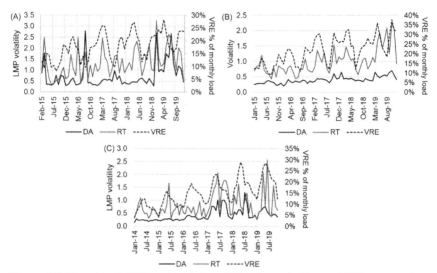

Figure 6.5 Day ahead (DA) and real-time (RT) price volatility and VRE penetration across time for ERCOT (A), SPP (B), and CAISO (C) systems in the United States.

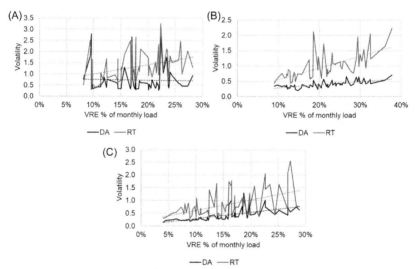

Figure 6.6 Day ahead (DA) and real-time (RT) price volatility as a function of VRE penetration within ERCOT (A), SPP (B), and CAISO (C) systems in the United States.

universal and here exemplified using data from three large system operators spanning wind and solar dominance. The rates of change for pricing and volatility are system- and market-dependent. For example, DA volatility in ERCOT and SPP appears to be relatively stable, while CAISO shows a greater increase, perhaps explained by CAISO being solar dominant, while the other two are more heavily dependent on wind. In all cases the RT volatility increases with greater renewable penetration, and at a much faster rate than DA.

Why would a utility planner or policy specialist care about increasing price volatility as more wind and solar are added to the system?

- Price volatility impacts which generators in the portfolio can serve load at any moment in time.
- Inflexible baseload or intermediate units may not be able to react fast enough in volatile hourly DA markets. While these inflexible units may be the most efficient, their lack of dynamic features requires them to miss profitable hours and to run during unprofitable hours, compromising their profitability.
- Low-cost inflexible units are incapable of starting or stopping to serve volatile RT net loads and pricing.
- Flexible units [energy storage, Recips, aero combustion turbines (CTs)] become more valuable in DA hourly markets as they have fast start times, minimal restrictions on operations, and are best able to thrive in a volatile price environment.
- Flexible units are the only resources capable of adequately serving the increasingly volatile RT market as VRE penetration expands.

Examples of variable renewable energy driving baseload and intermediate resources out of the market

While VRE penetrations (on an annual basis) have barely reached 30% in CAISO as of 2020, inflexible thermal plants are already facing pressure from falling prices and price volatility. For example, a large 750 MW state-of-the-art high-efficiency combined cycle combustion turbine (CCCT) that came on-line in 2009 was forced to retire in 2019, 20 years before the end of its economic life. Reasons cited include start times too long to capitalize on market pricing [8], because the profitable pricing periods were too short for the plant to complete its start sequence and then run profitably across established minimum run-times for the plant. Another state-of-the-art 1400 MW CCCT, this one in Germany, was forced to idle and seek retirement in 2015, less than 10 years after it was commissioned. Heralded as one of the most efficient CCCTs on the market, its closure was due to increasing VRE penetration, falling energy prices, and a dwindling number of profitable run hours [9]. Regulatory bodies are beginning to question the installation of large new CCCTs, instead urging utilities to seek a broader diversity of smaller, more flexible resources [10,11]. Inflexible baseload coal units, with even longer start, minimum run, and minimum down times will lose economy in systems with increasing VRE penetration [12], leading to accelerated retirements.

Resource planning considerations

Electric utility resource planners must leverage capacity expansion and dispatch simulation tools that can account for the complexities that VREs bring to the planning process. Levelized cost, screening curve, or load duration curve (LDC)-based tools are no longer adequate. Indeed, when the large CCCTs in California and Germany mentioned above were initially planned for, prior to the broad-scale emergence of chronological dispatch and capacity expansion tools, the legacy methods outlined a business case that spurred investment. If those same projects were evaluated using more advanced chronological assessments available to planners today, and knowing the volatility that accompanies VREs, different and more flexible technologies would have been considered more appropriate.

The expansion of VREs to meet decarbonization goals, and their ever-improving economics, will drive average energy pricing downward and "steepen" the supply stack. The low-cost end of the supply stack will consist of very low variable cost VREs. The middle of the supply stack, which used to consist of relatively low-cost thermal baseload or intermediate units, will disappear because of their inflexibility. And the right of the supply stack will consist of higher variable cost, but flexible, system balancers and peaking units, from energy storage to flexible thermal. In order for electric utilities to plan for portfolios that can support increasing VRE penetration 5, 10, or 20 years into the future, they need to use analytical approaches today that capture the complexities of this rapidly changing and increasingly volatile energy landscape.

1. Chronological expansion analyses inherently account for volatility in the supply stack and select optimal capacity mixes that include non-VRE flexible choices best able to support renewables while minimizing CO_2 emissions and ratepayer costs.

2. If portfolios are selected using LDC-based capacity expansion simulations, at a minimum the operating expenditures (Opex) from the simulations should be replaced with detailed chronological Opex estimates prior to final net present-value calculations.

3. If all-source approaches are used, where the utility identifies capacity shortfalls and then issues all-source requests for proposals, valuation of proposals should be performed using chronological dispatch models where selection is not made on optimal financials for the project, but on the optimal financials for the portfolio. Hourly time steps should be used at a minimum, subhourly is preferable.

Typically, RT costs and benefits are assessed together with AS only in the context of portfolio dispatch analyses, and not within the long-term capacity expansion phase. This is so because RT energy and AS in general are, at least at present, too computationally expensive to include in capacity expansion simulations except for small utilities with only a handful of generators.

Ancillary services

AS refer to functions utilities and grid operators use to maintain system reliability. AS are used to correct system imbalances, maintain grid voltage within certain bands, and allow for system recovery in the event a large perturbation occurs, from the largest plant in the system tripping off line to complete system blackout recovery. Power systems with increasing levels of VREs need expanded or additional AS to manage increased uncertainty and variability. Typical AS include the following;

- *Regulation/synchronized reserves*: Designed to preserve system frequency and voltage. Typically provided by on-line assets that can respond up or down within milliseconds.
- *Contingency reserves (spin)*: Designed for the largest contingency in the system, such as the largest generator. If that largest generator trips (worst-case scenario) enough reserve capacity must be available to quickly fill the gap and prevent system collapse. Typically provided by on-line connected assets that can ramp within seconds, of command.
- *Contingency reserves (nonspin)*: Backup reserve to support spin reserve. Served by nonspin assets that can provide MWh to the grid and ramp within a specified time frame, often 10 minutes.
- *Black-start reserves*: Black-start requirements that must be served by generators that meet certain criteria as specified by the grid operator. Typically served by nonspin assets that can provide MWh to the grid within a specified time frame of minutes to hours.
- *Load following reserves*: A reserve product designed to provide fast ramping to accommodate rapid swings in net load. Served by assets that can provide MWh to the grid within a specified time (market-dependent).

These definitions are often summarized internationally as primary, secondary, and tertiary reserves, with primary reserves allocated to frequency response, secondary reserves allocated to regulation (spin and nonspin contingency), and tertiary allocated to black-start and other supplemental reserves.

Typically, although not always, AS markets are cooptimized with energy markets. Cooptimization means the least-cost algorithm is searching for the lowest-cost way in each hour to provide both energy and AS. Power plants provide information to the grid operator regarding their complete operational costs and constraints. The solution algorithms then search for a specific combination of generators running at full load for energy and/or running at part load or in standby to serve AS needs. The DA hourly schedule then commits units to run for energy, AS, or some combination of the two. The entire process is repeated in RT to commit resources to supply least-cost cooptimized energy and AS as needed for discrepancies relative to the DA hourly schedule. Not all markets or utilities account for cooptimization in their planning or dispatch, but cooptimization does provide the true least cost approach and is preferred.

Flexible capacity in organized markets

The process outlined above for dispatching units to serve load and AS is simulated in chronological dispatch models. Resource planners supply all the relevant information to the software and the model chooses the optimal portfolio dispatch in the same way grid operators do so. Only in the planning process the goal is not operations, the goal is to determine least-cost operations moving forward in time. Typically, resource planners or developers use traditional valuation approaches or hourly simulations for energy only for capacity choices. This approach stands the risk of overvaluing inflexible assets and denying flexible capacity benefits that can only be visualized and quantified outside of the hourly energy paradigm. Finding valuation examples from the literature encompassing RT and AS was, until recently, a laborious process with little fruit. Today the references are growing. Examples are provided below across the New York Independent System Operator (NYISO), SPP, CAISO, and ERCOT markets in the United States. The following examples compare specific technologies; however, the reader is encouraged to understand references to recips as a proxy for flexibility. Energy storage or other flexible choices could provide similar advantages. Similarly, the drawbacks of frame CTs would apply to other inflexible technologies.

Example from SPP (2014)

Northwestern Energy is a utility that serves more than 700,000 customers across South Dakota, Nebraska and Montana in the United States. Their 2014 integrated resource plan (IRP) for South Dakota included an evaluation of potential thermal resources in the SPP market, specifically a recip facility and a frame CT [13]. The comparison showed that the more flexible recip solution was able to capitalize on RT and AS revenues in ways less flexible units could not (Fig. 6.7). This same sentiment is conveyed in the Northwestern IRP where it is stated [13]:

> *The SPP market places a substantial economic premium on flexibility to react to the 5-minute real-time market. In addition, flexible resources that can economically deliver regulation energy and 10-minute spinning reserves carry additional value... Peaking generation that can rapidly and efficiently respond to the SPP market price signals has substantial value over less flexible generation.*

This example from 2014 is an early demonstration of a utility IRP considering, through simulations, RT and AS revenue contributions to project economics.

Example from NYISO (2016)

In an early demonstration of AS and RT contributions to project economics for NYISO, in the eastern United States [14], market data including DA and RT energy and AS pricing were collected across the years 2011−14 for the New York City pricing zone in NYISO. A

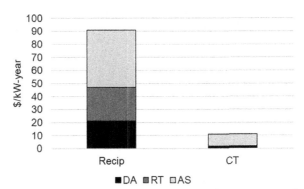

Figure 6.7 Estimate of revenue potential from DA and RT energy and ancillary services for two types of generators in the SPP market. *Data from 2014 South Dakota Electric Integrated Resource Plan, Chapter 4: Portfolio Modeling and Analysis.* < http://northwesternenergy.com/docs/default-source/documents/2014-south-dakota-electric-integrated-resource-plan/Chapter4 > , 2014.

chronological dispatch model was used to estimate the potential revenues from a hypothetical 200 MW recip plant and a 300 MW CCCT. Revenues were projected as being representative across the commercial lifetime of the facilities and weighed against investment costs and Opex to calculate leveraged internal rate of return (IRR). IRR is a metric used to estimate the profitability of investments; the higher the IRR, the more profitable the project. Assuming DA energy only, the two options were about equal. The CCCT had almost twice the run hours but also started close to 300 times per year, approximately once per day. When RT operations were added, the flexible units were able to increase IRR, while the CCCT IRR barely increased at all. AS provided a revenue boon to the recip option that was not available to the CCCT (Fig. 6.8). Regulatory agencies in the United States are increasingly calling for adding RT revenue streams to utility analyses [15].

Example from ERCOT (2016)

The city of Denton, Texas, has ambitious renewable energy targets. Energy in Denton is provided by the local utility Denton Municipal Electric (DME). With anticipated peak loads of approximately 200 MW, the city's 2015 "Renewable Denton Plan," pledged to move from roughly 40% renewable energy to 70% by 2019 [16]. The Brattle Group, a large international consulting firm, was engaged to evaluate technology choices and confirm the optimal pathway for DME to achieve its goals.

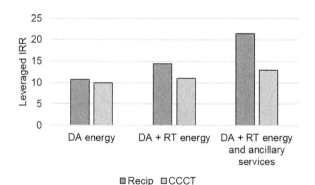

Figure 6.8 Potential IRRs for two types of capacity in NYISO. *Data from J. Ferrari, Get a higher return on investment with Wartsila. < https://www.wartsila.com/docs/default-source/smartpowergeneration/content-center/presentations/wärtsilä-ice-technology-out-performs-gas-turbines-in-the-nyiso-market.pdf >, 2016.*

Renewable energy was to be provided by wind and solar via power purchase agreements (PPAs) with IPPs. While the PPAs could secure the correct amounts of energy, 70%, on an annual basis, VREs generally produce when they can and are not strictly dispatchable. This means the remaining 30% of annual MWh would have to be purchased from the ERCOT DA and RT markets to meet load when VRE generation was insufficient. This exposure to market pricing can be considered a risk, as market pricing in ERCOT can be low on average, but experience periods of volatility (Figs. 6.5 and 6.6) where energy prices exceed thousands of dollars per MWh.

To counter market exposure risk, DME considered a 225 MW recip plant due to its attractive heat rate and excellent flexibility characteristics. The plant would be used as a hedge. Basically, when dispatchable MWh were needed and market pricing was low, DME would purchase MWh from ERCOT. When market pricing was higher than self-generation, DME would self-generate with the recip plant.

To evaluate options the Brattle Group did not rely on the traditional hourly energy approach. Instead they used a state-of-the-art dispatch optimization tool to model ERCOT pricing, the cost of MWh purchases, and revenue from sales to the ERCOT market [17]:

- Over the 20-year planning horizon
- Accounting for both DA hourly and RT 5-minute energy purchase and sales
- Accounting for AS sales

The Renewable Denton Plan evaluation is an early example of a utility considering RT and AS operations for investment decisions. The reason it was necessary to model to this level of detail was the variability and volatility of supply, in RT, from wind and solar assets. The analysis was made possible through use of dispatch simulation tools that account for full chronology in both DA and RT markets.

The final report from the Brattle Group indicated the self-generation hedge (225 MW recip plant, referred to as the Denton Energy Center, or DEC) would save the municipal utility of 975 million USD over the 20-year planning period relative to complete reliance on market purchase [17] and had this to say:

Both the renewable PPAs and the DEC are integral parts of the RDP. The DEC physically hedges the net load variability caused by the increased renewable resources that bring about the cost savings shown in the RDP-DEC Strategy. Without the DEC, or comparable flexible capacity, incorporating large amounts of intermittent resources would expose rate payers to the price volatility of the ERCOT wholesale energy market ... the DEC is the lowest cost option for "firming" the renewable energy.

Example from SPP (2018)

Public Service of Oklahoma (PSO) is an operating company of American Electric Power, one of the largest utilities in the United States. PSO's 2018 IRP [18] identified a need for peaking resources within a specific geographic region in the state of Oklahoma. The need (MW) was fixed and the goal was to find the optimal technology for the site based on largest net revenue, market revenue minus fixed and operating costs. The approach in the IRP was to first generate 20 + -year forward price streams for DA (hourly) and RT (5-minute) energy and AS (regulation up, regulation down, spin, and nonspin reserves) for three scenarios. The scenarios were high volatility, stable volatility, and high-low volatility. All three assumed pricing volatility at the start of the modeling horizon would be the historical average. Stable volatility assumed pricing would stay at 2018 volatility levels through the analysis horizon. High volatility scenario assumed that increasing wind and solar penetration would increase pricing volatility (e.g., Fig. 6.6 for SPP above). High-low volatility assumed volatility would initially increase, then decrease back to historical averages at the end of the horizon. This last scenario was done to represent the possibility that new technologies or transmission capabilities may emerge that could reduce volatility associated with increasing wind and solar penetration. All price stream scenarios were developed for a specific pricing node in Oklahoma near the site of the potential capacity addition.

Three peaking options were evaluated: industrial or frame type CTs, with 30%−35% efficiency, low capital cost, and start times of 10−30 minutes; aeroderivative CTs with 35%−40% efficiency, higher capital cost, and start times of 10−15 minutes; and recips with 40%−45% efficiency, start time of 5−10 minutes and capital costs similar to aero CTs. Recips also have lower minimum loads (10%−20%) allowing them to sell more capacity into the regulation and spin reserve markets. These resources were then simulated running against the price scenarios across the modeling horizon to determine the total revenues across DA and RT energy and AS markets. According to the IRP [18]:

With the development of Regional Transmission Organizations (RTOs) and actual pricing values for energy and ancillary services at both the Day-Ahead

Hourly level and Real-Time 5-minute level; as well as the development of modeling software and affordable computing power, the Company now has the ability to analyze generating resources with the consideration of additional revenue sources than energy with a combined Day-Ahead and Real-Time margin perspective... compared to the 'more traditional' IRP analyses that rely on hourly energy revenues to evaluate the cost effectiveness of the various resources considered in an IRP, this more granular analysis from both a time perspective and energy products perspective provides the Company and its stakeholders with additional information to assist in selecting new generating resources. The Company's approach was to consider this new modeling capability with respect to "peaking" resources that the Company considers in its IRP process.

The analyses showed recips to be the least costly option, continuing with [18]:

The results of the model showed the reciprocating engine was the least costly generating technology on a per kW basis across all three volatility scenarios... As mentioned earlier these results are based on a model of volatility of prices specific to the Comanche node in SPP. Based on the analysis it provides support for PSO's decision to add reciprocating engine generation.

The PSO IRP includes a rare explanation of their forward pricing methodology accounting for enhanced volatility due to increasing renewable penetration, and subsequent use of chronological dispatch models to evaluate assets against the full suite of revenue streams, including RT and AS.

Example from CAISO (2019)

Glendale Water and Power (GWP) is a municipal utility in California serving close to 90,000 customers [19]. In 2019 GWP completed an IRP [20] that covered a host of capacity and reliability concerns, ultimately recommending a portfolio that included a mix of VREs, battery storage, and recip engines for backup and flexible operation. The GWP IRP is among a growing number of IRPs quantifying RT energy revenues in addition to the traditional hourly energy-only paradigm. They evaluated four technologies against RT market pricing: batteries (Li-ion), recips, CTs, and CCCTs. Battery assets are referred to as battery energy storage system (BESS). The energy imbalance market (EIM) is the regional western RT balancing market (of which various utilities within and outside of California are a part). From the IRP [20]:

... Fast-ramping resources such as BESS and ICEs are able to respond to short-duration price spikes (prices between $100 and $1000 plus in 5 and 15 minute markets) and therefore have additional value in the real time market. To

capture this value, these fast ramping assets were modeled against the EIM market time scale to determine their average ancillary and energy value...

The reported RT energy and ancillary values (Fig. 6.9) show BESS providing the most value in this instance. The relative flexibility rank can be understood relative to the characteristics of the technologies considered (Table 6.4).

The 2019 Glendale IRP [20] is one of a small but growing number of resource plans including detailed RT comparative analyses across both thermal and energy storage technologies.

Resource planning considerations

The examples above demonstrate a growing trend for project valuation that considers AS and RT revenues within a centralized electricity

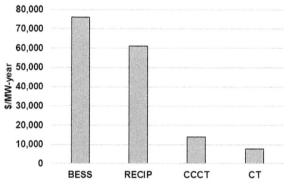

Figure 6.9 Annual real-time and ancillary benefits for four capacity choices in the CAISO/EIM market for a municipal utility in California. *Data from 2019 Integrated Resource Plan, City of Glendale Water & Power, Glendale, CA. < https://www.glendale-ca.gov/home/showdocument?id = 51814 >, 2019.*

Table 6.4 General characteristics of technologies, where flexibility rank is the $/MW-year benefit of each relative to that of battery energy storage system (BESS) as reported in [20].

Technology	Net efficiency	Full output to grid	Min run time	Min down time	Flexibility rank relative to BESS (%)
BESS	85%−90% (round trip)	Millisecond	0	0	100
RECIP	40%−45%	1−5 min	0	5 min	80
CCCT	50%−55%	30−90 min	2−4 + h	2−4 + h	18
CT	35%−40%	10−30 min	1 h	1 h	10

market. Utilities operating in such markets are increasingly aware that expanding VRE penetrations are driving up pricing volatility, placing greater emphasis on RT operations and AS. Capacity choices made on simplified levelized cost or revenues from DA hourly markets only are not the optimal capacity types for day-to-day operations; hence, resource planning must continue to include finer timescales in evaluation of individual projects.

What do these examples indicate for utilities that are not part of a centralized market, which must serve their own loads based on cost versus marginal price? These utilities will find that increasing VRE penetration increases volatility within the supply stack and has the same impact on dispatch and portfolio operations as VREs have on price signals in organized markets. Legacy baseload assets will become uneconomic. Flexible capacity, including energy storage, will be required to maintain voltage/frequency and attend to RT fluctuations in energy supply from VREs. Flexible capacity securing the largest revenues from organized markets will essentially be dispatched for islanded utilities in the same way, only instead of maximizing revenue, they will minimize cost at the portfolio level. This is why long-term capacity expansion planning tools with chronological capabilities tend to choose flexible capacity over baseload or intermediate assets for portfolios with any greater than 15%–20% annual VRE penetration. This is also why the World Economic Forum suggests flexible capacity as one of the major asset types a utility needs to future-proof against the growth of wind and solar, where they say [21]:

> With the expected growth of renewables, the grid of the future will experience higher levels of variability driven by the intermittent dispatch of renewable sources. Utilities will need to devise a strategy to offset the impact of variable generation from renewables in their business. Depending on the level of vertical integration of each utility, strategies range from incorporating flexible generation assets to partnering with other utilities or service providers that can offer this as ancillary services.

Note that none of the above examples show capacity selections based on a chronological long-term capacity expansion model. They all focus on evaluation of technologies using advanced chronological dispatch models. At present use of chronological expansion analyses has been restricted to third-party analyses showing the difference in outcomes legacy versus state-of-the-art (e.g., ref. [22,23]). The industry is gaining experience with advanced dispatch models, paving the way toward incorporation within capacity expansion modeling. At present there are a number of utilities with licenses to advanced planning software that are slowly but systematically moving toward full adoption in the IRP process.

Energy storage (and flexible capacity in general) in integrated resource plans

Energy storage is emerging quickly as a viable capacity choice, yet IRPs are, in general, ill-equipped to capture the full value of storage. On the one hand traditional LDC-based approaches simply cannot track the time-shifting aspect inherent in storage valuation. On the other hand, initial storage investments are typically made by utility systems with low (sub 30%) VRE penetration, in which their value is not in the hourly energy market. Experience is showing that storage investments at low VRE penetrations are acting as system balancers, providing AS and RT energy; two aspects of dispatch that fall completely outside of most capacity expansion simulations. So how can a utility value flexible capacity in general, and energy storage in particular, if their planning models cannot select them as part of a least cost plan?

One approach to flexible capacity valuation is to first calculate portfolio costs as-is, with no new capacity, for a given demonstrative year using a detailed chronological dispatch simulation, which may be subhourly. Then, the portfolio cost is recalculated with the addition of flexible capacity. In 2013 the National Renewable Energy Laboratory (NREL) in the United States performed such an analysis on a collection of balancing areas in the western United States encompassing the service territory of two utilities. The total combined generating capacity included approximately 6 GW of coal, 4 GW of CCCTs, 4 GW of CTs, 1 GW of hydro, 500 MW of pumped storage, and 4 GW of VREs (75% wind) [24]. They explored the annual production cost of providing hourly energy and AS for this base portfolio, then again adding 300 MW of Li-ion battery storage with 8-hour duration and compared production costs (Fig. 6.10).

As the NREL study [24] noted, at least half of the value of flexible capacity was in offsetting millions of dollars of start costs for thermal units. They also calculated the marginal price for each hour and the potential net revenue of the storage project, in essence simulating market revenues. Market revenues thus calculated were 5.2 MUSD. Thus if this storage project were evaluated on a project basis the revenues of 5.2 MUSD would need to exceed the costs for the project to see any profit. The portfolio analysis concerned with costs (and not revenues) shows the value being double that of the potential revenues. *This demonstrates that*

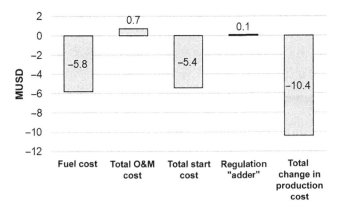

Figure 6.10 Production cost benefit (MUSD) reported by NREL [24] for a western utility system in the United States with addition of 300 MW of battery storage.

project-level revenue estimates alone do not capture the full benefit of flexible capacity within a portfolio.

Storage may not be the ideal solution for every need, hence the emergence of IRPs comparing, for example, battery storage against various thermal options. Direct comparison can be difficult given the wide disparity among thermal choices and the vagueness with which storage is often defined. For example, how to compare a battery storage system with a 200 MW CT? Does the storage project also have to be 200 MW? At what duration? One way to compare on an equal footing is to analyze on a "per kW" basis.

Puget Sound Energy (PSE) provided a demonstration of portfolio benefits in their 2017 IRP [25]. PSE is located in Washington State and serves approximately 1.1 million electric customers [26]. Like many utilities in the western United States, PSE anticipates rapid expansion of VREs and the consequent need for flexible capacity. Typical IRPs have new-resource tables illustrating several metrics, from engineering, procurement and construction (EPC) or installed cost to operations and maintenance (O&M) to efficiency. Thermal resources may include start time, min up/down time, etc. But there is little information available to planners to gage the flexibility benefits of any specific capacity type. To correct for this, PSE asked the following question in their 2017 IRP *"When new resources are added to the portfolio, what benefits do they have and do they help to reduce the operating cost of the portfolio?"* [25]. Similar to the NREL study [24], PSE performed a series of annual cost calculations using a comprehensive chronological dispatch model to calculate DA and RT Opex differences between the base portfolio and the same with additions of specific capacity types, ranging from CCCTs to flow batteries. Their results (Fig. 6.11) indicate that more flexible assets such as batteries provide greater Opex savings for the portfolio. PSE went one step further to calculate the additional savings when RT dispatch (5-minute) is accounted for.

The portfolio savings effect (Figs. 6.10 and 6.11) is an example of how resource planners can quantify and demonstrate the portfolio benefit of flexible capacity independent of an organized market. However, the total impact requires calculating the net cost of any capacity addition. This can be tricky when a utility is serving load directly and not receiving market revenues. For example, let us say a new capacity choice costs 100 $/kW-year. This is the annual fixed cost for capital recovery, fixed O&M, etc. Now let us say its addition to the base portfolio yields an annual reduction in portfolio operating costs of 60 $/kW-year. The portfolio Opex savings is the "operational benefit" of adding the new asset. The net cost is then the fixed cost minus the operational savings. If there are other assets the utility is considering, say a less flexible technology that is also lower fixed cost, comparative savings of one versus another, inclusive of all costs, can be determined as shown in Fig. 6.12. The capacity choice with the lowest net cost is the optimal choice. This comparative paradigm was first demonstrated in the 2016 Portland General Electric IRP [27] and is considered a "best practice" for assessing the benefits of storage in an IRP context [28,29].

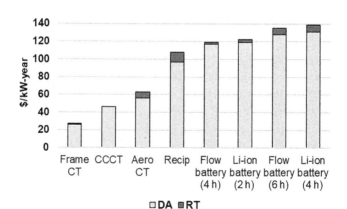

Figure 6.11 Portfolio savings effect per kW of capacity installed for several technology types as reported in an IRP in 2017 [25].

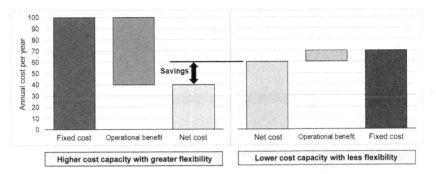

Figure 6.12 Flexible capacity may cost more to install but deliver superior operational benefits at the portfolio level, making it a better choice than less expensive and less flexible capacity, as quantified by comparison of net costs.

The future direction of integrated resource plans

Electric utility IRPs are the documents that identify bulk capacity decisions moving forward in time, often independent of the T&D planning process and without reference necessarily to the siting, permitting and development process. Once resource planning teams identify capacity needs in the IRP, those needs are communicated to a generation development (or similarly named) team in the utility who must go out, find sites, file interconnection documents to the appropriate authorities, secure environmental impact assessments, file for air permits and secure fuel agreements as necessary, issue RFPs, etc. The process can be time-consuming. In some instances, resource planners have information on a number of prescreened sites and interconnect costs as part of the IRP process, but this is typically limited to utilities with only a small number of projects to consider.

Some utilities, however, are moving toward consideration of a broader array of smaller projects, often referred to as distributed energy sources (DERs). The industry is moving away from GW scale central stations toward smaller sized projects located strategically. For highly developed areas, load growth can occur in pockets where upgrading or installing new transmission may be prohibitively expensive and difficult to site and permit. There might also be transmission bottlenecks that could leverage local flexible capacity for voltage and frequency support. Flexible thermal generation may be technically feasible but impractical due to emissions concerns near highly populated urban areas. Emissions-free energy storage can be sited in these instances, deferring costly T&D upgrades, providing grid support, and doing so in a way that minimizes local impact (and speeds up the permitting process). Understanding the locational impacts of resource additions, from thermal to renewable to storage, and the cost impacts or deferrals based on location requires planning to include T&D network topology.

This work has focused mainly on resource planning for generation capacity, independent of transmission. Upgrades to the transmission system can bring benefits as well, independent of capacity. These include new or increased access to other pools of generation and the potential for increased system flexibility and efficiency, reduced energy and AS costs, etc. In the United States at least, planning for capacity is often divorced from T&D planning. T&D systems are owned by different companies or by separate divisions within the same utility. Resource additions identified in an IRP are communicated to T&D planners, who then optimize T&D networks around known or expected resource additions.

Regardless of the reason, many utilities consider transmission topology to be fixed when trying to solve for new capacity additions. Within the United States there are a limited number that consider T&D upgrades simultaneous with capacity expansion, but the choices of T&D upgrades to be considered are often limited [30] and not necessarily representative of a true optimization of the entire T&D network and the capacity mix combined. The complexity of solving the capacity and T&D expansion problem simultaneously is one of the reasons utilities may avoid it, and to be fair, in the prior decades where the central-station large plant mindset was the rule, the T&D could at best have a limited number of options to be considered. But for future planning efforts considering a larger number of smaller distributed projects, the locational impact of capacity relative to T&D becomes extremely important.

In this context the IRP process will need to evolve to include elements of T&D planning. Two recent examples of utilities moving in this direction are Duke Energy and Hawaiian Electric Company. Duke Energy (Duke) is one of the largest electric utilities in the United States serving 7.7 million retail customers across six states, with approximately 51 GW of capacity [31]. In 2018 Duke outlined a new process, called the Integrated System & Operations Planning (ISOP) process, which blends traditional capacity planning with elements of T&D planning. The 2019 Duke IRP update for the Carolinas [32] explained the reason for this process as follows, in large part due to their anticipation of rapid expansion of VRE energy sources:

The anticipated growth of energy resources on (or closer to) the grid edge, particularly energy storage, will require utilities to move beyond the traditional utility distribution and transmission planning practice of analysis that considers only a few snapshots of system conditions at discrete points in time. Moving forward, analysis of the distribution and transmission systems will need to account for increasing volatility of net demand (load less variable distributed resources), which will require significant changes to modeling inputs and tools.

The ISOP process is, at the time of this publication, under active development, and includes projections of hourly load and potential DER contribution to the system at the distribution level. The purpose is to capture the benefits/tradeoffs of local DER generation versus T&D upgrades, ideally to solve for optimal cost minimization of electric generation capacity and T&D simultaneously. They note in the IRP that Duke is "...developing models to enable derivation of hourly forecasts for 4500 + distribution circuits in the Carolinas covering a ten-year horizon" [32].

Hawaiian Electric Company (HECO) provides electricity to the state of Hawaii. An island system traditionally reliant on imported fossil fuel, the state and its utilities are quickly moving toward a 100% RPS. With this change come new opportunities for everything from demand response to distributed energy resources. Recognizing the need for a more holistic approach, HECO released its Integrated Grid Planning (IGP) Report in March of 2018 [33]. The IGP intends to transform the traditional IRP process to produce an optimized portfolio that considers incremental generation and load, T&D resource additions simultaneously. Distributed generation is cited as a driving force [33]:

The growth of distributed generation in, for example, a location where a transmission or distribution upgrade is necessary to accommodate growing loads could both offset the need for large-scale generation and defer or eliminate the need for grid upgrades. In this case, one solution addresses two needs, thus directly benefiting customers. Similarly, customer adoption of solar-plus-storage systems may offset the need to increase hosting capacity through traditional distribution upgrades if these systems are operated to benefit the circuit.

Integrated grid planning in this context aims to replace the stacked overlay of capacity and T&D planning with a coordinated approach, as the two combined will yield optimal solutions that cannot be arrived at through consideration of one and not the other.

The two utilities mentioned above are not alone in striving toward more advanced integrated planning schemes; they were shown here as examples of a trend in the electric utility industry. Given practically all utilities are adding VREs to their portfolios and leaning toward distributed solutions, T&D cooptimization with capacity will benefit from capacity expansion approaches that recognize volatility and provide appropriate solutions, such as the newest class of chronological capacity expansion models. If the portfolio planning model cannot value flexible capacity, then by default it cannot appropriately value the interplay with T&D.

References

[1] J.H. Nelson, L.M. Wisland, Achieving 50 percent renewable electricity in California: the role of non-fossil flexibility in a cleaner electricity grid. <https://www.ucsusa. org/sites/default/files/attach/2015/08/Achieving-50-Percent-Renewable-Electricity-In-California.pdf>, 2015.

[2] P. Heptonstall, R. Gross, F. Steiner, The costs and impacts of intermittency − 2016 update. <http://www.ukerc.ac.uk/>, 2017.

[3] FERC. <https://www.ferc.gov/industries/electric/indus-act/rto.asp>, n.d. (accessed 16.02.20).

[4] ERCOT market data. <http://www.ercot.com/mktinfo/prices>, n.d. (accessed 07.01.19).

[5] SPP market data. <https://marketplace.spp.org/>, n.d. (accessed 07.01.19).

[6] CAISO market data. <http://oasis.caiso.com/mrioasis/logon.do>, n.d. (accessed 07.01.19).

[7] Personal communication with Gary Dorris, CEO, Ascend Analytics. <https://www. ascendanalytics.com/>, 2020.

[8] T. Hipple, K. Sanzillo, T. Buckley, New risk factors emerge as GE Shutters California Plant − 20 years early. <https://ieefa.org/wp-content/uploads/2019/07/New-Risk-Factors-Emerge-as-GE-Shutters-California-Power-Plant_July-2019.pdf>, 2019.

[9] C. Steitz, Update 2 − Germany's Irsching gas-fired power plant set to close, reuters. com. <https://www.reuters.com/article/e-on-irsching/update-2-germanys-irsching-gas-fired-power-plant-set-to-close-idUSL6N0WW1NB20150330>, 2015.

[10] J. Spector, Gas Plant Rejection Brings the Energy Transition Home to Indiana, GreenTechMedia, 2019. Available from: https://www.greentechmedia.com/articles/ read/the-energy-transition-comes-home-to-indiana.

[11] C. Morehouse, Minnesota Rejects Xcel's 720 MW Mankato Gas Plant Purchase Over Stranded Asset Concerns, Utility Dive, 2019. Available from: https://www. utilitydive.com/news/minnesota-rejects-xcels-720-mw-mankato-gas-plant-purchase-over-stranded-as/564029/.

[12] R. Smith, Analysis of hourly generation patterns at large coal-fired units and implications of transitioning from baseload to load-following electricity supplier, J. Mod. Power Syst. Clean Energy 7 (2019) 468−474. Available from: https://link.springer. com/article/10.1007/s40565-018-0470-9.

[13] 2014 South Dakota Electric Integrated Resource Plan, Chapter 4: portfolio modeling and analysis. <http://northwesternenergy.com/docs/default-source/documents/ 2014-south-dakota-electric-integrated-resource-plan/Chapter4>, 2014.

[14] J. Ferrari, Get a higher return on investment with Wärtsilä. <https://www.wartsila. com/docs/default-source/smartpowergeneration/content-center/presentations/wärtsilä-ice-technology-outperforms-gas-turbines-in-the-nyiso-market.pdf>, 2016.

[15] Resolution on modeling energy storage and other flexible resources, in: NARUC 2018 Annual Meeting Resolutions. <https://pubs.naruc.org/pub/2BC7B6ED-C11C-31C9-21FC-EAF8B38A6EBF>, 2018.

[16] E. Dearman, Denton announces renewable energy plan, The Texas Tribune. <https://www.texastribune.org/2015/10/06/denton-announces-renewable-energy-plan/>, 2015.

[17] I. Shavel, B.M.K. Tsuchida, Review of the Renewable Denton Plan, Final Report, The Brattle Group, 2016. Available from: http://files.brattle.com/files/5762_review_of_the_renewable_denton_plan_final_report.pdf.

[18] Integrated Resource Planning Report to the Oklahoma Corporation Commission. Public Service Company of Oklahoma, 2018.

[19] Glendale Water & Power. <https://www.glendaleca.gov/government/city-departments/glendale-water-and-power/about-us>, n.d. (accessed 22.01.20).

[20] 2019 Integrated Resource Plan, City of Glendale Water & Power, Glendale, CA. <https://www.glendaleca.gov/home/showdocument?id = 51814>, 2019.

[21] G. Nieponice, 5 Things Utilities Companies Must Do to Future-Proof Themselves, World Economic Forum. <https://www.weforum.org/agenda/2017/03/5-things-utilities-companies-must-do-to-future-proof-themselves/>, 2017.

[22] C. Nweke, F. Leanez, G. Drayton, M. Kolhe, Benefits of chronological optimization in capacity planning for electricity markets, in: 2012 IEEE International Conference on Power System Technology (POWERCON), Auckland, 2012, pp. 1−6.

[23] J. Ferrari, Incorporating Flexibility in Utility Resource Planning. <https://cdn.wartsila.com/docs/default-source/power-plants-documents/downloads/white-papers/americas/wartsila-bwp---incorporating-flexibility-in-utility-resource-planning.pdf?sfvrsn = 63b6f145_8>, 2014.

[24] P. Denholm, J. Jorgenson, M. Hummon, T. Jenkin, D. Palchak, B. Kirby, et al., The value of energy storage for grid applications. NREL/TP-6A20-58465. <https://www.nrel.gov/docs/fy13osti/58465.pdf>, 2013.

[25] 2017 Final Integrated Resource Plan, Puget Sound Energy (Chapter 6). <https://pse-irp.participate.online/>, 2017.

[26] Puget Sound Energy. <https://www.pse.com/about-us>, n.d. (accessed 07.02.20).

[27] Integrated Resource Plan, Portland General Electric. <https://www.portlandgeneral.com/our-company/energy-strategy/resource-planning/integrated-resource-planning/2016-irp>, 2016.

[28] Advanced Energy Storage in Integrated Resource Planning (IRP). 2018 Update. <https://energystorage.org/wp/wp-content/uploads/2019/09/esa_irp_primer_2018_final.pdf>, 2018.

[29] A.L. Cooke, J.B. Twitchell, R.S. O'Neill, Energy storage in integrated resource plans, Pacific Northwest National Laboratory PNNL-28627. <https://energystorage.pnnl.gov/pdf/PNNL-28627.pdf>, 2019.

[30] F. Kahrl, A. Mills, L. Lavin, N. Ryan, A. Olsen, The future of electricity resource planning, Lawrence Berkeley National Laboratory 1006269, Report No. 6. <https://emp.lbl.gov/sites/all/files/lbnl-1006269.pdf>, 2016.

[31] Duke Energy. <https://www.duke-energy.com/our-company/about-us>, n.d. (accessed 22.02.20).

[32] Duke Energy Progress, 2019 Integrated Resource Plan Update Report. <http://www.energy.sc.gov/files/2019DEPIRPDocument-PUBLIC2.pdf>, 2019.

[33] Planning Hawaii's Grid for Future Generations: Integrated Grid Planning Report. Hawaii Electric Company (HECO). <https://www.hawaiianelectric.com/documents/clean_energy_hawaii/integrated_grid_planning/20180301_IGP_final_report.pdf>, 2018.

CHAPTER 7

Pathways to 100% decarbonization

The ideal characteristics of the future power system can be defined in a number of ways. Here we will identify at least three criteria that must be considered: affordability, reliability, and sustainability. Affordability reflects the need to minimize ratepayer costs. Low energy prices are important for individual citizens and help local businesses and industries remain competitive. Reliability is just as important as power loss can negatively impact people and industry. Sustainability is a bit harder to define, but in today's climate it would be safe to say sustainability includes minimizing and eventually eliminating fossil-fuel use, minimizing carbon and other emissions, and minimizing land development. With the advance of 100% renewable portfolio standard (RPS) mandates electric utilities are being forced to focus on reducing fossil-fuel use often at the expense of affordability and the land use, or conservation part of sustainability. Here we look at some prior history of minimizing emissions and how this relates to decarbonization. The semantics of what "100%" means is explored to illustrate how definitions shape the trajectory and ultimately how a utility balances affordability, reliability, and sustainability.

Learning from the past

Decarbonization is an attempt to limit carbon emissions in much the same way societies have limited other emissions in the past. Some of the first emissions restrictions were put in place in the 1970s to limit nitrogen oxides (NO_x) and sulfur dioxide (SO_2), when coal and oil were primary fuels for power generation. Restrictions were put in place, at least in part, to limit or reverse the impacts of acid rain. Understanding why these limits were put in place, how the utility industry responded, and the outcome may provide some context for today's challenge related to decarbonization.

Combustion of fossil-fuels generates NO_x and, depending on the fuel, SO_2. Combustion requires air as a source of oxygen, and air is almost 80% nitrogen. Nitrogen in air combines with oxygen during combustion

Electric Utility Resource Planning
DOI: https://doi.org/10.1016/B978-0-12-819873-5.00007-1

to form NO_x, which means that any combustion, even of hydrogen, will generate NO_x. The amount of NO_x in an exhaust stream is dependent on many factors, including the amount of excess air needed for complete combustion, combustion temperature, and combustion efficiency. This allows for engineering/design changes to minimize NO_x such that emissions for modern recipes and combustion turbines (CTs) are far lower today than they were in the 1970s. On the other hand, the amount SO_2 found in exhaust is directly related to the sulfur content of the fuel.

Broad-scale historically uncontrolled coal and oil combustion led to increasing atmospheric NO_x and SO_2 concentrations, which in turn combined with water, oxygen, and other chemicals to form sulfuric and nitric acids, the source of acid rain. Over the course of decades, acid rain—reduced soil pH at global scales, leading to ripple effects in soil chemistry and nutrient and water uptake abilities for trees. This severely compromised forest health and caused deforestation. For example, the famous Black Forest in Germany is reliant on soils with a neutral pH. By the mid-1980s more than half of the trees in the forest were dead or dying due to the change in soil acidity caused by acid rain. Similar impacts were observed globally and went well beyond forest health. Acid rain changes the pH of lakes and streams, disturbing ecosystem equilibrium as many aquatic species are sensitive to pH. Over time, society placed greater restrictions on NO_x and SO_2 to prevent acid rain and reverse, or at least halt the damage.

Fuels are required to have a low or zero sulfur content, otherwise scrubbers are required to remove SO_2 from combustion exhaust. Means to reduce NO_x to acceptable levels in exhaust streams include various postproduction reactors. Today, even the most advanced natural gas—fired generators may require NO_x controls, but do not need SO_2 scrubbers because pipeline-quality natural gas is processed to remove sulfur. Permitting and regulatory agencies may also limit the run hours or starts per day of various generators to further limit emissions. As a result, in the United States SO_2 emissions have fallen 91% from 1980 to 2018 [1] and NO_x emissions fell 51% from 1990 to 2014 [2]. The positive benefit of limiting these pollutants is now measurable. Forest health complications due to acid rain are now being reversed, with large areas of the northeastern United States and Canada showing improved soil conditions and a comeback from acid rain—related problems [3].

The above example of power generation impacts on the environment and the subsequent societal response is a positive one. It shows that we can communicate concerns from broad stakeholder groups and iterate toward solutions, using various policy and technology advancements to achieve the desired outcomes which balance the need for affordable and reliable energy with preservation of human and ecological health. These types of successful processes teach us that we can and should be proactive. We do not need to wait until forests or rivers are dead to take notice and do something about the cause. Big data and advances in computational power mean we are now able to measure, visualize and quantify impacts of power generation on our lives and natural resources at scales and to a depth not considered possible even 20 years ago.

Today's great concern is the increasing CO_2 concentration in the atmosphere. Considered a greenhouse gas, CO_2 is a key driver in the Earth retaining greater amounts of incident solar radiation, leading to what was once called "global warming." The precise impacts, however, are not necessarily increasing temperatures everywhere, but rather an alteration of global energy budgets that manifest as higher overall average temperatures, which can lead to more extreme weather events, melting of glaciers, sea-level rise, and many other effects that can have profound effects on human populations and natural systems. Hence the phenomenon is more recently referred to as "climate change," or more specifically "anthropogenic climate change," implying that human-related CO_2 emissions are driving the process.

The impacts of increasing atmospheric CO_2 concentrations are perhaps not immediately obvious and the cause-effect relationships are more subtle than those observed with acid rain. Indicators such as frequency of extreme weather events are not as definitive as soil pH measurements. Regardless, many believe it is necessary to limit, if not entirely curb, CO_2 emissions from all sources, not just power plants. The Intergovernmental Panel on Climate Change (IPCC) has advocated the need to become net-zero on CO_2 by 2050 [4] to prevent irreversible negative climate change outcomes. Net-zero here means no further increase in atmospheric CO_2 concentrations from any sources, going well beyond power infrastructure to include air and sea transportation, cars and trucks, home heating and cooking, and industrial processes.

There are no carbon-free fossil-fuels. There is no way to reduce CO_2 from combustion by optimizing elements of the combustion process itself. Carbon capture technologies are available, similar to SO_2 scrubbers, but capture technologies are complex and in most cases require an offtaker of the byproduct to improve economics. Many environmentalists oppose carbon capture from fossil-fuel power generation because it supports the continued consumption of fossil-fuels and, by extension, the extraction of those fuels via drilling, hydraulic fracturing, and mining.

Ultimately, utilities and society at large are now considering generation sources that either do not need fuel at all (renewables) or are considered carbon-neutral (renewable power to gas, biofuels) or carbon-free (nuclear energy, renewable hydrogen). The big question looming for policymakers and electric utilities is how to proactively plan to reduce carbon emissions while being sensitive to a host of other concerns, such as affordability, reliability, and sustainability. As we shall see, the final outcomes are dependent on how targets are defined.

The definition of "100%": the importance of semantics

Targets declare 100% renewable or 100% decarbonized or 100% "clean energy" and so on, but proposed plans are often short on details and there is no common understanding of what this means in the electric utility industry. Even in academia and in public discourse there is little distinction between these definitions. People intuitively understand 100% renewables to mean all energy will come directly from renewable sources. Difficulties in understanding and implementation occur when it becomes apparent that directly serving load with wind and solar around the clock may be impractical, necessitating energy storage or other firm sources of energy, including burning some sort of fuel. And it is counterintuitive to consider that as societies transition from fossil-based to renewable energy, it may be necessary to build new thermal plants (burning fossil-fuels) to support renewables during the transition.

Regardless of ambiguities, governments at all levels are declaring mandatory targets for 100%. They are understood as renewable mandates and wind, solar, hydro, and other renewable energy sources are expected to replace fossil-fuels to eliminate carbon emissions. Germany [5], Scotland [6], and Denmark [7] have 100% commitments. As of 2018 more than 100 cities internationally obtained at least 70% of their energy from renewable sources [8], and more join the list regularly, striving for 100%. The capital city of Australia, Canberra, announced starting January 1, 2020, that they would produce or purchase the equivalent of their annual electricity needs from renewable sources [9]. The island state of Tasmania announced a 200% renewable goal, with plans to take excess renewable energy for bulk hydrogen production [10]. Several Caribbean islands have plans to reach 100% targets [11]. In the United States, as of early 2020 more than 130 municipalities have committed to 100% renewable energy [12] as well the District of Colombia, Puerto Rico, and seven states. In addition, investor-owned utilities in the United States are independently committing to 100% targets whether the states they do business in require it or not [13−15], as are some utilities in Europe [16]. The references provided above are indicative and do not represent the full magnitude of 100% commitments, which are evolving rapidly.

One thing the majority of declared targets have in common is compliance in the 2040−2050 timeframe. It is not a coincidence that these dates align with reporting by the IPCC that in order to prevent negative impacts of anthropogenic climate change "Global net human-caused emissions of carbon dioxide would need to fall by about 45 percent from 2010 levels by 2030, reaching 'net zero" around 2050" [4]. The IPCC recommendations apply to all of society, not just electric utilities. Accordingly, there are efforts to decarbonize transportation and other sectors through electrification, which will place increasing emphasis on electric utilities.

To this end it is imperative to discuss what is meant by 100% renewable versus 100% carbon-free versus 100% carbon-neutral. A tabular format of technology classes and their applicability in various definitions of 100% is provided in Table 7.1. Note that biofuels classification is dependent on local definitions. Some jurisdictions consider biofuels to be renewable or admissible in a carbon-free context even though they are carbon-neutral. Similarly, some may assume energy storage is admissible in a "100% renewable" system, although they should recognize then that they are not actually serving load directly with renewables. These may seem like minor distinctions, but the semantics are important and do have consequences.

Pathways to 100%

Generally, a 100% renewable mandate is the most restrictive, carbon-free is intermediate, and carbon-neutral is the least restrictive based simply on the number of choices (Table 7.1), or degrees of freedom, available to the resource planner. The definition, and the subsequent choices available for utilities to serve load, defines the pathway one can take while making the transition from today to the 100% ideal state, however defined (Fig. 7.1). Each pathway will involve a different trajectory and cost.

Table 7.1 Classification of power generation technologies and their applicability according to how a power system is defined: 100% renewable, 100% carbon-free, or 100% carbon-neutral.

Classification technology			Power system definition		
			100% renewable	100% carbon-free	100% carbon-neutral
Renewable		Wind	Yes	Yes	Yes
		Solar	Yes	Yes	Yes
		Hydro	Yes	Yes	Yes
		Geothermal	Yes	Yes	Yes
Carbon-free		Nuclear	No	Yes	Yes
		Energy storage	No	Yes	Yes
	PtG hydrogen	Allowed?	No	Yes	Yes
		Use existing infra?[a]	No	No	No
		Use existing assets?[b]	No	No	No
Carbon-neutal	PtG methane	Allowed?	No	No	Yes
		Use existing infra?[a]	No	No	Yes
		Use existing assets?[b]	No	No	Yes
		Biofuels	Depends	Depends	Yes

[a]Refers to ability to use existing gas-fuel infrastructure for storage and delivery of fuel.
[b]Refers to ability to burn the fuel in existing thermal technologies designed to burn natural gas, including those already installed, without modification.

The path to 100% renewable

A 100% renewable system is one in which load is directly served by hydro, geothermal, and VREs (Table 7.1). Countries such as Iceland provide 100% of their energy with hydro and geothermal already [17], but hydro and geo-thermal are not available to all utility systems, or may not be available in suffi-cient quantity, so these must be supplemented with VREs or other forms of generation. And here we must differentiate between a large utility securing 100% renewables versus the claim by some industrials and smaller municipal utilities doing the same. In the latter case it is possible to secure annual MWh needs via contractual renewable energy arrangements, but the electricity coming across the wires is from a larger pool of energy sources and their load

Figure 7.1 Potential pathways toward 100%.

is not directly served by renewables. Here we are talking about large utility systems with requirements for reliability such as capacity reserve margins. Can these utilities realistically be 100% renewable?

100% renewable leads to oversupply

Some have argued that 100% renewable targets at the large utility or regional scale are indeed feasible (e.g., [18–21]). However, the cost of these systems may be impractical, in large part due to the tremendous waste associated with overbuild and curtailment. For example, the state of California has aggressive renewable targets and provides detailed information on overgeneration/curtailment to the public (Fig. 7.2A) [22]. It is difficult for most people to grasp the magnitude of curtailment in GWh, so let us calculate it in terms of something more tangible. Take the average GWh curtailment for each year, divide by 8760 hours per year, then again by the average capacity factor of solar in California, 28.4% [23]. The result is the average MW of solar capacity that is effectively completely unutilized (Fig. 7.2B). That is, in 2019 the amount of renewable energy wasted by the CA system was the equivalent of a 400 MW utility-scale solar installation generating MWh for an entire year, and as of 2019 California was still very far from 100% renewable. If past trends hold (Fig. 7.2A and B) the amount of overgeneration will increase dramatically

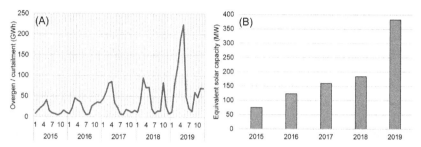

Figure 7.2 (A) Historical overgeneration from solar and wind in California [22] and (B) equivalent solar capacity that is completely unutilized due to curtailment.

as more VREs are added to the system. The CA experience is indicative of what can be expected for any system with growing VRE penetration. The more you add, the more that is wasted.

Another way to look at this issue is to consider the hypothetical utility system from Chapter 2, Influx of Variable Renewable Energy Sources, the Way Things Are Going, for the 900 MW peak load day in June. To provide every MWh of energy from wind and solar throughout the day means there must be enough wind capacity to meet all nighttime loads and enough solar and wind capacity to meet daytime loads which, in this example, happen when wind generation is minimal.

It turns out that using the data from Chapter 2, Influx of Variable Renewable Energy Sources, the Way Things Are Going, Fig. 7.9B there are hours at night with no wind generation. So, no amount of VRE capacity can serve the needs across all 24 hours of the peak day load, even if there is enough generation to meet the peak. If we calculate the proportion of load served by renewables as a function of the amount of renewables installed (Fig. 7.3) we see that there are rapid gains up to approximately 5x (Fig. 7.3), when VRE capacity is five times the peak of 900 MW, and serving approximately 73% of the daily load. Tripling the VRE capacity to 15x only gets to 80% of the load served by VREs, and the curve asymptotes to a maxima in the 84% range.

Solar and wind generate independent of need, so the higher the amount of VRE capacity as the curve in Fig. 7.3 asymptotes, the greater the amount of oversupply and curtailment. For example, at 16x only 16% of the VRE generation is used to serve load, 84% of VRE generation is curtailed, and the utility must still get 20% of its daily MWh from some other source. It is possible of course for a utility to supply 100% of its load from renewables for specific days, and this is more likely to occur for

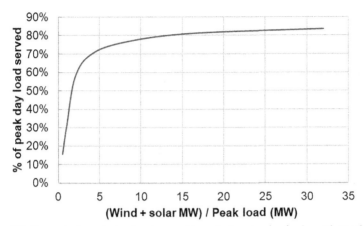

Figure 7.3 Percent of peak day load served by wind and solar for hypothetical utility as a function of the amount of wind and solar capacity available relative to peak load MW.

shoulder month low load days. This brief example illustrates how it is possible to have a situation where meeting 100% of the load for every day of the year solely with VREs may not be possible.

Wasting oversupply weakens the economic case for variable renewable energy

VRE oversupply it can become low-cost energy for export to neighbors. This has great potential early in the game when neighboring utilities may have a need and can take the energy. But as the utility industry, as a whole, moves toward 100% targets, they will be dealing with their own oversupply issues happening at the same time and will be unable to absorb oversupply from neighbors. In addition, reliability requirements often mandate that each utility maintain its own capacity reserve margins to assure security of supply islanded from neighbors (and for actual island utility systems, this is the reality they live with every day).

Even so, there is a sentiment that VREs are falling so rapidly in price that it makes no sense to ever build thermal again. For example, "Lazard's Levelized Cost of Energy Analysis—13.0" [24], gives a wide range of levelized cost of energy (LCOE) costs for unsubsidized solar capacity across crystalline and thin film, fixed and tilt axis, across a range of capacity factors. The lower end of the range, or best case for solar LCOE is 32 $/MWh, the higher end is 42 $/MWh. In comparison the lowest LCOE for gas generation was estimated as 44 $/MWh. So, obviously, solar is less expensive than gas generation, or so it seems. The LCOE calculations do not account for portfolio dynamics that may lead to curtailment. If solar is forced to curtail 25% of its generation, 32 $/MWh becomes 43 $/MWh, very close to the best case for gas generation. If 50% of solar is curtailed, the LCOE is 64 $/MWh and it is no longer clear that solar is less expensive than thermal generation.

Land requirements for variable renewable energy development

At this point it is helpful to define an upper limit for wind and solar capacity, however arbitrary, to demonstrate a point about land use. Referring to the example above (Fig. 7.3), a VRE deployment of 16x (16 times the 900 MW peak load) gives 7200 MW each of solar and wind (assuming equal amounts of each) and meets 80% of MWh for the peak load day. Assuming 5 acres/MW (2 ha/MW) of land for utility-scale solar [25] and 0.75 acres/MW (0.3 ha/MW) for onshore wind [26] gives a combined total of 41,400 acres of land needed for VRE development (equivalent to 65 sq. miles or 168 sq. km). Doubling the VRE capacity only pushes the VRE penetration on the peak day to 84% yet now requires 336 sq. km. Of course, the example here is demonstrative, and one could carefully optimize the proportions of wind and solar to more perfectly match the needs, use ensemble data to achieve more favorable wind and solar outcomes, or simply choose other data sets for hypothetical examples that demonstrate 100% of load met on peak days by VREs. But this example does illustrate a fundamental truth: A 100% renewable system (defined in Table 7.1) will need massive overbuilds of VRE capacity that require a tremendous amount of land.

In terms of cost, the land requirements for VREs are mostly ignored in power system planning analyses. Most sources of cost for various generation technologies refer to the EPC or installed cost of the equipment but do not account for owners' costs (which include land, interconnect, and permitting). Ever-increasing reliance on solar and wind will require utility resource planning teams to carefully account for the complexities and costs of vast amounts of land and of building the transmission capability to connect VREs to load.

Opposition to land use for variable renewable energy development

At a conceptual level, the amount of available land required to power the majority of countries with wind, water, and solar has been estimated as less than 1% [27]. Society can spare 1% of its landmass to provide clean energy, right? Yes and no.

Development of large tracts of land for wind and solar development is just that, development. This development is land-use change and in effect, habitat-loss, which according to numerous scientists is the greatest threat to biodiversity on the planet. The United States National Wildlife Fund says "Habitat loss—due to destruction, fragmentation, or degradation of habitat—is the primary threat to the survival of wildlife in the United States." [28], and a report by the United Nations [29] that listed the five major causes of accelerating species extinction rates considered "changes in land and sea use" as the leading cause. Accordingly, environmental permitting often requires expensive and detailed environmental impact assessments and must, on occasion, weather criticism and protest from environmental groups. Wind and solar projects have faced opposition from environmental groups in the United States (e.g., [30−36]), while similar resistance does not seem to be so prevalent in other parts of the world. However, we are only recently beginning the mass deployment of VREs on a global scale and environmental factors of little concern today can be expected to garner more attention as impact becomes apparent.

The mass addition of VREs will inevitably require land development in close proximity to people who, for any number of reasons, do not want these projects in their communities. Their objections can range from indigenous/tribal issues related to the land in question [37] to local concerns over excessive renewable development altering their communities irreversibly [38]. Even offshore wind faces opposition by coastal populations who want to protect the viewsheds and maintain tourism and by shipping and fishing concerns. Local opposition exists to varying extents globally but can be expected to increase as broader tracts of land are required to meet 100% targets (however defined).

The pushback on siting poses additional challenges to utilities. Building thousands of MW of VREs will require multiple project sites which must be independently sited, developed, and permitted. Transmission corridors will also require land, additional permitting, and development. The process can take years for each project in question, and opposition can kill a project several years into the process, wasting the time and resources of the utility and potentially putting needed capacity increases behind schedule. While these issues are considered part of the price of doing business in the industry, alternate pathways to 100% may offer a way to minimize the amount of solar and wind needed, and by extension the amount of land that needs to be developed.

Resource planning considerations

VREs must be major contributors toward deep decarbonization. However, project-level economics used to justify 100% renewable systems provide a distorted picture of reality. Overgeneration can only be sold if there is a buyer, and the purchase price may be near-zero. Without system-level considerations the very real aspects of overgeneration and its subsequent cost impacts are ignored. Utility resource planners must account for all impacts, including land use, and attend to them in a cost-optimal way. One way to do this is to shift attention from "100% renewable" to "100% carbon-free," as this allows for additional degrees of freedom and less costly options that work to maximize the utility of solar and wind, as opposed to passively wasting the energy they generate.

The path to 100% carbon-free

The major difference between a 100% renewable and 100% carbon-free power system is that the latter pathway allows for energy storage and hydrogen combustion. Certainly, most proponents of "100%" do not mean to exclude storage, but as noted, the semantics matter. A carbon-free system is not strictly 100% renewable in that load is not entirely served directly by renewables. Instead, a carbon-free system allows for storage to time-shift VRE overgeneration for use at a later time. In this case, renewable production no longer needs to meet real-time demand. Rather, renewable production + storage must meet aggregate demand, with storage providing firm power when VREs are not available.

At this point one must step away from simplistic LCOE or project-level comparisons because we are not talking about one asset versus another; we are talking about providing firm energy for an entire utility system. This involves the interplay among numerous assets of different technology types that are producing and now, with storage or hydrogen production, consuming energy at various and often overlapping times.

Carbon-free power systems reduce oversupply and require less land

The hypothetical utility on its peak day and with installed VRE capacity $32 \times$ the 900 MW peak (Fig. 7.3) cannot meet its load continuously throughout the day with VREs alone. Even with thousands of MWs of VREs installed, the energy produced is far in excess of the load but cannot be utilized effectively because energy production is out of phase with demand. But what if the utility had access to energy storage with an 85%

Table 7.2 Calculated values of generation, storage potential, and load-serving capability for hypothetical utility on June day with peak load of 900 MW, as a function of the amount of wind and solar capacity installed.

Wind capacity (MW)	900	1800	3600	7200	14,400
Solar capacity (MW)	900	1800	3600	7200	14,400
GWh load	16.7	16.7	16.7	16.7	16.7
GWh served directly by wind and solar	9.6	11.7	12.8	13.6	14.0
Meet 100% from wind and solar?	No	No	No	No	No
GWh oversupply	0.8	9.2	28.9	69.8	152.8
GWh storage potential (assuming 85% round trip efficiency)	0.7	7.8	24.6	59.3	129.9
GWh met by wind and solar, plus storage	10.3	19.5	37.4	72.9	143.8
Meet 100% from wind, solar, and storage?	No	Yes	Yes	Yes	Yes

round trip efficiency that could store overgeneration for later use? Table 7.2 compares outcomes across VRE installed capacities considered thus far. These are daily energy balances for the peak day in June. Installing a total of just 3600 MW (1800 MW each of wind and solar) provides ample stored energy potential for this utility to be 100% carbon-free on the peak day. If 3600 MW of VREs were installed, a total of (16.7−11.7) 5 GWh of storage would be needed (Table 7.2). A total of 900 MW of Li-ion batteries with 6-hour duration would be more than sufficient. If 5 GWh of energy were stored on this day, it would absorb 5.9 GWh of oversupply (assuming 85% efficiency). The oversupply was 9.2 GWh and is now reduced to (9.2−5.9) 3.3 GWh as the majority of oversupply is now used directly for storage charging, which acts as a new load. Rather than 168 sq. km to install 14,400 MW of VREs that cannot supply 100% of load, allowing energy storage drops the land requirement to 42 sq. km for VREs and allows the utility to be 100% carbon-free.

The simple addition of energy storage as an allowable technology dramatically reduces the amount of VRE capacity needed and maximizes the utility of VREs by minimizing oversupply. It is unknown whether this arrangement would serve load for all other days of the year, but the example illustrates a major point. *Carbon-free allows for a broader array of technology choices and results in more efficient, smaller power systems that require dramatically less land than a strictly 100% renewable power system.*

Hydrogen and nuclear in carbon-free power systems

VRE oversupply can be used to power electrolysis systems to produce hydrogen from water, thus using hydrogen as a form of long-term energy storage. Hydrogen infrastructure is, at present, lacking in most of the world and its cost to support GWs of thermal and fuel cell power generators is unclear [39]. The Fuel Cell and Hydrogen Energy Association, together with 19 companies and organizations, produced a report for the United States [40] indicating the first dedicated hydrogen pipelines could come to market in the United States by 2030. According to the International Energy Agency, as of 2019 there were in excess of 50 targets, mandates, and policy incentives in support of hydrogen investment, but "The development of hydrogen infrastructure is slow and holding back widespread adoption" [41]. They suggest four near-term opportunities to expand hydrogen use, one of which is to leverage existing gas infrastructure by blending hydrogen with natural gas streams to "significantly boost demand for hydrogen and drive down costs" [41].

Rather than relying on a new-built hydrogen pipeline infrastructure, utilities with access to nearby natural gas storage structures may be able to leverage hydrogen sooner. Existing natural gas assets can operate on methane-hydrogen blends, but there is an upper limit to the hydrogen fraction. Combustion assets which can operate at higher fractions or burn pure hydrogen are in development, and some projects are including them in their plans. For example, a 1 GW project called the Advanced Clean Energy System (ACES) is in planning for a site in Utah (western United States) that intends to use salt domes, large underground caverns, for storage of hydrogen produced on site [42]. The caverns are located close to a large coal-fired power plant scheduled for retirement, which provides energy to the municipal utility that serves the city of Los Angeles (Los Angeles Department of Water and Power, LADWP). LADWP plans to replace the coal capacity with a large combined cycle combustion turbine (CCCT) that will initially run on natural gas, but will ultimately transition to 100% hydrogen [43] supplied from the ACES hydrogen fuel storage nearby.

Nuclear power generation is also zero carbon but is expensive and difficult to site, permit, and develop. What is more, added VREs yield volatile net loads for which nuclear is not well-suited. Baseload nuclear facilities, however, can be converted to hydrogen production, a concept being explored by utilities in the United States [44] and Europe [45]. If mass volumes of hydrogen can be produced economically by baseload nuclear, utilities able to gain access to this fuel can store it indefinitely and burn it at will to fill in the gaps when load is not being served directly by VREs.

Resource planning considerations

The details of the final cost optimal buildout for any specific utility will be unique to their load profiles, geographic location, wind/solar potential, and availability of other carbon-free sources such as nuclear, geothermal, etc. Regardless of the specifics, the example here provides some universal truths: allowing for carbon-free storage and generation will:

1. reduce the total amount of VRE capacity needed,
2. reduce the amount of land that must be developed for VREs, and
3. increase the utilization of VREs by minimizing overgeneration and curtailment.

Technology valuations using LCOE or similar project-level analyses are of little value. Planning for a 100% carbon-free system is reliant on long-term capacity expansion plans, preferably chronological, as well as detailed (even subhourly) dispatch simulations. This is so because of the interplay between load, generation, storage charging, and discharging. Each type of capacity has benefits and costs that are impossible to quantify without analyzing the portfolio across annual or longer timescales. This is very similar to how utilities today plan for reservoir hydro. Annual energy budgets are dependent on rainfall, temperature, ice-melt, and more from the prior year as well as the year in question. Optimal discharge of reservoir hydro (and the benefits it brings to power systems) cannot be valued or understood using simple approaches, and neither can energy storage.

Carbon-free systems will be expensive, and a huge proportion of the cost will come toward the end, as systems transition from 80% to 100%. A major challenge will be the way in which long-term storage is developed and utilized. One study by Jenkins et al. in 2018 [46] reviewed 40 studies of deep-decarbonization pathways (80%—100% decarbonization) published between 2014 and 2018. They stated [46]:

"Prolonged periods of calm wind speeds lasting days or weeks during winter months with low solar insolation are particularly challenging for VRE-dominated systems. These sustained lulls in available wind and solar output are too long to bridge with shorter-duration batteries or flexible demand... Power systems with high VRE shares consequently require sufficient capacity from reliable electricity sources that can sustain output in any season and for long periods (weeks or longer)."

In looking at the United States they estimated that if Li-ion batteries were 100 $/kWh it would cost seven-trillion US dollars to install enough batteries to power the United States for one week "... or nearly 19 years of the total United States electricity expenditures" [46]. Granted, estimates like these can be contingent on a number of assumptions and analytical approaches, and it is unlikely the entire United States would ever need a week of nationwide stored energy. But it is realistic to expect that individual utilities will experience multiday to multiweek periods of low to no VRE generation, and they must plan for these contingencies independent of how their neighbors are preparing for the same.

Another study by Blanco and Faij that same year [47] reviewed 60 studies assessing expanding renewable penetrations (up to 100%) and the role of storage, and noted;

"As expected the role of storage becomes more relevant for high VRE penetrations. Below 30% penetration, curtailment (if any, depending on the system) is the best option, since the number of hours where there is a surplus are not enough to justify an investment in any asset. To reach fractions > 80%, storage (and specifically long-term) plays a key role and reduces the overall system cost..."

Long-term carbon-free storage options are rather limited, at least until the proposed hydrogen infrastructure is realized. At this point it is worth exploring the ramifications of allowing additional long-term storage technologies, such as carbon-neutral power to methane (PtM), into the analytical framework.

The path to 100% carbon-neutral (net-zero)

A carbon-neutral approach involves an "all of the above" mindset, and we will see below just how critical asset diversity is to grid reliability. Renewables of all types, including VREs, as well as energy storage, biofuels, and PtM can work together to form an optimal power system. Biofuels are, in some jurisdictions, considered "renewable" already. They are indeed renewable and are considered carbon-neutral since, when combusted, they emit CO_2 which was originally harvested from the atmosphere. Likewise, PtM systems that use direct air capture for CO_2 feedstock are carbon-neutral. Carbon-neutrality is important as it is considered an acceptable pathway for addressing climate change concerns [4]. With so much focus on decarbonization and use of carbon-free energy sources, one may forget that carbon-neutral options are a valuable, perhaps even vital, part of the mix (Table 7.3).

Table 7.3 Comparison of pathways to 100%.

Where on the path?	Percentage of energy from renewables	Pathway to		
		100% carbon-neutral	100% carbon-free	100% renewable
Across entire path	0−100	Decreasing fossil generation leads to falling CO_2 emissions through time.	Same	Same
Early to midway	0−60	New flexible thermal generation replaces aging inflexible fossil resources. Flexible thermal supports renewable integration.	Generally a commitment to 100% carbon-free is perceived as a commitment to no new fossil. Accelerated retirement of existing thermal capacity.	Same as 100% Carbon-free
Early to midway	20−60 +	Opportunities for traditional energy storage increase with renewable penetration.	Same	No storage
Toward end	80−100	Install power-to-fuels resources, retain thermal capacity and infrastructure.	Hydrogen infrastructure and generation capacity added.	No firm capacity or storage
At the end	100	Thermal assets fully transition from fossil to renewable carbon-neutral or biofuel equivalent, act as firm capacity and long-term storage.	All thermal assets and infrastructure "climate-stranded" with the possible exception of resources using biofuels. Hydrogen provides long-term storage and firm capacity.	All thermal assets and infrastructure "climate-stranded."

Utilities can generally reach 50% or more of energy supply from carbon-free sources without facing dramatic challenges, especially if they allow flexible fossil-based generation to play a flexibility/support/

reliability role (as opposed to a primary generation role). Traditional energy storage will then gain momentum as VRE penetrations increase, while fossil generation and CO_2 emissions continue to decline. Major challenges arise when utilities are facing the 100% target date, transitioning from "almost there" to the final state, and these challenges are mainly related to reliability.

Planning for reliability

Most utilities follow the "best practice" of maintaining a capacity reserve margin. Many utilities recognize a reserve margin of 15% (15% is a common value, utilities may calculate and maintain other values). They want to have at least 15% more capacity than their peak load. This ensures that they will have enough capacity to meet all load conditions even if maintenance outages or other loss of capacity occurs. Because wind and solar are "variable" it is not possible to consider them as 100% firm resources. Accordingly, utilities generally assign an "Effective Load Carrying Capacity" (ELCC) to them, a percentage of resource capacity that the utility considers available to meet peak loads. If the peak load for a utility happens at night, the ELCC for solar is zero. The calculation of ELCC can be quite complicated and involve reliability indices such as loss of load expectation or similar [48], but the main outcome is that wind and solar capacity used for reserve margin calculations is often substantially less than the nameplate capacity. The ELCC for any VRE resource is region dependent. For example, the PJM market in the eastern United States reports average ELCC for wind and solar at 11.5% and 42.5%, respectively [49], while the SPP market in the central United States reports 24% and 62%, respectively [50]. Individual utilities often calculate or assign ELCCs based on data from their own VRE assets.

An interesting facet of ELCC calculations for VREs is that their ELCC is generally considered to decrease as VRE penetration increases. The first MWs of solar and wind could have relatively high ELCCs, but the addition of more solar and wind will generally yield progressively lower aggregate ELCCs for those capacity types. Why would the ELCC for VREs decrease as more are added? In part, this is due to geographic diversity. Recall from Chapter 2, Influx of Variable Renewable Energy Sources, the Way Things Are Going (Figs. 2.15 and 2.16) that as more solar and wind sites are added, the peak average output from the aggregate is lower than their collective nameplate capacity. This is so because at any point in time utility-scale solar facilities spaced far apart from each other are not all generating their maximum at the same time, similar for wind farms. As more solar and wind projects are added to a portfolio, their average aggregate "peak output" will continue to go down relative to their aggregate nameplate capacity, which directly impacts ELCC. For example, the SPP report on ELCC [50] shows wind ELCC at 24% when the amount of wind capacity is 20% of peak load, falling to 14% when wind is 75% of peak load; solar at 62% ELCC at 5 GW of solar capacity falls to 15.5% at 40 GW.

Energy storage such as batteries exhibits the same ELCC decline as more distributed assets are added to the system. The California Public Utility Commission 2019 Integrated Resource Plan for the state provides documentation of how ELCC can be assigned to energy storage [51]. Four-hour Li-ion and flow batteries were considered to have 100% ELCC when their installed capacity was less than 20% of peak load, falling to less than 10% as battery capacity exceeded 45% of peak load. These values were determined using subhourly reliability analyses. The reason storage ELCC falls as storage capacity increases is that adding storage tends to flatten the net load peak and lengthen its duration. It becomes more challenging to have fleets of short duration storage devices all prepared at full charge for peak conditions and have enough energy (MWh) to serve the peak.

In contrast, conventional thermal plants are considered to have ELCCs at or near 100%. If there is a 1000 MW peak load to be served by 1150 MW of thermal capacity, there is a true 15% capacity reserve margin. To have the same reserve margin with solar at 15% ELCC, the system would require 7667 MW of solar capacity ($7667 \times 0.15 = 1150$). The long-term planning exercise for 100%, however defined, will need to add capacity in a cost-optimal way that also respects ELCC's for each technology considered and their contribution to capacity reserve margin. These are considered constraints the simulation must maintain while converging toward a solution

This is where PtM can help power systems. A 100% carbon-neutral system will allow traditional thermal assets, like recips and CTs with ELCCs at or very close to 100%, to remain in the system. This includes legacy assets the utility owns, and any new flexible thermal additions installed along the path to 100%. Once the target dates are met, fossil-fuels are disallowed but renewably sourced synthetic methane is not a fossil-fuel and can still be used. Generation from thermal assets will produce no net increase in atmospheric carbon (the fuel is carbon-neutral).

Fuel stores can be stocked up throughout the year taking advantage of oversupply from VREs, allowing for long-term time shifting of energy, with durations of days to weeks as opposed to hours (Fig. 7.4). Another advantage of PtM is that it allows thermal units to avoid being climate-stranded (e.g., becoming stranded assets due to climate change concerns).

Resource planning considerations

Given the above considerations of ELCC and capacity reserve margins it would make sense for utilities to seek energy sources that are:

- flexible, to work with VREs to optimize power system dispatch;
- responsive, able to use oversupply from VREs and minimize waste;
- clean, not increasing atmospheric CO_2 levels;
- secure, not at risk of becoming "climate-stranded" assets; and
- firm capacity, with high ELCC to help maintain reliability without a need for massive overbuild.

Utilities with flexible thermal generation already have capacity that meets the first and the last criteria above. Transitioning to carbon-neutral fuels, either biofuels or renewable-powered PtM (or methanol or synthetic diesel), converts these thermal assets to a piece of the 100% carbon-neutral capacity mix.

At least one utility, Hawaiian Electric Company (HECO) has invested in this approach using biofuels. Their Power Supply Improvement Plan for reaching what they call a 100% renewable energy future is actually a carbon-neutral approach. To reach a 100% state they take full advantage of demand response, renewables such as wind and solar, and battery energy storage, but they also intend to keep thermal resources that are, at present, running on fossil-fuels. When 100% target dates approach they will transition to clean, renewable biofuels, for the following reliability reasons [52] (author emphasis added):

> Load shifting energy storage with variable renewable energy such as wind and solar can have an important role in the 100% renewable energy future. **Conventional thermal generating resources will still be required to meet the load during seasonal low renewable energy production or unpredicted weather-related events** (such as the 6 weeks of consecutive rainy days in 2006).

Consider the wide breadth of renewable fuel options, in particular those that mimic fossil-fuels. Any natural gas—fired generator installed today can burn synthetic methane, and any oil-fired generator (common

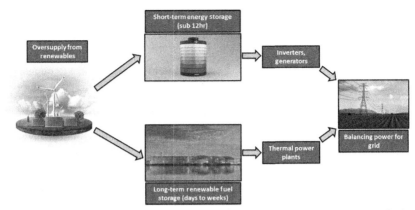

Figure 7.4 The symbiotic roles of short-term energy storage and renewable fuels (biofuels, power-to-methane, hydrogen, methanol, etc.).

on island systems) can be transitioned to biodiesel, methanol, or other form of synthetic renewable diesel. This strategy future-proofs utility investments and removes the risk of the assets becoming climate-stranded. Even if such fuels are more expensive than their fossil-counterparts, in a 100% end-state combustion of fossil-fuels is disallowed. Carbon-neutral fuels and thermal generation in this context must be valued for the reliability they bring (high ELCC) and their utility as long-term storage, offsetting costly overbuilds of storage technologies best suited for short (sub 12-hour) durations.

Summary of the pathways to 100%

The discussions and examples in this section highlight the attributes and characteristics of the different targets that define the pathways utilities must take. The least-cost pathways utilities propose in the integrated resource plans (IRPs) will be dependent on target definitions, the technologies available, their cost, and their ELCCs. Considering what has been presented thus far each pathway is assessed against the primary goals of affordability, reliability, and sustainability (Table 7.4). This assessment may change with time as hydrogen infrastructure and the various capacity types that can generate with hydrogen mature. Hydrogen could supplant renewable hydrocarbons for long-term storage. This would allow the carbon-free system to enjoy some of the advantages of the carbon-neutral system.

Table 7.4 Utility planning criteria and the nature of different definitions of 100%.

Criteria	Attribute	Power system definition		
		100% renewable	100% carbon-free	100% carbon-neutral
Affordable	Cost to ratepayer	High	Medium	Medium to low
Reliable	Meets capacity reserve margins?	Required	Required	Required
	Capacity overbuild	High	Medium	Low
	Percentage of energy from renewables	100%	80 + %	80 + %
Sustainable	Percentage of energy from carbon-free sources	100%	100%	80 + %
	Net zero on carbon	Yes	Yes	Yes
	Land use	High	Medium	Low

A comparison of different pathways using capacity expansion analyses

There are a growing number of analyses in the literature looking at the cost of traveling the path to 100%, mostly from a regional perspective. Few studies look at the problem from an electric utility planning perspective, accounting for reserve margin considerations and the like. To be sure, no example will answer all questions for any specific utility as each one has unique situations and challenges. The goal here is to explore different approaches and ideas.

To that end, let us look at a generic utility (the Utility) whose trend in capacity mix is similar to that of utilities in the United States in general. In the United States, nuclear capacity is stable in recent times, while coal is decreasing, and gas is increasing (Fig. 7.5A). The Utility has legacy stable nuclear, a rapidly declining amount of coal capacity, increasing natural gas reliance, and is adding wind and solar (Fig. 7.5B).

A paper titled "Pathways Towards 100% Carbon Reduction for Electric Utility Power Systems" [57] addressed the following scenarios/questions using the Utility as a test case (Table 7.5), and provided the basis for the numbers and data presented in this section, with additional discussion and analysis provided by the author.

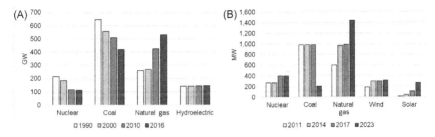

Figure 7.5 (A) Capacity mix of utilities in the United States 1990 to 2016 [53], and (B) capacity mix for sample utility 2011 and projected through 2023 [54—56].

Table 7.5 Scenarios addressing questions about varying pathways addressed in [57].

Scenario	Question being addressed
Unconstrained	What would the utility build and how would its CO_2 trajectory look if it were unconstrained by RPS or other mandates?
Carbon-free	How would the buildout and cost differ if the Utility had to be carbon-free at the end of the planning horizon?
Carbon-neutral	Same as carbon-free scenario, but allowing for power to methane (PtM)?

The following approach was used by [57] to address the questions (Table 7.4):

- commercially available chronological capacity expansion planning tool;
- 20-year planning horizon (2020—2040);
- integer build for new thermal options, restricting new-build thermal to unit sizes available on the market;
  - Frame CTs at 600 $/kW, 34% HHV efficiency, $15,000 per start;
  - Recips at 800 $/kW, 42% HHV efficiency, $0 per start;
- linear build for solar, wind, battery storage, and PtM options, allowing optimal capacities of each per scenario;
- integer unit commitment in dispatch simulations at 1-hour time step;
- forward pricing curves for solar, wind, battery storage, and PtM from publicly available sources
- load profiles, fuel prices, and additional coal retirement dates as per the IRPs published by the Utility; and
- 15% capacity reserve margin across the planning horizon.

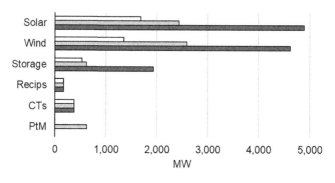

Figure 7.6 New capacity added to the Utility across the planning horizon (2020−2040). *Data from J. Ferrari, Pathways towards 100% carbon reduction for electric utility power systems. <https://www.pathto100.org/2020/02/pathways-towards-100-carbon-reduction-for-electric-utility-power-systems/>, 2019.*

New-build capacity by scenario

The resultant new-build capacity (Fig. 7.6) shows increasing VRE capacity and battery storage going from unconstrained to carbon-neutral to carbon-free, with carbon-free having almost double the VRE capacity of carbon-neutral. The carbon-free scenario had close to 2 GW of storage (4−6-hours duration) and firm nuclear capacity. In the carbon-neutral scenario approximately 600 MW of PtM capacity was installed. This acts as a 600 MW load powered by excess renewable energy and produces carbon-neutral fuel in the final year when fossil-fuel is disallowed. Due to cost and the prevalence of low-cost fossil-fuels, power to fuels was not installed by the model until the final year of the horizon. Interestingly, all three scenarios install similar amounts of thermal capacity, the only difference being whether they run and fuel choice at the end of the planning horizon.

Land use

The wind and solar capacities installed (Fig. 7.6) coupled with estimates of 5 and 0.75 acres per MW of solar [25] and wind [26], respectively, provide ranges of land use by scenario. For the unconstrained scenario 9405 acres (3806 ha) are needed for VRE development. The C-neutral scenario needs 14,130 acres (5718 ha) and C-Free needs 27,880 acres (11,284 ha).

The costs of land were not explicitly considered in the analysis so these results reflect artificially depressed installed cost of VREs. Ignoring land cost is a common and useful simplifying assumption in these types of comparisons but must be avoided in actual utility planning. In any scenario, the first sites for VRE development will be chosen based on proximity to load and lowest cost for land, permitting, and interconnect. Every additional project site to be developed will be further away from load and more expensive and time consuming to build, permit, and interconnect. The carbon-neutral scenario requires approximately 50% more land than the unconstrained case, while the carbon-free scenario requires 200% more land. If local opposition against land-use change has any chance of thwarting renewable development, the carbon-free pathway has the greatest risk of facing cost overruns and delays.

Generation, load, curtailment, and air emissions

While consumer load remained constant, the Utility load increased with battery charging (all three scenarios) and PtM systems (carbon-neutral scenario). Annual energy needs were 14.3 GWh (unconstrained), 17.9 GWh (carbon-free), and 17.4 GWh (carbon-neutral). The amount of VRE generation serving load directly was maximized in the carbon-neutral scenario (Fig. 7.7).

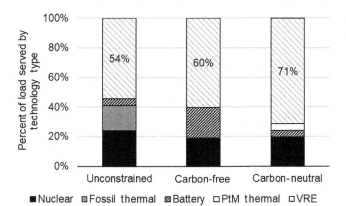

Figure 7.7 Percent of load served by technology class across scenarios in last year of horizon. Numbers in chart indicate the percentage of load served directly by VRE's (solar and wind). *Data from J. Ferrari, Pathways towards 100% carbon reduction for electric utility power systems. <https://www.pathto100.org/2020/02/pathways-towards-100-carbon-reduction-for-electric-utility-power-systems/>, 2019.*

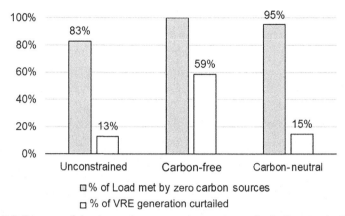

Figure 7.8 Percent of load met by zero-carbon sources (including nuclear) across scenarios, and percent of VRE generation curtailed in last year of horizon. *Data from J. Ferrari, Pathways towards 100% carbon reduction for electric utility power systems. <https://www.pathto100.org/2020/02/pathways-towards-100-carbon-reduction-for-electric-utility-power-systems/>, 2019.*

Carbon-free generation served 100% of load in the carbon-free scenario, but both the unconstrained and carbon-neutral pathways had more than 80% of load served by carbon-free sources (Fig. 7.8) as well. In the carbon-neutral scenario only 5% of load was served by thermal generators in the final year, running on renewable methane from power-to-gas (PtG) processes. This is important, as it shows thermal generation is being used as a reliability backstop, complementing battery storage in the management of both load and VRE utilization. Without PtM the carbon-free pathway wasted more than half of VRE output. Ratepayers are paying for this renewable capacity even if most of the energy is wasted. PtM provides a flexible load designed to absorb this oversupply, maximizing the value of installed VRE capacity.

Timing of use of power to methane in the 100% carbon-neutral scenario

PtM processes consumed VRE oversupply to generate fuel in the first 6 months of the year and in the final three (Fig. 7.9). Consumption of fuel, indicated by falling fuel levels, occurred midyear through September when the capacity factors of solar and wind were at their lowest.

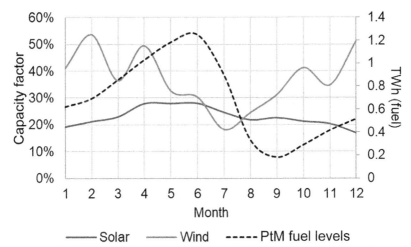

Figure 7.9 Final year of horizon for carbon-neutral scenario. Monthly capacity factors for solar and wind as well as fuel storage levels from power to methane process. *Data from J. Ferrari, Pathways towards 100% carbon reduction for electric utility power systems. <https://www.pathto100.org/2020/02/pathways-towards-100-carbon-reduction-for-electric-utility-power-systems/>, 2019.*

Long-term storage potential of power to gas

Economically and reliably serving load during the months-long mid-year lull in wind (Fig. 7.9) requires longer term storage, such as PtG (or PtH). In the final year of the horizon, the carbon–neutral scenario had retained 1370 MW of gas-fired thermal capacity (all coal capacity had been retired). Of that 1370 MW only the most flexible and efficient thermal capacity was dispatched to serve load: 415 MW of CCCTs, 166 MW of Recips, and 374 MW of frame-type CTs, running at 17%, 7%, and 1% capacity factors, respectively. The remaining 415 MW was held as "cold reserve," to be started only when necessary for reliability purposes.

The duration of the thermal fleet when afforded 1.25 TWh$_{fuel}$ (Fig. 7.9) is dependent on the thermal capacity considered. For high-level screening purposes let us assume an average thermal efficiency of 45%, which yields an electrical energy budget of (1.25 TWhfuel × 45% conversion efficiency) 562,500 MWh$_{electric}$. If all 1370 MW thermal capacity is considered, the duration is 410 hours (17 days) (Fig. 7.10, point "A"). If cold reserve capacity is excluded, the duration of the 955 MW of active capacity is 589 hours (24.5 days) (Fig. 7.10, point "B").

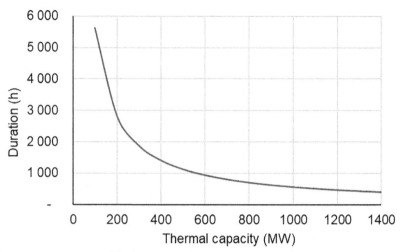

Figure 7.10 Duration of fuel as renewable energy storage for the Utility in carbon-neutral scenario. If all 1370 MW of thermal capacity considered (A), duration is 410 h (17 days). With cold reserve excluded and only considering the remaining 955 MW of active capacity (B), duration is 589 h (24.5 days).

Costs

As discussed in previous chapters, utility cost calculations are often expressed as net present value (NPV). The NPV was calculated for each scenario in the example above using a 6% discount rate (Fig. 7.11). The unconstrained scenario provided at least 83% of MWh from clean energy sources in the final year of the horizon but was reliant on fossil-fuels at market prices. This scenario assumed business as usual across a 20-year horizon taking advantage of falling VRE and storage pricing, with a final NPV of 7.06 BUSD and an average generation cost in the final year of 37 $/MWh ("generation cost" being the total undiscounted final year annual cost, Opex, and Capex, divided by total generation in MWh to serve load). For the carbon-free scenario NPV rose to 9.49 BUSD with a final year generation cost of 70 $/MWh. While the carbon-free scenario is not reliant on fossil-fuels at all in the final year, the large amounts of VREs and storage increase the Capex (Annualized build cost in Fig. 7.11) and fixed operations and maintenance (FOM) considerably.

The carbon-neutral scenario has the lowest NPV (6.91 BUSD) and the lowest generation cost in the final year, 35 $/MWh. Having avoided the mass overbuild, the FOM and Capex are considerably lower than in the carbon-free case. It is also less expensive than the unconstrained case

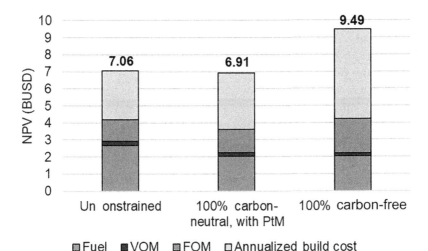

Figure 7.11 Twenty-year net present value (NPV) of costs (BUSD) broken into major components, and accounting for end-effects. *Data from J. Ferrari, Pathways towards 100% carbon reduction for electric utility power systems.* <*https://www.pathto100.org/2020/02/pathways-towards-100-carbon-reduction-for-electric-utility-power-systems/*>, *2019.*

because it uses no fossil-fuel in the final year of the planning horizon. All three scenarios have the same nuclear fuel cost as fuel costs are carried into perpetuity.

Summary

The study performed by [57] and reviewed here provides a validation of the characterizations in Table 7.4. Carbon-free systems cost more, install more capacity, and require more land than carbon-neutral. What is more, the study provided an example of what it could take to achieve deep decarbonization from a long-term capacity expansion perspective in the absence of RPS mandates. The expected falling prices of solar, wind, and energy storage will provide a landscape in which unconstrained least-cost analyses select carbon-free over fossil generation, but only to a certain point. Other studies indicate similar findings (e.g., [58]).

Moving from the unconstrained state to 100% will not come naturally unless additional technologies are considered and constraints added to the model, such as RPS compliance dates. If the system is constrained with RPS mandates that only allow carbon-free portfolios, in the absence of firm generation from something other than sub-12-hour storage or VREs, the amount of capacity needed to meet reserve margins is excessive.

The necessary overbuild increases oversupply from, and curtailment of, VREs when coupled with traditional storage. Similar findings have been reported in analyses of California [59] and the Pacific Northwest of the United States [58].

In the absence of access to new hydro, nuclear, or geothermal generation, many utilities will be left with few choices for meeting 100% carbon-free conditions other than costly overbuild of capacity types with low ELCCs. Hydrogen production coupled with fuel cells, recips, or CTs could provide firm capacity to offset the need for dramatic overbuilds, but the cost and timing of the necessary hydrogen infrastructure buildout are highly uncertain and thus carry significant risk at this time.

Final thoughts on pathways to 100% and the importance of resource planning

We have learned a great deal in the past decades and new analytical approaches and technologies are emerging that continually redefine what is possible. Renewable energy sources have fallen dramatically in price and are quickly becoming the new baseload, providing the majority of MWh generated by a growing number of electric utilities. Advances and economies of scale are quickly improving the economics of traditional storage technologies such as batteries. All of this indicates that electric utilities can, in an unconstrained manner and without too much trouble, reach 60%—80% of their energy needs from renewables. However, it is not as simple as just adding VREs, as the transition takes time. As older fossil assets are retired, reliability analyses help to drive new capacity selections. Large centralized fossil generation is more often replaced by numerous projects of different sizes using different technologies. The pace of change is contingent on many factors, including the price of fossil-fuels. Island systems paying a premium for liquid fuels may see a better business case for a quick transition than a large utility with access to very low-cost fossil-fuels.

As utilities install enough VRE capacity that pricing volatility becomes an issue, traditional IRP valuations, from annual cost curves to LCOE, and/or use of load duration curve based capacity expansion models (CEMs), quickly become inadequate. Loss of time dependence in these approaches tends to overvalue VRE and baseload, inflexible resources, which leads to suboptimal outcomes and higher utility costs once these resources are deployed. Utilities around the world are experiencing this now as CCCT or similar resources, once considered the most cost-effective thermal on the market, are being pushed aside in dispatch in favor of flexible assets which better supports VREs.

Selecting the proper amounts of capacity types with the correct capabilities, including adequate flexibility, is the domain of more complicated chronological long-term CEMs, or Chrono CEMs. Chrono CEMs retain the time dependence of load and VRE output and tend to select a more diverse array of flexible resources designed to mitigate volatility in the supply stack brought by VREs. In order for utilities to continue along the path to 100% in a cost-optimal way, they need to transition to Chrono CEMs and adopt new ways of characterizing risk associated with the vagaries of weather that drive the availability of hydro and VRE resources.

Some utilities do not select capacity but rather issue requests for proposal for specific capacity amounts, however the same concepts apply. In this case, rather than a CEM, chronological dispatch simulation tools should be used to compare portfolio costs for different capacity choices being considered. As demonstrated in Chapter 6, Illustrating Concepts with Examples, the net benefit of an asset at the portfolio level (relative to other potential choices) is the best metric for technology selection. Only in this manner can the value of flexibility be truly understood, as attributes of a flexible asset can change the dispatch of other generation assets in the portfolio.

Additional elements are being considered as utilities understand the interplay between transmission and distribution (T&D) planning and integrated resource planning (for electric generation capacity). With growing restrictions and barriers to expansion of T&D, utilities are seeing the benefit of distributed generation alleviating T&D expansions. To date much of this work has been ad hoc and on a "project by project" basis, but it is becoming clear that economies can be gained by combining elements of T&D and capacity expansion analyses. As noted prior, the portfolio benefits of flexible generation are paramount and can only be understood using hourly or even subhourly chronological analyses. Understanding the correct capacity types needed to efficiently support renewables will also optimize the interplay between capacity and T&D expansion analyses.

However policymakers or electric utility management define future targets for decarbonization, the utility IRP forms the vision statement and backbone of future capacity installations needed for the utility to meet the challenge. Utility resource planning staff and regulatory agencies should be staffed and trained on the most advanced analytical approaches and afforded the capabilities to use them to full effect. Newer Chrono CEM approaches, and portfolio analyses versus project-level comparisons are computationally intensive but could save the utility, and ultimately ratepayers, millions if not billions of dollars over the planning horizon. Allowing the broadest range of technologies to meet load will help maintain reliability, while decarbonization that respects conservation of land will maximize sustainability.

References

[1] US Environmental Protection Agency, Sulfur dioxide trends, 2020. <https://www.epa.gov/air-trends/sulfur-dioxide-trends> (accessed 4, 2020).

[2] US Environmental Protection Agency, Nitrogen oxide emissions. <https://cfpub.epa.gov/roe/indicator_pdf.cfm?i = 15>, 2018.

[3] G.B. Lawrence, P.W. Hazlett, I.J. Fernandez, R. Ouimiet, S.W. Bailey, W.C. Shortle, et al., Declining acidic deposition begins reversal of forest-soil acidification in the Northeastern U.S. and Eastern Canada, Environ. Sci. Technol. 49 (2015) 13103−13111. Available from: https://pubs.acs.org/doi/pdf/10.1021/acs.est.5b02904.

[4] Intergovernmental Panel on Climate Change, Summary for policymakers of IPCC special report on global warming of 1.5°C approved by governments. <https://www.ipcc.ch/2018/10/08/summary-for-policymakers-of-ipcc-special-report-on-global-warming-of-1-5c-approved-by-governments/>, 2018.

[5] United Nations, 100% renewable electricity supply by 2050. <https://sustainabledevelopment.un.org/index.php?page = view&type = 99&nr = 24&menu = 1449>, 2019.

[6] T. Love, Scotland will run on 100% renewable energy by 2020, GreenMatters.Com. <https://www.greenmatters.com/renewables/2017/11/08/Z2rjgAy/scotland-2020-solar>

[7] M. Fraende, Denmark aims for 100 percent renewable energy in 2050, Reuters. <https://www.reuters.com/article/us-denmark-energy/denmark-aims-for-100-percent-renewable-energy-in-2050-idUSTRE7AO15120111125>, 2011.

[8] The world's renewable energy cities. <https://www.cdp.net/en/cities/world-renewable-energy-cities>, (accessed 22.02.20).

[9] B. Nogrady, Australia's capital city switches to 100% renewable energy, Nature (2019). Available from: https://www.nature.com/articles/d41586-019-02804-0.

[10] C. Keating, Tasmania eyes 'battery of the nation' ambitions with 200% green energy goal, PV-Tech. <https://www.pv-tech.org/news/tasmania-sets-target-of-200-renewables-by-2040>, 2020.

[11] International Renewable Energy Agency, Latin America and the Caribbean announce ambitious new renewables target. <https://www.irena.org/newsroom/articles/2019/Dec/Latin-America-and-the-Caribbean-Announce-Ambitious-New-Renewables-Target>, 2019.

[12] 100% commitment in cities, counties and states. Sierra Club. <https://www.sierraclub.org/ready-for-100/commitments>, (accessed 19.04.15).

[13] M. Coren, Two US electric utilities have promised to go 100% carbon-free—and admit it's cheaper, Quartz, 2018. <https://qz.com/1490832/two-utilities-promised-to-go-100-carbon-free-last-week/>.

[14] S. Ptacek, S. Carter, More utilities make big commitments to climate action, Natural Resources Defense Council. <https://www.nrdc.org/experts/sophia-ptacek/more-utilities-make-big-commitments-climate-action>, 2019 (accessed 19.06.11).

[15] APS voluntarily commits to 100% carbon-free electricity by 2050, 45% renewables by 2030. Sierra Club. <https://www.sierraclub.org/press-releases/2020/01/aps-voluntarily-commits-100-carbon-free-electricity-2050-45-renewables-2030>, 2020.

[16] J. Hodges, EON switches all U.K. Customers to 100% renewable power, Bloomberg News. <https://www.bloomberg.com/news/articles/2019-07-09/eon-switches-millions-of-u-k-customers-to-100-renewable-power>, 2019.

[17] P. Gipe, Iceland: a 100% renewables example in the modern era, RenewEconomy. <https://reneweconomy.com.au/iceland-a-100-renewables-example-in-the-modern-era-56428/>, 2012.

[18] M.Z. Jacobson, M. Delucchi, Z. Bazouin, C.C. Bauer, E. Fisher, S.B. Morris, et al., 100% clean and renewable wind, water, and sunlight (WWS) all-sector energy roadmaps for the 50 United States, Energy Environ. Sci. 8 (2015) 2093−2117. Available from: https://pubs.rsc.org/en/content/articlelanding/2015/ee/c5ee01283j#!divAbstract.

[19] R. Perez, K. Rabago, A radical idea to get a high-renewable electric grid: Build way more solar and wind than needed, GreenBiz (2019). Available from: https://www.greenbiz.com/article/radical-idea-get-high-renewable-electric-grid-build-way-more-solar-and-wind-needed.

[20] M. Perez, R. Perez, K.R. Rabago, M. Putnam, Overbuilding & curtailment: the cost-effective enablers of firm PV generation, Solar Energy. 180 (2019) 412−422. Available from: https://www.documentcloud.org/documents/6111597-Solar-Energy-Journal-study.html.

[21] S. Roth, California has too much solar power. That might be good for ratepayers, LA Times, 2019. <https://www.latimes.com/business/la-fi-solar-batteries-renewable-energy-california-20190605-story.html>.

[22] California ISO managing oversupply. <http://www.caiso.com/informed/Pages/ManagingOversupply.aspx>, 2019 (accessed 22.01.20).

[23] Southwestern states have better solar resources and higher solar PV capacity factors. Today in Energy. <https://www.eia.gov/todayinenergy/detail.php?id = 39832>, 2019.

[24] Lazard's Levelized Cost of Energy Analysis − Version 13.0. <https://www.lazard.com/media/451086/lazards-levelized-cost-of-energy-version-130-vf.pdf>, 2019.

[25] Solar farm land requirements: how much land do you need? Green Coast, 2019. <https://greencoast.org/solar-farm-land-requirements/>

[26] R. Gaughan, How much land is needed for wind turbines?, 2018 <https://sciencing.com/much-land-needed-wind-turbines-12304634.html>.

[27] M.Z. Jacobson, M.A. Delucchi, Z. Bauer, S.C. Goodman, W.E. Chapman, M.A. Cameron, et al., 100% Clean and renewable wind, water, and sunlight all-sector energy roadmaps for 139 countries of the world, Joule 1 (2017) 108−121. Available from: https://web.stanford.edu/group/efmh/jacobson/Articles/I/CountriesWWS.pdf.

[28] Habitat loss. National Wildlife Foundation, 2020. <https://www.nwf.org/Educational-Resources/Wildlife-Guide/Threats-to-Wildlife/Habitat-Loss> (accessed 20.02.20).

[29] UN Report: nature's dangerous decline 'unprecedented'; species extinction rates 'accelerating'. The United Nations. <https://www.un.org/sustainabledevelopment/blog/2019/05/nature-decline-unprecedented-report/>, 2019.

[30] T. Maddox, Available from: https://www.bnd.com/news/local/article222260280.htmlA wind farm could be coming to Southern Illinois. Why are environmentalists trying to stop it? Belleville News-Democrat, 2018.

[31] T. Woody, Sierra Club, NRDC sue feds to stop big California solar power project, Forbes. <https://www.forbes.com/sites/toddwoody/2012/03/27/sierra-club-nrdc-sue-feds-to-stop-big-california-solar-power-project/#714312f81d65>

[32] R. Chason, Georgetown wants to raze 210 acres of trees to meet green-energy goals. Environmentalists are crying foul, The Washington Post, 2019. Available from:

https://www.washingtonpost.com/local/md-politics/georgetown-wants-to-raze-210-acres-of-trees-to-meet-green-energy-goals-environmentalists-are-crying-foul/2019/02/17/428c22f2-2584-11e9-ad53-824486280311_story.html.

[33] M. Harrington, Coalition opposes proposed solar power plant in Shoreham, Newsday, 2017. <https://www.newsday.com/long-island/suffolk/coalition-opposes-proposed-solar-power-plant-in-shoreham-1.13183967>.

[34] J. Russell, Environmentalists fight Alliant energy's new community solar plan, Iowa Public Radio, 2017. <https://www.iowapublicradio.org/post/environmentalists-fight-alliant-energy-s-new-community-solar-plan#stream/0>.

[35] S. Baars, Environmentalists say new farm is bad for the birds, C-Ville, 2017. <https://www.c-ville.com/environmentalists-say-new-farm-bad-birds/>.

[36] B. Cohen, Available from: https://www.heartland.org/news-opinion/news/environmentalists-sue-to-block-oregon-wind-projectEnvironmentalists sue to block Oregon wind project, The Heartland Institute, 2012.

[37] J. Trinastic, A matter of scale: the cultural and environmental impact of big solar, Nature (2015). Available from: https://www.nature.com/scitable/blog/eyes-on-environment/a_matter_of_scale_the/.

[38] A. Maiorino, How moratoriums pose a risk to renewable projects and how to avoid them, Renewable Energy News (2019). Available from: https://www.renewable-energymagazine.com/al-maiorino/how-moratoriums-pose-a-risk-to-renewable-20190705.

[39] D.A. Garcia, F. Barbanera, F. Cumo, U. DiMatteo, B. Nastasi, Expert opinion analysis on renewable hydrogen storage systems potential in Europe, Energies. 9 (2016) 963.

[40] Fuel Cell & Hydrogen Energy Association. Road map to a US hydrogen economy. <http://www.fchea.org/us-hydrogen-study>, 2020.

[41] The future of hydrogen. International Energy Association (IEA), Paris. <https://www.iea.org/reports/the-future-of-hydrogen>, 2019.

[42] S. Patel, MHPS, Magnum will build 1-GW renewable energy storage facility in Utah, Power. (2019). Available from: https://www.powermag.com/mhps-magnum-to-build-1-gw-renewable-energy-storage-facility-in-utah/.

[43] C. Morehouse, Natural gas plant replacing Los Angeles coal power to be 100% hydrogen by 2045: LADWP, Utility Dive. <https://www.utilitydive.com/news/natural-gas-plant-replacing-los-angeles-coal-power-to-be-100-hydrogen-by-2/568918/>, 2019.

[44] S. Patel, Three more nuclear plant owners will demonstrate hydrogen production, Power (2019). Available from: https://www.powermag.com/three-more-nuclear-plant-owners-will-demonstrate-hydrogen-production/.

[45] A. Lee, EDF plans vast hydrogen production at UK nuclear plants, Recharge (2020). Available from: https://www.rechargenews.com/transition/edf-plans-vast-hydrogen-production-at-uk-nuclear-plants/2-1-763048.

[46] J.D. Jenkins, M. Luke, S. Thernstrom, Getting to zero carbon emissions in the electric power sector, Joule 2 (2018) 2498−2510.

[47] H. Blanco, A. Faaij, A review at the role of storage in energy systems with a focus on power to gas and long-term storage, Renew. Sustain. Energy Rev. 81 (2018) 1049−1086.

[48] The economic ramifications of resource adequacy white paper. NARUC. <https://pubs.naruc.org/pub.cfm?id = 536DBE4A-2354-D714-5153-70FEAB9E1A87>, 2013.

[49] T. Falin, Effective load carrying capability (ELCC) analysis for wind and solar resources. <https://www.pjm.com/-/media/committees-groups/committees/pc/20190110/20190110-item-14a-elcc-analysis.ashx>

[50] C. Haley, Solar and wind ELCC accreditation. <https://www.spp.org/documents/61025/elccsolarandwindaccreditation.pdf>, 2019.

[51] California Public Utilities Commission, 2019–20 IRP: Proposed reference system plan, 2019. <https://www.cpuc.ca.gov/uploadedFiles/CPUCWebsite/Content/Utilities Industries/Energy/EnergyPrograms/ElectPowerProcurementGeneration/irp/2018/2019 IRPProposedReferenceSystemPlan_20191106.pdf>.

[52] Hawaiian Electric Companies' PSIPs Update Report, Filed December 23, 2016, Book 1 of 4. <https://www.hawaiianelectric.com/documents/clean_energy_hawaii/grid_modernization/dkt_2014_0183_20161223_companies_PSIP_update_report_1_of_4.pdf>, 2016.

[53] U.S. Energy Information Agency, Electricity data. <https://www.eia.gov/electricity/data.php#gencapacity>, 2019 (accessed 19.02.04).

[54] Public Service of New Mexico, Electric integrated resource plan, 2011–2030, 2011. <https://www.pnm.com/documents/396023/396193/2011_IRP_final/af9ea6f6-59e2-4a29-aca9-26bde3cd4b03>.

[55] Public Service of New Mexico, Integrated resource plan, 2014–2033, 2014. <https://www.pnm.com/documents/396023/396193/PNM + 2014 + IRP/bdccdd52-b0bc-480b-b1d6-cf76c408fdfc>.

[56] Public Service of New Mexico, Integrated resource plan, 2017–2036, 2017. <https://www.pnm.com/documents/396023/396193/ PNM + 2017 + IRP + Final.pdf/eae4efd7-3de5-47b4-b686-1ab37641b4ed>.

[57] J. Ferrari, Pathways towards 100% carbon reduction for electric utility power systems, 2019. <https://www.pathto100.org/2020/02/pathways-towards-100-carbon-reduction-for-electric-utility-power-systems/>.

[58] D. Aas, O. Sawyerr, C. Kolster, P. O'Neill, A. Olsen, Pacific northwest zero-emitting resources study, 2020. <https://www.ethree.com/wp-content/uploads/2020/02/E3-Pacific-Northwest-Zero-Emitting-Resources-Study-Jan-2020.pdf>.

[59] Path to 100% renewables for California, Wartsila, 2020. <https://www.wartsila.com/docs/default-source/power-plants-documents/downloads/white-papers/americas/path-to-100-renewables-for-california.pdf>.

Index

Note: Page numbers followed by "*f*" and "*t*" refer to figures and tables, respectively.

A

AC. *See* Annual cost (AC)
ACCs. *See* Annual cost curves (ACCs)
ACES. *See* Advanced Clean Energy System
    (ACES)
Adsorption, 127–128
Advanced Clean Energy System (ACES),
    216
Aero CTs, 11
Aeroderivative CTs. *See* Aero CTs
Affordability, 139
Affordable electricity, 1, 33
Air emission standards, 2–3
Aircraft propulsion, 11
Alkaline electrolyzers, 117–118, 119*t*
"Alkaline" batteries, 85
Ancillary services (AS), 179, 185–196
Annual cost (AC), 26, 33, 148–149
Annual cost curves (ACCs), 148–149, 150*f*
Arbitrage, 73–74
ARCO. *See* Atlantic Richfield Oil
    Company (ARCO)
Argon, 81–82
Arizona Public Service, 4–6
AS. *See* Ancillary services (AS)
Atlantic Richfield Oil Company (ARCO),
    44
Australian Renewable Energy Agency, 126

B

Baseload, 67–69
    renewables impose on baseload
        generators, 61–62
Battery energy storage system (BESS),
    82–88, 191–192
    flow batteries, 86–88
    lead-acid, 83
    lithium-ion, 86
    NaS, 85
    Ni-Cd and Ni-MH, 83–85
Battery-storage system, 75–77

BC Hydro, 30
BESS. *See* Battery energy storage system
    (BESS)
Bio-feedstock, 114–115
Bio-methanation, 114–115
Biofuels, 2–3, 112–115
    direct combustion, 113–114
    electricity generation, 39
    recycled biofuels, 114
    resource planning considerations, 115
    synthetic biofuels, 114–115
Biological methanation, 114–115, 130
Biomass, 10
Black liquor, 113
Black-start reserves, 185
Blending hydrogen with natural gas,
    125–126
Bromine, 87–88

C

CAES. *See* Compressed air energy storage
    (CAES)
California Independent System Operator
    (CAISO), 59–60, 67*f*, 87–88,
    179–180, 191–192
Candles, 4
Capacity, 7
    expansion analyses, 224–232
    expansion planning, 20–21, 20*f*, 139
        approaches, 25, 33–35
    factors, 147–148
    fade, 94
    markets, 52
    reserve, 156
Capacity expansion model (CEM), 20, 29
Capacity expansion planning, 20–21
    major approaches to, 25
    timeline of, 33–35
Capex, capital cost, 26
Capex. *See* Capital expenditures (Capex)
Capital costs, 3, 25–26, 33

Capital expenditures (Capex), 31, 140−142
Carbon, 129−131
Carbon dioxide emissions
    (CO_2 emissions), 1
Carbon-free
    energy, 39
    power systems, 214−218
        hydrogen and nuclear, 216−217
    resources, 1
Carbon-neutral, 126−127
    approach, 218−223
    fuel, 112
    power systems, 112
    scenario, 228
Catalytic/thermochemical methanation,
    130
CCCT. See Combined cycle combustion
    turbine (CCCT)
CEM. See Capacity expansion model
    (CEM)
Central Vermont Public Service
    Corporation, 46−47
Chile, 40
Chrono capacity expansion model,
    101−102
Chronological CEMs, 32−33
    to value flexibility, 99−103
Chronological long-term planning models,
    163−167
Chronological subhourly valuation, 99
"Clean" sources, 41−42
Climate change, 114, 205
Coal boiler plants, 9−10
Coal plants, 10
Coal-fired boiler plant, 9
Coal-fired generating station, 4−6
Coal-fired power
    generation, 9
    plants, 9
Combined cycle combustion turbine
    (CCCT), 11−12, 183−184, 216
Combustion, 203−204
    gases cool, 8−9
Combustion turbines (CTs), 8−11, 110,
    120, 183, 203−204
Commercial maturity, 27
Compliance costs, 3

Compressed air energy storage (CAES),
    77−78, 88−89, 89f
Compressed air storage, 88
Compression ignition, 12−13
"Constant pressure" CAES air storage, 88
"Constant volume" CAES air storage, 88
Contingency reserves, 155, 185
Convergence contingent, 155−156
Cost approaches, evolution of, 7−8
CTs. See Combustion turbines (CTs)
Curtailment of renewables, 60, 73

D
DAC. See Direct air capture (DAC)
Day ahead (DA), 178−179, 181f, 182f
Day-ahead forecasting, 142−143
DEC. See Denton Energy Center (DEC)
Decarbonization, 42, 203
    comparison of pathways to 100%, 219t
    comparison of pathways using capacity
        expansion analyses, 224−232
    definition of "100%", 206−207
    pathways to 100%, 207−223
    power generation technologies, 208t
Degradation
    issues, 91−95
    solar and wind degradation rates, 65−67
Demand-side management, 18−19
    participation rates, 24−25
Denton Energy Center (DEC), 189−190
Denton Municipal Electric (DME), 188
Deployment of ES, 90−91, 91f
    battery energy storage technologies, 93t
    cumulative battery-storage capacity, 92f
DERs. See Distributed energy sources
    (DERs)
Direct air capture (DAC), 110, 128
Direct air carbon capture, 126−129
    HTAS DAC, 127−128
    LTSS DAC, 128
    resource planning considerations for
        DAC, 128−129
Direct combustion, 113−115
Dispatch models. See Production cost
    models
Dispatch simulators, 153−154

Distributed energy sources (DERs), 197−198
Distribution, 6
DME. *See* Denton Municipal Electric (DME)
Dynamic features, 160−162, 161*t*

E

Economic dispatch, 51
Effective Load Carrying Capacity (ELCC), 220
Efficiency, 7
EGEAS. *See* Electric generation expansion analysis system (EGEAS)
EIM. *See* Energy imbalance market (EIM)
ELCC. *See* Effective Load Carrying Capacity (ELCC)
Electric generation expansion analysis system (EGEAS), 156
Electric Reliability Council of Texas (ERCOT), 179−180, 188−190
Electric utilities, 2−4, 50−51, 109, 139
  chronological, 164*f*
  display in lobby of Arizona Public Service headquarters, 5*f*
  early history, 4−7
  early stages of evolution of cost approaches, 7−8
  five-step process, 163*f*
  long-term capacity expansion planning, 153*f*
  LRP, 16−33
  resource planners, 95−96
  timeline of capacity expansion planning approaches, 33−35
  varying technology types, 8−16
    CCCT, 11−12
    coal boiler plants, 9−10
    CTs, 10−11
    hydro, 14
    nuclear, 14−15
    other, 16
    reciprocating engines, 12−14
Electric voltage, 43−44
Electrical conversion efficiency, 124
Electricity, 1, 39
  generation, 39

load forecasting, 19
Electro-osmotic flow, 118
Electrochemical battery-storage systems, 91−93
Electrolysis, water consumption for hydrogen production from, 123−124
Electrolytic hydrogen production, 117
Electrolyzer costs, 124−125
Energy, 7
  density, 121−122, 122*f*
  devices, 77
  production, 1, 81
Energy imbalance market (EIM), 59−60, 191−192
Energy storage (ES), 1, 70, 73, 109, 194−196
  BESS, 82−88
  CAES, 88−89
  degradation issues, 91−95
  from energy source to energy potential, conversion, storage, 76*f*
  flywheels, 79−81
  LAES, 89−90
  metrics for common forms, 95, 96*t*
  PH, 78−79
  principles, 74−75
  resource planning considerations, 95−104
  size and duration, 75−78, 77*f*
  thermal energy, 81−82
  thermal storage, 81
  "time-shifting" excess renewable generation, 74*f*
  trends in deployment, 90−91
Energy-Saving and Pollution Reduction Comprehensive Action Plan, 81
"Engines", 13
ERCOT. *See* Electric Reliability Council of Texas (ERCOT)
ES. *See* Energy storage (ES)
Evolutionary scale, 3−4
Excess renewable energy, 112, 125−126

F

"Fifty horsepower" unit, 4−6
Fischer-Tropsch process, 114−115

Fixed cost, 149
Fixed load forecast, 23—24
Fixed operations and maintenance (FOM), 140, 230
Fixed-fee revenues, 51—52
Flames, 1
Flexibility
  reducing curtailment and maximizes value, 173—177
  value, 99—103
Flexible capacity, 32, 52, 97, 99—102, 176t
Flow batteries, 86—88
Flywheels, 79—81
FOM. See Fixed operations and maintenance (FOM)
FOR. See Forced outage rate (FOR)
Forced outage rate (FOR), 22
Fossil fuels, 4, 109
Frame CTs, 11
Fuel, 3, 7
  cells, 119—120
  combustion, 8
  production processes, 110

G

Gas/kerosene lamps, 4
Gasoline engine, 12—13
Gasoline-fired generator, 46
Gasoline-type engine, 12—13
General Electric (GE), 12
Generation, 6
  mix of utilities, 8—16
  technology, 65—66
Generic five-step capacity expansion framework, 153—162
  attempted fixes, 162
  convergence contingent, 155—156
  dynamic features, 160—162, 161t
  of electric utility long-term capacity expansion, 163f
  electric utility long-term capacity expansion planning, 153f
  production cost models, 157—158
  traditional approaches, 158—160
Geographic diversity effect, 62—63, 63f, 64f
Geothermal, electricity generation, 39

Glendale Water and Power (GWP), 191—192
Global hydrogen production facilities, 124—125, 125t
Global warming, 205
Globally installed renewable energy, 50
Gorges Dam, 14
"Grid-scale" ES, 73—74
Gross efficiency, 9
GWP. See Glendale Water and Power (GWP)

H

Hawaiian Electric Company (HECO), 199, 222
Heat exchangers, 8—9
Heat recovery steam generator (HRSG), 9
Heating value, 121—122, 122f
HECO. See Hawaiian Electric Company (HECO)
HHV. See Higher heating value (HHV)
High-renewable power systems, 31
High-speed machines, 13
High-temperature aqueous solution (HTAS), 127
High-temperature aqueous solution direct air capture (HTAS DAC), 127—128
Higher heating value (HHV), 121
Hoover Dam, 14
HRSG. See Heat recovery steam generator (HRSG)
HRSG/steam turbine, 12
HTAP. See Hydrogen Technical Advisory Panel (HTAP)
HTAS. See High-temperature aqueous solution (HTAS)
HTAS DAC. See High-temperature aqueous solution direct air capture (HTAS DAC)
Hybrid systems, 87—88
Hydro, 14, 111
Hydrocarbons, 116—117
Hydroelectric generator, 4
Hydroelectric power plant, 14
Hydrogen, 115—127, 129—131
  in carbon-free power systems, 216—217

hydrogen-oxygen fuel cell, 119
to power, 119—120
    combustion turbines and reciprocating
        engines, 120
    fuel cells, 119—120
    power to hydrogen, 116—118
    production from electrolysis, 123—124
    resource planning considerations for,
        121—126
Hydrogen Technical Advisory Panel
    (HTAP), 116
Hydropower, 14, 39

I

Ice production, 81
IGCCs. *See* Integrated gasification
    combined cycles (IGCCs)
IGP. *See* Integrated Grid Planning (IGP)
Incentives driving change, 41—43
Independent Power Producers (IPPs), 97,
    140
Independent system operators (ISOs), 178
Insofar, 18—19
Installed solar and wind capacity and
    pricing, 47—50, 49*f*
Integrated gasification combined cycles
    (IGCCs), 129
Integrated Grid Planning (IGP), 199
Integrated resource planning. *See* Long-
    range planning (LRP)
Integrated resource plans (IRPs), 1—2,
    95—96, 187, 223
    energy storage in, 194—196
    future direction, 197—200
    storage in, 96—97
Integrated System & Operations Planning
    process (ISOP process), 198—199
Internal rate of return (IRR), 187—188
International Panel on Climate Change
    (IPCC), 110, 205
International Renewable Energy Agency
    (IRENA), 116
Investor-owned utilities (IOUs), 2—3
IOUs. *See* Investor-owned utilities (IOUs)
IPCC. *See* International Panel on Climate
    Change (IPCC)

IPPs. *See* Independent Power Producers
    (IPPs)
IRENA. *See* International Renewable
    Energy Agency (IRENA)
Iron solutions, 86—87
IRPs. *See* Integrated resource plans (IRPs)
IRR. *See* Internal rate of return (IRR)
ISO-NE. *See* New England Independent
    System Operator (ISO-NE)
ISOP process. *See* Integrated System &
    Operations Planning process (ISOP
    process)
ISOs. *See* Independent system operators
    (ISOs)

J

Jet engine, 11

K

Kinetic energy, 79—80

L

LADWP. *See* Los Angeles Department of
    Water and Power (LADWP)
LAES. *See* Liquid air energy storage
    (LAES)
Land-based power generation, 11
LCOE. *See* Levelized cost of energy
    (LCOE)
LDC. *See* Load duration curve (LDC)
LDC-SCA. *See* Load duration curve-
    screening curve approach
    (LDC-SCA)
Lead-acid batteries, 83
Least-cost
    dispatch planning software, 69—70
    economic dispatch principle, 50—51
    planning principles, 16—17, 41—42
    principles, 21
Levelized cost, 149
    of electricity. *See* Levelized cost of
        energy (LCOE)
Levelized cost of energy (LCOE), 26—27,
    52, 148, 150*f*, 175—176
LFP. *See* Li-ion phosphate (LFP)
LHV. *See* Lower heating value (LHV)
Li-ion phosphate (LFP), 86

Light sensitive device, 43—44
Liquid air energy storage (LAES), 89—90
Lithium cobalt oxide, 86
Lithium-ion (Li-ion), 86
  manganese oxide, 86
  system, 75—77
  technology, 91, 92*f*
Lithium-manganese oxide (LMO), 86
Lithium-nickel-manganese oxide (LNMC),
    86
Lithium-titanate oxide (LTO), 86
LMO. *See* Lithium-manganese oxide
    (LMO)
LMP. *See* Locational marginal price (LMP)
LNMC. *See* Lithium-nickel-manganese
    oxide (LNMC)
Load, 55—61, 56*f*, 57*f*, 58*f*, 59*f*
  forecasting, 18—19
  Loa following reserves, 185
Load duration curve (LDC), 27, 28*f*,
    151—153, 184
  LDC-based capacity expansion models,
    29—31
Load duration curve-screening curve
    approach (LDC-SCA), 27
Locational marginal price (LMP), 144—145
LOLE. *See* Loss of load expectation
    (LOLE)
LOLP. *See* Loss of load probability (LOLP)
LOLP/LOLE. *See* Loss of load probability/
    loss of load expectation (LOLP/
    LOLE)
Long-range planning (LRP), 1—2, 16—33
  annual cost, 26
  basics of utility LRP, 18—25
    capacity expansion planning, 20—21
    load forecasting, 18—19
    risk/uncertainty assessment, 21—25
  capacity expansion planning, major
    approaches to, 25
  capital cost, 25
  chronological CEMs, 32—33
  LCOE, 26—27
  LDC-based capacity expansion models,
    29—31
  LDC-SCA, 27
  modified LDC-CEMs, 31—32

source-LDC approach, 27—29
Long-term capacity expansion planning
  capacity factors, 147—148
  chronological long-term planning
    models, 163—167
  costs in capacity expansion, 140—142
  Generic five-step capacity expansion
    framework, 153—162
  LDC, 151—153
  models for regional and policy initiatives,
    167—168
  net load and supply stack, 145
  optimization problem, 139*f*
  real-time dispatch, 145—147
  screening curves, 148—151
  supply stack and marginal cost, 142—145
Long-term planning. *See* Long-range
    planning (LRP)
Long-term storage potential of power to
    gas, 229
Los Angeles Department of Water and
    Power (LADWP), 216
Loss of load expectation (LOLE), 22
Loss of load probability (LOLP), 22, 155
Loss of load probability/loss of load
    expectation (LOLP/LOLE), 22—23
Low-temperature solid sorbent (LTSS), 127
Low-temperature solid sorbent direct air
    capture (LTSS DAC), 128
Lower heating value (LHV), 121
LRP. *See* Long-range planning (LRP)
LTO. *See* Lithium-titanate oxide (LTO)
LTSS. *See* Low-temperature solid sorbent
    (LTSS)
LTSS DAC. *See* Low-temperature solid
    sorbent direct air capture (LTSS
    DAC)

M
Mandates and subsidies, 103—104
Marginal cost, 142—145
Mean time to repair (MTTR), 22
Methanation, 126—127, 129—131
  biological methanation, 130
  catalytic/thermochemical methanation,
    130

resource planning considerations for, 130–131
Methane (CH_4), 110
Minimum net load bound, 60–61
Modified load duration curve-based capacity expansion models (Modified LDC-CEMs), 31–32
MTTR. *See* Mean time to repair (MTTR)

N

NARUC. *See* National Association of Regulated Utility Commissioner (NARUC)
NaS. *See* Sodium-sulfur (NaS)
National Association of Regulated Utility Commissioner (NARUC), 32
National Renewable Energy Laboratory (NREL), 53, 130–131, 194
Natural disasters, 21–22
Natural gas, 2–3, 10
blending hydrogen with, 125–126
Natural Resources Defense Council (NRDC), 115
Net load, 55–61, 57f, 58f, 59f, 145, 173–175
Net present value (NPV), 26–27, 230
Net revenue, 144–145
Net-zero approach. *See* Carbon-neutral, approach
New energy-consuming devices, 18–19
New England Independent System Operator (ISO-NE), 61, 67–68
New York Independent System Operator (NYISO), 186
market, 187–188
Ni-MH batteries. *See* Nickel—metal hydride batteries (Ni-MH batteries)
Nickel cadmium batteries (Ni-Cd batteries), 83–85
Nickel-hydrogen (NiH), 85
Nickel-iron (NiFe), 85
Nickel-zinc (NiZn), 85
Nickel—metal hydride batteries (Ni-MH batteries), 83–85
Nitrogen oxides (NO_x), 203
Nonrenewable technologies, 70
NPV. *See* Net present value (NPV)

NRDC. *See* Natural Resources Defense Council (NRDC)
NREL. *See* National Renewable Energy Laboratory (NREL)
Nuclear in carbon-free power systems, 216–217
Nuclear power, 14–15. *See also* Energy
NYISO. *See* New York Independent System Operator (NYISO)

O

Objective function, 154–155
OEMs. *See* Original equipment manufacturers (OEMs)
Oil-fired Recip plants, 13
Operating costs, 26
Operating expenditures (Opex), 101, 140, 142
operating costs, 26
Operational cost, 7
Operational reserves, 155–156
Opex. *See* Operating expenditures (Opex)
Original equipment manufacturers (OEMs), 22
Overestimation, 18–19
Overgeneration storage, 73–74
'Owners' cost, 7

P

Paper/pulp processing, 113
Percolation theory, 44
PH. *See* Pumped hydro (PH)
PHES devices. *See* Pumped Heat Electrical Storage devices (PHES devices)
Phoenix Electric Light Company, 4–6
Photovoltaic effect, 43–44
Photovoltaic power devices, 44
PLEXOS chronological dispatch simulations, 102
Policy and incentives driving change, 41–43
Portfolio optimization, 102
Portfolio planning, 20
Potassium hydroxide (KOH), 127–128
Pouch factor, 86
Power devices, 77
Power purchase agreement (PPA), 48–49, 49f, 189

Power to hydrogen (PtH), 116–118, 131
  alkaline electrolyzers, 117–118
  comparison of alkaline and PEM
    electrolyzers, 118
  PEM electrolyzers, 118
Power to methane (PtM), 131
Power to X (PtX), 112
Power-to-gas processes (PtG processes),
    129, 228–229
  facilities, 132–133
Power-to-liquid process (PtL process), 129
PPA. See Power purchase agreement (PPA)
Pricing
  installed solar and wind capacity and,
    47–50
  solar and wind impact dispatch and,
    50–52
Prismatic form factor batteries, 86
Production cost models, 157–158
Production tax credits (PTCs), 42–43
Profit-making businesses, 2–3
Proton exchange membrane (PEM)
  electrolyzers, 118, 119t
  technology, 117
PSCO. See Public Service of Colorado
    (PSCO)
PSE. See Puget Sound Energy (PSE)
PSO. See Public Service of Oklahoma
    (PSO)
PTCs. See Production tax credits (PTCs)
PtG processes. See Power-to-gas processes
    (PtG processes)
PtH. See Power to hydrogen (PtH)
PtL process. See Power-to-liquid process
    (PtL process)
PtM. See Power to methane (PtM)
PtX. See Power to X (PtX)
Public sentiment, 27
Public Service of Colorado (PSCO), 29
Public Service of Oklahoma (PSO), 190
Public Utility Commissions (PUCs),
    16–17
Puget Sound Energy (PSE), 195–196
Pumped Heat Electrical Storage devices
    (PHES devices), 81–82
Pumped hydro (PH), 73–74, 78–79, 79f
Pure water electrolysis, 117

R
Ramifications for resource planning,
    69–70
Rational planning techniques, 17–18
Real time (RT), 178–179, 181f, 182f
  considerations, 97–99
  dispatch, 145–147
Real-time pricing, 177–185
Reciprocating engines (Recips), 8–9,
    12–14, 100, 110, 120
Recycled biofuels, 114
Reduction-oxidation processes (Redox
    processes), 86–87, 87f
Regeneration, 127–128
Regional Transmission Organizations
    (RTOs), 190–191
Regulation, system-wide ancillary service,
    98
Regulation/synchronized reserves, 185
Reliable electricity, 1
Renewable energy, 39, 109. See also
    Variable renewable energy (VREs)
  sources, 46–47
Renewable fuels, 112–113, 131–134
  liquid fuels, 112
  as long-term RS, 110–112
    annual capacity factor, 112f
    biofuels, 112–115
    direct air carbon capture, 126–129
    hydrogen, 115–126
    methanation, 129–131
Renewable Portfolio Standard (RPS), 2–3,
    41, 42t, 133, 203
Renewables, 67
  impose on baseload generators, 61–62
  resources, 1
  synthetic fuel production, 77–78
Request for proposals (RFPs), 25, 96–97
Residual loads, 67–69
Residual net load, 68–69, 68f
Resource planning, 95–104, 115, 173,
    184–185, 192–194
  case for real-time considerations, 97–99
  chronological capacity expansion to
    value flexibility, 99–103
  for DAC, 128–129
  for hydrogen, 121–126

blending hydrogen with natural gas, 125−126
  electrical conversion efficiency, 124
  global hydrogen production facilities, 124−125
  heating value and energy density, 121−122
  storage and transport, 123
  water consumption for hydrogen production, 123−124
  mandates and subsidies, 103−104
  for methanation, 130−131
  storage even in IRP, 96−97
Reversible heat pump/heat engine, 81−82
RFPs. *See* Request for proposals (RFPs)
Risk assessment, 21
Risk/uncertainty assessment, 21−25
Round-trip efficiency, 74−75
RPS. *See* Renewable Portfolio Standard (RPS)
RT. *See* Real time (RT)
RTOs. *See* Regional Transmission Organizations (RTOs)

S

Sabatier process, 130
Scenario analysis, 23−25
Screening curves, 148−151
Semantics, 206−207
Size and duration, 75−78, 77*f*
Small modular reactors (SMRs), 15
Smith−Putnam turbine, 46
SMRs. *See* Small modular reactors (SMRs)
Sodium hydroxide (NaOH), 127−128
Sodium-sulfur (NaS), 85
SOECs. *See* Solid oxide electrolysis cells (SOECs)
Solar
  degradation rate, 65−67
  plants, 40−41
  potential, 40
  power, 43−45, 45*f*
  and wind impact dispatch and pricing, 50−52
    hypothetical utility fleet with only thermal, 50*t*
    hypothetical utility fleet with thermal and renewable assets, 51*t*

Solid oxide electrolysis cells (SOECs), 117
Source-LDC approach, 27−29
Southwest Power Pool (SPP), 179−180
  market, 187, 190−191
Spark-ignited internal combustion engines, 12−13
SPP. *See* Southwest Power Pool (SPP)
Steam reformation, 116−117
Storage in integrated resource plan, 96−97
Subsidies, 103−104
Sulfur dioxide (SO_2), 203
Supply stack, 142−145
Synthetic biofuels, 114−115
Synthetic fuels, 110, 126−127

T

T&D. *See* Transmission and distribution (T&D)
Texas plant, 89
Thermal energy storage, forms of, 81−82
Thermal plants, 8
Thermal storage, 81, 90−91
Thermal units, 62
Time scale, 63−65
Time-shifting, 73−74
  excess renewable energy, 73
Traditional fossil-fueled generation, 2
Transmission, 6
  constrained load pocket, 20
Transmission and distribution (T&D), 173

U

Uncertainty analysis, 21, 23−24
Uninterruptable power supplies (UPS), 82
US Energy Information Agency, 111
Utility long-range planning, 18−25
  capacity expansion planning, 20−21
  load forecasting, 18−19
  risk/uncertainty assessment, 21−25

V

Value of lost load (VOLL), 22−23
Vanadium, 86−87
  flow battery energy, 87−88
Variability of solar and wind, 53−55, 53*f*, 54*f*

Variable operations and maintenance
(VOM), 50–51, 140
Variable renewable energy (VREs), 24–25,
111, 142–143, 173. *See also*
Renewable energy
economic case for, 211–212
flexibility reduces curtailment and
maximizes value, 173–177
land requirements for, 212
opposition to land use for, 212–213
penetration on day ahead and real-time
pricing, 177–185
sources, 39, 73
baseload going away, enter residual
loads, 67–69
effect of geographic diversity, 62–63
global solar potential map, 40*f*
global wind potential map, 41*f*
net load *vs.* load, 55–61
policy and incentives driving change,
41–43
ramifications for resource planning,
69–70
renewables impose on baseload
generators, 61–62
solar and wind degradation rates,
65–67

solar and wind impact dispatch and
pricing, 50–52
solar power, 43–45
time scale, 63–65
trends in installed solar and wind
capacity and pricing, 47–50
variability of solar and wind, 53–55
wind power, 45–47
VOLL. *See* Value of lost load (VOLL)
VOM. *See* Variable operations and
maintenance (VOM)
VREs. *See* Variable renewable energy
(VREs)

W
Water battery. *See* Pumped hydro (PH)
Water consumption for hydrogen
production from electrolysis,
123–124
Wind
capacity factor, 53
degradation rate, 65–67
potential, 40
power, 45–47, 48*f*
"Wind Corridor", 40
Wood products, 113